DAVE BROCK POSED A QUESTION ON

"Other than making the number, what i front line sales managers?"

C000175559

AMONG THE RESPONSES:

"Empowerment to think outside of the box and not get caught in the trap of because it always been done this way." **James Perkins**

"If as a sales manager, if you want excellence, then show what excellence looks like. Then manage the activity and coach to improve weak competencies within the process." **Dylis Guyan**

"Building a framework for success that advances the skills of both the top and average performer." **Doug Nyberg**

"I'm going to say it is either unteachable sales reps, or the lack of resource support from upper management that does not invest in a sales team, resulting in high turnover." **Deric Mills**

"But the biggest challenge I see is adaptability. … there is not a cookie-cutter model that you can coach your sales team to follow. Great sales managers will focus on situational awareness and use data and insights to prioritize and coach their teams…" **Hank Barnes**

"How to balance their time between customers, sales team and management activities." **Pascale Hall**

"How to coach, who, when and about what. " **George Bronten**

"Right people, in the Right role doing the Right things, effectiveness in the key to success and Good Growth." **David Leaver**

"Execution!! (Well thought out, customer focused) Plan > Process > Praxis If you fail the first two you're out. Fail the latter - all will fail." **Patriek van Eijck**

"Sales managers need relevant metrics to assist in coaching that are leading indicators instead of only trailing indicators; need to have visibility into dips to coach proactively." **Tim Preston**

"Talent, talent, talent! From scouting to acquisition to development. I typically have evaluated my front-line sales manager's talent pipeline along with the more popular deal pipe!" **Art Petty**

"Tough to pick just one but I'd say effective pipeline and opportunity reviews/coaching along with forecasting which is interdependent. Very few I've worked with do it well." **Don Mulhern**

DAVE'S BOOK ADDRESSES THESE CHALLENGES— AND MORE!

SALES MANAGER SURVIVAL GUIDE

Lessons from Sales' Front Lines

David A. Brock

KCD PRESS
2016
http://salesmanagersurvivalguide.com

For Dad and Mom, Harold and Janellen Brock, without whom I wouldn't be, both figuratively and literally, where I am.

And for my wife, Kookie. As you will discover reading this book, Kookie has been my mentor in many ways, and is one of the most inspirational sales leaders I have ever known.

CONTENTS

FOREWORD

My thoughts about Dave's book are inseparable from my thoughts about Dave.

Dave Brock has street cred! No BS, no hype, no simple theory. Dave has knowledge gathered from real life as a salesperson and leader. Like Dave, with his multiple decades of direct experience, I too have more time in this role than most of our audience has in life. Does that just make us old? It might. But not in this case.

In this case, Dave leads the evolutionary thinking about the forever-changing business world and the implication that this evolution is having on the role of the salesperson and their leadership. Dave is one of a handful of sales professionals around the world who truly grasps what we need to do TODAY to succeed, versus continuing to do what worked once.

Over the last few years Dave and I have had many conversations about the "new world" and how it affects our passionate pursuit of excellence in the art and science of selling. We are in violent agreement in almost everything. In fact, as I think of it now, I don't recall what we did not agree on.

Above all, we agree on the critical impact and importance of the role of the sales leader who is in direct support of the individuals that make up the client-facing team. It does not really matter much what the industry, the products, or services sales people are focusing on. It does not really matter what the "size of the deal" is or where in the world we are working. The simple matter is the singular most important role in any sales team, anywhere around the world, is that of their Front Line Sales Manager.

Now, I will give Dave a little grief here, and take the position that words are everything and that Manager is too tactical a word. Leader is a more accurate description of the role Dave writes about... But at the same time, I understand most corporations around the world will not accept that differentiation in title. Too bad: their loss.

In any case, Leader or Manager title aside, the role and its application is the matter at the heart of Dave's book. He does a masterful job of spelling out the needs and the actions every rookie and seasoned pro trying to guide a sales team should dig into and understand in total.

This is a Survival Guide for one of the most challenging positions you will ever tackle in the sales arena. And Dave Brock gives you the knowledge, the tools, and the answers (even though he may not think so,) needed to master one of the most satisfying roles you will ever have.

So, let's all go out and make a difference with those whom we serve, and the clients whom they serve. We really can create a better world! It's a great calling. Have fun with it!

Mitch Little
Vice President, Worldwide Sales and Applications,
Microchip Technology, Inc.

INTRODUCTION

Sales Manager Survival Guide is intended to take you on a journey some of you have already begun. The journey starts the day you are named as a Front Line Sales Manager. I'll take you through the critical first 30-60-90 days, then move you through your life as a manager, all the way to the point you are looking for a more senior sales management role.

Before I go further, I hope you are asking yourself this question: "Why should I trust you?"

This book is data driven. Not in the sense of rigorous market surveys, but it is the result of literally tens of thousands of experiences and lessons learned over my career, the careers of my colleagues and clients in Partners In EXCELLENCE.

These lessons were learned the hard way. Some I was proud of, and others not so much, but sometimes, even in the mess made by a terrible mistake, I've been able to find insights that help me achieve future successes.

Let's look at some of the data. I've been involved in selling and sales management for over 35 years—yes, some of you guessed right, I started when I was 5 years old—would you believe… Over that time, I've participated in more than 30,000 deal and sales call reviews, over 9,000 pipeline reviews, and tens of thousands of one-on-ones.

Cumulatively, in my responsibilities as a line manager/executive, and through our clients at Partners In EXCELLENCE, we've been involved in producing over $67 billion in revenues. I've been directly involved in interviewing, hiring, and firing hundreds of sales people and managers, as well as and developing over 100,000 sales professionals.

I've worked for and with some of the top corporations of the world. I've also worked for and with some of the hottest start-ups in the news. I've worked with family-owned, small and mid-sized businesses. This work has taken me to dozens of countries, working with teams in Sub-Saharan Africa, Asia, Latin/South America, India, Europe, Australia, the Middle East, Eastern Europe, and, naturally, North America.

Through my travels I've picked up tens of thousands of experiences. The lessons I've learned have been instrumental in shaping me both personally and professionally. There are things I wished I'd done better, but had to learn through sometimes tough experience before I could improve. Layer onto this the experience of the people on my team and our clients—we have a collective data base of hundreds of thousands of reviews, meetings, hiring/firings we've learned from—and there is plenty of wisdom and insight to draw from.

Global spending in Sales Training is $4-6 billion a year. Yet we spend less than 5% ($200-300 million) of that on formal training for sales managers. It's a huge difference in investment, yet the front line sales manager is the most important person in driving day to day sales performance.

There aren't a lot of resources available to managers who want to learn and develop. Just a quick search of Amazon, shows over 16,000 titles related to sales and selling, yet only 1,700 titles related to sales leadership.

Where do sales managers go for answers and ideas for even the most basic issues they face every day? How do managers "hack" sales management, learning the things critical to them and their teams, without having to go through the 30,000 deal reviews, call reviews, and endless pipeline reviews? I hope to help you accelerate your growth, avoid some of the mistakes I've made, and contribute more quickly to the success of your team, your manager, and your own.

This book focuses on the *Front Line Sales Manager*, but is a resource to all sales managers. By front line sales manager, I mean managers who have sales people reporting directly to them but have no managers among their own direct reports. I'll use the terms front line and first line sales manager interchangeably.

I believe the front line or first line sales manager is one of the most important and most difficult jobs in sales. Front line sales management is the point where we translate strategies, ideas, programs into tactical day to day execution.

If you'll excuse the military analogy, the front line sales managers are the sergeants of today's sales armies. They are the people who make things happen, and upon whom executive, corporate and sales management depend to get things done.

Despite—or perhaps because of—the importance of this mission, the front line sales manager is often caught between a rock and a hard place. You already know what I mean. You aren't a salesperson, and so, unless you also carry a personal territory, you aren't directly responsible for finding and closing deals.

You aren't responsible for driving the strategies of the company. Unless you are "the sales manager" in a very small company, you aren't even responsible for driving the strategy and priorities of the sales organization—though you contribute to the development of these.

The Front Line Sales Manager, particularly in any company over roughly $50 million in sales, is given their "marching orders" and expected to lead their team in sharp execution.

The role is even more difficult for someone new to the position. For most, this may be the first management/leadership role they have ever had. There's always that difficult transition from individual contributor—managing one's own territory, being accountable for their own results—to managing a team accountable for the results they must produce.

So this book is intended as a guide to helping the front line sales manager do the things that are most critical both for his or her personal success and that of the team.

I've tried to write the book in a simple, very direct manner. I won't cloud it with a lot of stories or examples, but will offer simple explanations of things you will encounter as a manager, and the issues you must be attentive to. It is my hope the book will help you identify land mines and challenges that can derail you or your team.

I won't necessarily provide answers. In reality there is never a "right answer." Each situation will be different. But I'll help you identify the issues you should be thinking about and how to figure out the answers most relevant to you and the specific situation you face.

I'll provide tools to help apply some of the things we talk about in this book. Among these tools will be checklists, templates, and references to other materials. There will also be a website, salesmanagersurvivalguide.com, where I will provide more tools, as well as generating discussion and idea sharing, with you and your peers from around the world.

The first section of this book will cover your initial days as a front line sales manager and how to have a great start in your new role. But the bulk of the book is intended to be a comprehensive reference guide to any sales manager. While I believe even seasoned front line sales managers and sales executives can benefit from the material in the opening chapters, for those of you with more experience, feel free to skip to the chapter most relevant to what you need right now.

Keep this book on your desk, or bookmarked on your computer or tablet. Highlight it, annotate it, bend the corners of pages down for reference. Use it as a quick reminder of how to excel in your role. For example, if you are coaching a deal, skim through that chapter to remind yourself about what you want to accomplish. If you are hiring, read those chapters to look at how you search, recruit, interview, hire, and onboard new sales people. Use the Sales Competency Model to help identify your ideal candidate.

A few notes about what this book isn't:

- This book won't give you the answers. It will help you identify the questions you should be asking, those you should be answering, and things you should be considering in developing the answers. But every manager's situation is different. It's *your* job to figure out the answers most important to you. **It's mine to help you become confident that you've considered all the**

possibilities and consequences of the professional challenges you'll face. If you want "the answers," this book probably isn't for you. Then again, if you want someone *telling* you the answers, rather than helping you develop the capabilities to figure things out for yourself, you won't be successful in sales management.

- This book focuses on the tactical day to day leadership required to execute these strategies and plans, and to get each salesperson contributing to the highest levels. This book doesn't address a number of very important issues that concern top sales executives or CEOs. I only touch lightly on the development of overall sales strategies, the organization and effective deployment of people and resources, the "business of selling," and a whole lot of other strategic topics. I'll be writing another book to address those issues. For some of you, in very small organizations, this will leave you in a bit of a tough spot because in addition to the day to day tactical execution, you are responsible for the overall strategy. As I mentioned, in later sections of the book I'll provide some thoughts—hopefully to help you until you read the next book.

- This book is not a book about the latest cool ideas and pop culture in sales management topics. It's a "down and dirty, let's get the job done" book. It's about the hard work of selling and sales leadership. If you want to be titillated by the latest hot and cool ideas, this definitely isn't for you.

Every day, there are new tools and technologies being announced that help sales people and sales managers. But without rock solid operating principles, great thinking, and relentless execution, these tools are worthless. They are, in fact, often distractions that divert your concentration from the basics of your job and its responsibilities.

One of the things I hope you get out of the book is the pure joy and fun of being a front line sales manager. This might seem an odd thing to say, particularly when your boss is hammering you for forecasts, budgets, and your team is struggling to make the numbers.

This may seem odd, especially when you look at your own career and want to advance and develop as much as possible. Many view the front line sales manager position as a stepping-stone, rather than a role filled with joy and fun.

Perhaps it takes some years and reflection to understand this. In my own career, I have been very ambitious—moving from front line sales manager to SVP or EVP of sales roles, moving further to General Management and CEO roles in both large (Fortune 100) and start-up organizations.

Don't get me wrong, there's a lot of fun in those roles, as well. But the greatest joy I've ever experienced came from working every day with sales people. Helping them perform at the highest levels possible, helping them think about deals and their territory, getting out and making calls on customers, feeling bad when we've lost, feeling the exhilaration when we've won.

Despite everything else, the real action in selling comes from working with sales people and customers. The real action in sales management is not sitting in a conference room figuring out next year's plan, but working with the sales people who work with customers every day.

I hope this book helps you with the details and challenges of those days—but I also hope that it helps you recognize and appreciate the joy your days as a front line sales manager can contain.

PART ONE

THE NEW SALES MANAGER

1

SO NOW YOU ARE A NEW SALES MANAGER. WHAT'S DIFFERENT?

First, congratulations! Your first job as a front line sales manager is a huge step forward in your career.

Now, don't screw it up—you'll get a lot of people who will immediately congratulate you, shake your hand heartily, and smile widely as they say:

"What have you done for me lately?"

Before we get on with getting in shape to answer that question, let's backtrack a little bit.

How did you get here? Probably one of a couple of things happened. You are working for the same company and have gotten a big promotion, moving from an individual contributor role to the front line sales manager role.

Alternatively, you were employed by another company, applied for this job and were hired.

In either case, you probably got the role for a number of reasons:

- You were a top performer as an individual contributor. You consistently met your numbers and did a great job.

- Your peers and your management may have considered you a role model.

- As a top performing salesperson, you may have mentored and coached your peers. Management became aware of your potential for leadership and promoted you.

- You may have had a management role at another company and been recruited by your new employer.

- Someone may have died, been promoted, or left the company, and you were the most "painless candidate to select."

Don't get me or my humor wrong. No matter how you got the role, congratulations are in order. You were made a sales manager because you earned it and deserve it.

But…

What you did, and how well you did, in your previous job has little to do with your new job as front line sales manager! Your past glory and awards don't count!

Being a great sales manager is different from being a great salesperson.

You are a newbie!

You are starting fresh!

It's a great opportunity—if you make the most of it!

The BIG change with becoming a front line manager is now your job is to get things done through your people.

Your past success was based on your ability to get things done yourself. Whether it was your adeptness in developing and executing winning deal strategies, or getting partners and others in your organization to help you, your success primarily rested upon what you did and how you performed.

As a sales manager, your success will be based on your ability to get each person on your team to perform to their fullest potential. If you can't get each of them to be successful, then there is no way you can be successful.

However great you were in making sales calls, closing and negotiating deals is relatively meaningless in your new position. Your own personal sales ability doesn't count. What matters now is your ability to get each member of the team doing the right things with the right people at the right time.

Don't get me wrong, **you have great experience in doing all these things yourself, and that experience will serve you well.** Your experiences and the seasoning they gave you will provide a strong foundation for the teaching, coaching, and development of your people.

You know all the what, how, why—the trick is how you get your people to know the what, how, why, and to execute it as well or better than you did.

How do you help them see the things that maximize their performance and results they produce?

How do you get them to execute consistently, at a cadence that supports the attainment of the overall team goals?

Answering these questions (and hundreds more)—and putting your answers into action—is the heart of your new job.

Some things you need to know are true, whether you want the knowledge or not:

- **You can't tell your people what to do.** Think back to when you were a salesperson not so many days ago. How did you react to someone *telling* you what to do?

- **You can't do the selling for them—there just aren't enough hours in the day.** Let's do some quick math. Say you produced $1M a year, consistently. (Yeah, I know you did much more, but humor me.) You know that you worked full-time to do that—and probably worked evenings and a little on the weekends, as well. So now you have 10 people, each with $1M to achieve. If you try to do it yourself—they may be glad to let you do it—the math works against you. It's simply impossible as long, as you are managing any more than one person.

- **You can't do nothing,** sit behind a desk, producing reports and trusting that your team will produce the numbers. What happens when they don't?

- **You can't swoop in as "Super Sales Manager,"** closing the deals yourself. Go back to 1 and 2—re-read that.

There are some things that will frustrate you:

- **Much of the time, you know you can do better and work faster than any person on your team.** You may be right, but that doesn't help them improve and perform. Besides, you've already done the math: You don't have enough hours in the day to do their jobs for them.

- **Sometimes, your team members just seem too slow; they don't have the urgency you do.** It's your job to figure out how to light a fire within each of them and, if necessary, *under* them.

- **Sometimes your temperamental 4-year-old at home will seem to have more sense and maturity than people on your team.** There have been many times when I've been tempted to tell a whining salesperson to go to his desk for a "time-out." There are times when they just don't seem to "get it." It's your job to figure out how to overcome this.

- **Sometimes, you will discover you have the wrong people.** They simply won't be able to get the job done, no matter how well you teach, coach, and develop them.

- **You will always be caught between a rock and a hard place.** Your management has high expectations of your performance—and you are dependent on your team to get the job done. Sometimes the directions provided by your management and what you need to do will be in conflict.

- **There are no easy answers.** Sales management is a thinking person's job. There is no magic, there are no tricks or techniques, there are no short cuts. You have to do the work. Suck it up, that's what management is all about!

But you'll quickly learn that part of the job and joy of being a manager is—figuring it out!

- **Figuring out who each person is on your team,** what they are good and bad at, what their capabilities are, what their aspirations are, and what makes each of them tick.

- **Figuring out how to inspire and light a personalized fire in each**—getting each to perform to their full potentials.

- **Figuring out the right systems, tools, processes, programs, and training** to provide to help your people be successful.

- **Figuring out how to get your people what they need to be successful**—and what to do when you can't.

- **Figuring out how to manage your manager,** getting her out of your way so you can do what you need to do, but getting her support through the process.

Being a sales manager, especially the first time, is like working a puzzle, without knowing the picture, and being certain a couple of pieces may be missing.

For now:

- **Be proud you are a front line sales manager.** It is the toughest sales job in the world, but it's through you things happen.

- **Know your job is different.** The one lesson to take from this article is: "Your job is to get things done through your people!" (Write this down and keep it on your desk, read it 3 times a day.)

- **Right now, don't rush to change anything.** Get to know your people and what they face. Get to know your company and how it works. Get to know your customers and what they think of your people and accompany.

- **And don't screw up**—you'll have unlimited opportunities to do that later!

The next few chapters will explore your first 30, 60, 90 days in the job. As you'll see, the job doesn't necessarily get any easier—after all, you didn't take the job because it was going to be easy.

But, trust me, it does become far more fun the better you get at it.

2

YOUR FIRST 30 DAYS:
SLOW DOWN, DON'T MOVE TOO FAST

No, I'm not channeling Simon and Garfunkel's "59th Street Bridge" song or Tyga's "Movin 2 Fast."

I'm talking about your first 30 days as a new manager.

It's human nature, particularly if you are in sales and very action oriented, to start doing things.

We feel compelled to take action, to start solving problems, to get things going—after all, it's that proclivity to take action that probably contributed to getting the job in the first place.

Sometimes, we feel we have to make a mark or set a tone of some sort. (Actually not much different than a dog marking its territory.)

Often, when we are hired as a new manager in a new/different company, we tend to think "something's broken, I have to fix it." Even when we are replacing a manager who has been promoted, we have the same thoughts.

That's the single biggest mistake we can make—despite anything the hiring manager may have said about needing to take action.

Here's the issue, "How do we know what action to take? How do we know the most important things we should do?"

The most important thing for a new manager to do—regardless of the situation—is to do *nothing!*

No, I don't really mean do nothing. I mean don't rush into changing things.

I've been involved as a CEO or top executive in a number of turnarounds. In many cases, the situations have been quite dire, with the company on the brink of failure. But even in those times, the worst thing to do is to start making changes. (Toward the end of this chapter I'll talk about triage: dealing with immediate critical distractions, so you can take your time with important, but less urgent challenges more systematically.)

The most critical things you need to do in your first 30 days as a new manager is figure out what drives your people, how they work, what's going on, how things get done, what people think, why the organization is where it is, and where you can have the biggest impact on the people and organization.

Until you do these, you don't know what actions—if any—you need to take, or which may have the highest priority.

Slow down! Even if the hiring manager has told you, "You need to fix these problems!"

So how do you figure things out?

1. **Your frame of reference is very important.** It's important to look at things through fresh eyes, as if you are the new kid on the block. If you are new to the company, this is easy: You actually are the new kid on the block! The biggest challenge is if you have been with the company for some time and have been promoted into a role. Too often, you become a prisoner of your own experience. Because you've been involved in the company, perhaps years of service, you make assumptions based on your experience, or the way things have always been done—and these may be entirely wrong.

2. **You don't have to prove anything.** You already have the job! So resist the temptation to try to prove yourself by taking quick actions, or by any kind of posturing you might do. It doesn't help you—in fact it probably hurts you.

3. **Focus on learning everything you can from anyone who's willing to talk to you**—yes, I mean the receptionist in the front and the janitor too! There's a checklist for your first 30 days at salesmanagersurvivalguide.com, but here's a starting point:
   - **Visit or talk to 30 customers, prospects, past customers.** You aren't there to sell them; you are there to ask them their views: What do they think about your company? What do they think about your competitors? What do they think about the sales people who support them? What about the other people from your company? What would they like to see different, why? Why do they, or why would they, do business with you? What company has the sales people they like the best and why? There are a lot of other questions. Go on many of these visits without the sales people so the customer can be open.
   - **Spend good quality time with each of your people.** Ride along with them, go on calls, listen as they are on the phone. Here you'll get to "visit" another 30 customers. Get to know your people as human beings. Get to know their aspirations and dreams. Learn how they do their jobs, ask about their frustrations. Get into the weeds with them, look at details—

how do they use the CRM system, how do they prepare for a call, how do they put together a proposal, how do they research, how do they prioritize and manage their time, what resources do they leverage to get things done, do they understand/own their metrics/numbers, do they have a growth or fixed mindset, what's their orientation to learning? *Don't critique or try to correct anything you see going on.* Ask lots of questions, listen, ask more questions, observe, ask more questions—and take plenty of notes! You'll have time to correct and improve them later, once you've figured out what you need to do.

- **Do similar things with the people and organizations in your company that support your team.** There may be a pre-sales group, there may be customer service, sales operations, sales enablement, marketing, lead gen, legal, finance, HR and others. Learn their roles, learn their opinions of the sales team, and their views of customers.
- **Get to know your peers in the organization.** Ask lots of questions, get to know your peers, get their perspective on how things work. Just listen, observe, take notes.
- **Do the same with your manager, and if possible with your manager's manager.** You may have to be a little more structured in your questioning and your use of their time, but spend time with them. Understand what's important to them. And while it's become unfashionable to ask this question, "What keeps them up at night?" (You'll want to make sure it isn't you or your team.) Understand their perspectives on your team, but take that as input to consider, not what must be done.
- **Find people who may know your people and organization but may not be directly involved with them.** Ask their opinions of the team and how things are done. Remember the lowest level people in the organization often have the most astute and pragmatic assessments of what's going on.
- **Spend time analyzing data**—look at what's available to you, understand it, analyze it, drill down to make sure you really get what's going on. Learn how good the data is, learn where you can get the data you need, understand the systems available to provide the data and analysis. Understand the key goals and metrics, look at performance trends. But do this in off hours and on the weekend. During the work week, spend all your time with people.

4. **Realize, as you do all of the above, you are killing a number of birds with one stone:**
   - **You are figuring out what's going on, how things get done, what people's attitudes and opinions are, and where the problems and challenges are.**
   - **You are starting to build relationships and trust with your people and across the organization.** When you figure out what you need to do, you have to have strong trusted relationships.
   - **You are starting to let people to get to know you—as a person.**

5. Take lots of notes. While I've said it before, it bears repeating. Your objective, right now, is not to solve problems and make changes, your objective is to collect as much information as you can. Resist the tendency to critique or challenge—even if someone is doing something wrong. Correcting their mistakes, for now, is not critical to figuring out what you need to do.

- **Every evening, sit down, review your notes.** Start developing some ideas or premises about issues or problems. These may form great questions you may ask in subsequent meetings. They may give you ideas about new things to look for.
- **You may want to go back to some people and "playback" what you have observed or heard.** Do it in neutral—don't express an opinion, positive or negative, just use the playback to validate what you heard or observed.

In most cases this will take you 30 days. Sometimes, you may be forced to do it faster—but, even with the direst of turnarounds I've done, this first 30 days of wandering around, learning, understanding, and building your network/support system is the most important thing to do to set up your future success.

Sometimes it may take more than 30 days—but that's probably rare, unless you have hundreds or thousands of people reporting to you. And if you do have a huge number of people reporting to you, you probably don't need to be reading this book: you probably have extensive management/leadership experience.

Earlier I mentioned "triage." Triaging is fixing some immediate problems. Usually the fix is for something simple or to deal with a single critical issue. For example, in emergency rooms, doctors want to stop the bleeding, get someone's heart beating, or get them breathing. They don't want to diagnose and fix the underlying problems, they just want to get the person to survive long enough to start the diagnostic process.

So in your first days as manager, you may have to triage a few things. Keep them to a minimum—otherwise you get consumed with Band-Aid fixes and never get around to doing what you were hired to do.

But sometimes, one of your people may be having difficulty getting something approved, or getting some support. You might help by making a phone call. Or they might need someone to help open doors with a customer, you might do that, but let them run the show and support them on what they need.

The biggest thing to remember about triage is it is very seductive. You are doing things,you are solving problems. It's what you have fun doing, you want to be doing more of it. Be very careful. Sometimes a paper cut won't cause the patient to bleed to death, so don't worry about it.

The problem with just triaging problems or issues is that you aren't addressing the root problems; you are just addressing the symptoms. If you want to drive sustained high performance in the organization, you have to identify and address the root problems.

Don't get caught up in the excitement and adrenalin rush that comes with "fixing" problems. Just do enough to eliminate the distractions so you can identify and focus on the real issues.

You now have some ideas for your first 30 days.

Since I've been using medical analogies, remember the first oath doctors take is to "**Do no harm**." It's good advice for sales managers as well.

How much and how well you learn in your first 30 days is key to your success. If you don't take the time to do this, you are putting your future—and that of your team at great risk.

In the next chapters, I'll focus on what you do next—how to handle your next 30-60 days, how to start taking action.

3

30-60 DAYS:
FIRST, YOUR PEOPLE

After 30 or so days in your new job, you're no longer a newbie, but you're still in your honeymoon period—at least for a while.

If you've done things right, you've spent your first 30 days learning obsessively. You've spent time with customers, your people, your peers, and anyone else willing to listen to your questions.

You've started getting some ideas about what's going on, what's wrong, what needs to be changed, what needs to be fixed, how to start moving the people on your team forward.

And this is the time to stop, at least briefly, and take a look at something all new managers experience…

"I gotta fix something!"

Yes, I'm repeating myself! I've mentioned this a couple of times already, but I know you are just itching to make your mark! It's natural; I felt the same way in my first management job.

Too often, when we move into a management job, particularly your first sales management job, we assume something's wrong, something needs to be fixed, big changes need to be made.

As a new front line manager, that's probably not true.

In the majority of cases, particularly if you are working for a larger company, you may be replacing a manager who has done a great job and gotten promoted.

You don't want to undo all the great stuff that manager has done, but you do want to build upon it, continue the great performance—and find ways to improve even further.

Even if the prior manager was not great, it is unlikely that your first management job will arrive in a time of crisis for the company, or even the sales department. The reality for most companies is that the hiring manager isn't going to hire a brand new, first time, front line sales manager to do a turnaround. They will want a grizzled veteran, not a newbie, however promising and enthusiastic you are.

This doesn't mean there aren't opportunities to make your mark, to continually drive improvement and build the capabilities of your team.

I just want to get past the feeling too many new managers have (particularly in the U.S.) that they have to make radical changes and "fix" something.

Some of you may be moving into a new job in a much smaller company—perhaps one that has never had a sales manager before, one where the owner/founder may have run sales, or where the previous manager may not have been the best.

In this case, there may need to be more "fixing." But again, speed is probably not critical. Take enough time to develop your priorities. If you don't, you may actually do the wrong things and have to spend time and resources unwinding the mistakes—and don't forget the hit on your reputation within the organization.

In short, be realistic and pragmatic. You may have inherited a wonderful organization, or an OK organization that has some problems. You are unlikely to be in a turnaround situation.

THE WORLD HASN'T STOPPED
JUST BECAUSE YOU ARE A NEW MANAGER

Let's continue this pause to look at another thing. By now, you are probably getting involved in doing things, not just learning. You're starting to hold pipeline reviews, deal reviews, territory reviews, and one-on-ones. You are, hopefully, spending time with your people calling on customers, helping them move deals forward.

Your management is asking for reports, maybe sucking you into a lot of the mind numbing internal stuff managers tend to do (try to minimize this—you can't avoid it).

Your key goal here is, "How do I help?" Remember help always comes in the form of coaching not telling. Help comes in the form of empowering your people to figure things out and perform, not doing it for them.

We'll spend a lot of time later on this stuff, but for now...

IT'S ALL ABOUT YOUR TEAM

So let's move on, now that I've gotten your heads into the right frame of mind. There are a lot of things you need to do, but your first, second, and third priorities are your people. So let's address them first.

You've spent your first 30 days doing a number of very important things:

- **Learning as much as you can from everyone.**

- **Getting to know your people, the business, and your customers.**

- **Getting to know how things get done in the organization.**

- **Building your own network and support system.**

- **Building relationships and trust with your people and others in the organization.**

By now, you probably have a lot more questions, but you are starting to have ideas.

Take some time, closet yourself away—maybe in the evening or on the weekend. Review your notes, start developing some ideas of things you think need to be done.

Look at each of your people.

- **What are their strengths, weaknesses?**

- **What are their skills and competencies? Are there any gaps?**

- **How well are they meeting their goals and objectives? Here you'll look at the metrics, pipelines, prospecting, and all sorts of normal sales stuff.**

- **How are they doing against their performance objectives? Hopefully they do have performance objectives in place?**

- **What are their goals and aspirations? Are they realistic?**

- **Look at their behavioral styles. This is critical; understanding their behavioral style is the key to connecting and communicating with them in the most impactful manner possible.**

- **How do they spend their time?**

- **How well are they using the systems, tools, programs, and processes in the organization?**

- **How do they interact with their peers in the organization? How do they interact with and engage their customers?**

- **How focused are they in creating value in every customer interaction?**

- **How do others interact with them? How do their customers interact with them?**

- **What do their customers think of them?**

- **What are their attitudes, behaviors?**

- **How much management time and attention do they want? How much do they need?**

With each of your people, take all that information, and ask yourself, "How can I help them perform at the top of their game?" "How can I help develop them to their full potential?"

Think about your top two priorities with each person.

It may not be big changes. It may be supporting the hell out of them, staying out of their way, but not ignoring them (I'll come back to this later.).

There may be some that need to be stirred up, refocused. They're B players, but they can perform better.

Then, inevitably you will have some challenges. Every organization has C players. These will be challenges; they are a time drain, but they can destroy you if you don't do anything about them.

Before you do anything, if you can, sit down with your manager. Use her as a sounding board for your impressions and ideas. Talk about your ideas for how you can best develop your team to their full potential.

Take your manager's input and counsel, but make sure you decide your priorities and plans.

Talk to each of the people, make them part of the process. After all, if they aren't engaged and owning what's going on, nothing you do will be effective.

Do this in an interactive, give and take. Share your observations—don't overwhelm them with everything—that's why focusing on your top 2 priorities is most important.

Be sure to listen to them, probe and drill down. Push back and challenge them a little. Make sure you agree on the top two areas you can be most helpful in performing at the top of their game.

You may come up with a specific action plan, or you may just have some focus areas, "I'd like to help you strengthen your deal strategies," "Let's focus on prioritizing your time to get more done," "You're struggling with prospecting, let's figure out how to be better at it."

YOU WILL GET RESISTANCE

Some of your people will resist; they'll say "Stay out of my way, leave me alone, I don't need a manager, particularly a newbie!"

This is unacceptable. Everyone needs a manager and coach. I've been Chairman and CEO of organizations, and in those roles I relied on my Board of Directors as my managers and coaches. Talk to any top level, high performing executive, they always have coaches and mentors (Well, then there's Donald Trump...)

The people who want you to stay out of their way are likely to fall into two categories:

- **Lone Wolves:** These may or may not be reasonable performers—probably not high performers. They typically work on their own, not with the team. They think they don't need help or support. They want to do their own thing. There may be some businesses where Lone Wolves can thrive and "fit in well." I've actually never seen one. Today's business and customers are too complicated; no one can do it alone. Everyone needs support from peers within the organization. Collaboration, within the organization, with partners, and with customers is the reality of today's and tomorrow's business.

    As a result, Lone Wolves don't do as well as they may think. In fact they are terribly destructive.

    I don't believe there is a case for a Lone Wolf in most organizations. I'll spend more time on Lone Wolves later, but for the time being, do what you can with them. To the degree they accept ideas and coaching, help them develop. But don't force yourself on them. (Remember, you are still pretty new in your job.)

- **Mediocre and Bad Performers:** The mediocre and bad performers may claim they don't need management help or support—when they are the ones who most need it. There are probably two reasons they will resist.
    - **They don't realize they are mediocre or bad performers,** and are blissfully ignorant.
    - **They are hiding out.** They probably know their performance isn't great and want to keep below the radar. No one gets to hide out!

    With mediocre and bad performers, you will probably have to be more directive in the improvement areas. You will want to be more explicit in the action plans and next steps. They need the teaching, discipline, focus and accountability.

    There are likely a lot of things they need and that you want to do, but stay focused on the top two priorities. No one, particularly mediocre and bad performers, can manage more than two major change areas at one time.

- **What About the Others?** The good news is your top performers—even some who aren't quite top performers, will welcome your support and coaching. They realize they need a sounding board to test ideas. They will leverage you as a resource to help get things done. They realize they need to continually learn and improve, so they will look for your coaching.

    With them, you need to be very collaborative. But it will be a pure joy. Hopefully, each of you takes advantage of your respective strengths, leveraging them, brainstorming and figuring out how they can accomplish more.

    That's what they want to do—in fact are driven to do—it's your job to help them do it.

I'll stop here; we'll dive into these issues later in the book as we look at coaching, leveraging business reviews, managing performance, development, and so on.

But remember, this is about day 31 in your job as manager. Make sure you have identified the top two areas you want to focus on with each person, gain their agreement and ownership, work with them in developing a plan, get started in executing it.

There are a lot of other areas you need to focus on as well, and we'll be addressing these in the next chapters.

4

30-60 DAYS:
YOUR COMPANY/SALES ORGANIZATION

If you've done things right, you've spent your first 30 days learning obsessively. You've spent time with customers, your people, your peers, and anyone else willing to listen to your questions.

Your highest priority is going the next step with your team. I covered some of the starting points in the previous chapter. .

Even as you're getting to know your team, you have to really understand your company and how the sales organization fits into the overall operation. It's critical that you get yourself wired into these, they are essential to getting things done.

Some of the things you need to make sure you both understand and know how to leverage are:

1. **Company strategy and how it translates into sales priorities.** Sales is responsible for executing the company's strategy. Are you targeting the right customers and markets? Are you focusing on the right products, solutions? Are you presenting the company the way the company wants to be perceived in the market place? How does your company create value for its targeted customers?

    If you don't really understand these and what drives the strategy and priorities, you can't make sure you are coaching your people to focus on the right things.

    There are some more subtle things that are a little more difficult: What's the culture in the company? How do they feel about themselves? How does that manifest itself? What are acceptable and unacceptable behaviors? (Not the big ones—but the smaller ones.)

One of the biggest mistakes I've made, is when I moved from one company to another at a high executive level. The culture of my previous company was very tough minded, assertive, and direct—bordering on appropriate confrontation. The culture of the new company was very collegial and collaborative. Until I realized the difference, I was inadvertently upsetting a number of people in the organization.

I wasn't aligned with the company culture. As a result, I wasn't getting the support I needed or getting things done as effectively as possible. Once I understood this, leveraging the company culture, my ability to get things done skyrocketed.

2. **How do things get done in the organization?** Every organization has its own way of getting things done. Some have very formalized processes and procedures, clearly defined roles and responsibilities, clearly defined reporting requirements. Others are less formal and others may be chaotic.

Unfortunately, there is probably no onboarding program to tell you this stuff, no guidebook, so you have to figure it out yourself. Some things to look at:

- **What is the reporting cadence in the organization?** For example, pipeline, forecasting, etc. How do they do these? What do they do with the information? What expectations does your manager have with respect to these?
- **How much individual autonomy and decision making capability do you have?** What do you have to get approval for? Do you merely have to inform management about what you are doing, or can you make the decisions yourself?
- **How are decisions made within the company?** Just as it's important for us to understand our customers' decision making processes, we need to understand that within our own company.
- **How do you get resources to help your people?** This is why you want to cast a wide net in getting to know people. Don't just stay within the sales organization; look at marketing, customer service, admin/operations, product management, finance, and others.
- **How do people communicate with each other?** Is it very formal? Are things in writing? Do they get things done in casual conversations?
- **What are their attitudes toward time?** It's interesting how much you can tell about an organization by their time integrity. I have a client that starts and ends every meeting right on time. People are always prepared; they are highly effective. This ripples through everything they do. On the other side, I have a number of clients that have very bad time integrity. I see them constantly missing deadlines, slipping, and far less effective than they should be. You should always be focused on the highest levels

of performance possible, you should seek to meet all your commitments on time, but you need to know what you are up against.

- **Naturally, if you are new to the company,** you want to understand the products, solutions, positioning, competition, markets, differentiation, value propositions, and so forth.

3. **Remember, there are "formal" and "informal" ways of getting things done.** You have to understand both. The formal is required to keep your job; the informal is critical because it's the way real work gets done. On the informal way of getting things done, it's important to understand the "grapevine" and how to tap into it. I'm not talking about gossiping—that's destructive. But there's an informal way people communicate within organizations. Understanding the grapevine and learning how to leverage it is important.

4. **Who's important to you in getting things done?** Clearly, your people and your boss are important to you. You need to make sure you are well aligned with both. But there are other people who may be very important. Some to consider:
   - **Your manager's assistant.** If your manager has an assistant, he is probably one of the most important people to get to know and to develop a close, genuine relationship with.
   - **Your manager's manager.** This may or may not be important. You don't want your manager to feel that you are going around her, but sometimes it's useful to have a relationship with your manager's manager.
   - **Your peers.** You have to work with them every day, it's critical to get to know them.
   - **Some others:**
     - **Human resources:** You will be involved in hiring, firing, and a number of personnel/people related things. Having someone in HR who can coach and advise you is very important.
     - **Financial/controller staff:** Money is important, how you get money, how investments are evaluated, pricing/discounting. They can also tell you about critical reporting requirements—all of those are important.
     - **Marketing:** Understanding the key marketing strategies and marketing programs, knowing how you can leverage them for your team will be important to getting things done.
     - **Product Management/Customer Service/Order Entry/Order Management.** For reasons similar to Marketing.
     - **Sales Operations/Enablement:** If you are in a larger organization, you can leverage many of your support programs and much of the sales analysis.
     - **Legal:** Yes, I can't believe I'm saying this, but legal may be important, particularly if you want to do "creative" deal making with your people and customers.

- **Partners:** If your company leverages partners as part of its go-to-customer strategies, you want to start working with those most important to you.

Now a note of caution! You can—and some organizations encourage this—end up spending all of your time with people in the company. There is no end to internal meetings you can attend. But for the most part, this isn't where you have the most impact on your people and in helping them get things done.

For new managers, these internal meetings often prove seductive. You participate in meetings with other managers, sometimes much more senior than you. You talk about strategies and all sorts of "interesting" internal topics. You can fool yourself into thinking this time is useful and what managers should be doing.

You'd be dead wrong. As a front line sales manager, the majority of your time must be spent working with your people, coaching them, developing them, helping them develop stronger deal strategies, making key customers calls with them.

Remember:

Make sure you're spending your time where it really counts!

In case you haven't gotten my message yet, this is **ALWAYS** with your people and their customers!

5

30-60 DAYS:
PROCESSES, SYSTEMS, TOOLS, AND METRICS

One of the final areas you need to make sure you understand, and are leveraging, is the range of your company's Processes, Systems/Tools, and Metrics. I'll go into a lot more detail on these in later sections of the book. Right now, I want to provide enough guidance for you to exploit them for yourself and your team.

SALES PROCESS

The cornerstone of sales performance is the Selling Process. It's critical that you understand the sales process, and that your people are leveraging the sales process in all their deal strategies and pipeline management.

Research shows those organizations using a sales process consistently outperform those who don't have a process or aren't using it.

If there is no sales process, then make sure you put one in place. If your people aren't using a sales process, then this should be one your highest priorities.

Without a sales process that your people are actively and consistently using, it is impossible for you to be able to make sure they are performing at their best possible levels. You will be unable to develop and manage a strong pipeline or commit to a forecast that has any level of integrity.

More than that, it will be literally impossible for you to do your job! Without a sales process that makes sure your people have things under control, you will have to inspect every deal. Let's look at how the numbers might work out.

Say you have 10 people reporting to you. Each has 20 active deals, but there's not activity on each of them each week, so let's say you have to check progress on "only" five deals per salesperson a week. That means, you are reviewing 50 deals a week. What does it take for to review a deal? 30 minutes? 60 minutes? Let's use 30 minutes, which means you will be spending *25 hours a week* just doing deal reviews!

If you really want to know what's going on, since they aren't using a sales process, you have to actually spend time reviewing every single deal and thing they are doing! That's 100 hours a week!

Something seems wrong about this doesn't it? But that's the way things work out. Without a sales process, the only way you have of knowing things are under control is to inspect/review every deal!

It simply impossible—don't forget you have a lot of other responsibilities to take care of at the same time.

The beauty of the sales process is that if people are using it, you only have to inspect a few deals to ensure they are doing things right. It they are, it's likely they are doing all the deals well. This frees you up to focus on the most important deals and helping your people figure out how to move those forward.

We'll spend more time on sales process later in the book. For now, bear in mind that sales process is probably the single most powerful element for driving sales effectiveness, both at an individual and organizational level.

The sales process is very closely tied to your Deal/Opportunity Management and Pipeline Management Processes.

SALES METHODOLOGY

Your company may have a sales methodology (Challenger, Solution Selling, or any of the dozens of methodologies on the market) it has committed to. You'll want to know the methodology your company has selected; make sure you are knowledgeable in the methodology, and leverage it in coaching and training with your people. The sales methodology needs to complement your sales process, not displace it!

OTHER PROCESSES

There are a lot of other business processes you have to make sure you understand and can leverage effectively. You company may have:

- **Quoting/Pricing reviews:** Usually these are processes or reviews you go through to take special pricing actions or even to quote a piece of business.

- **Proposal/RFPs:** How does your company manage these?

- **Forecasting:** How do we set the expectations on business volumes?

- **Lead management:** There is probably a lot of talk about the "L's," MQLs, SQLs, but this is probably an important process for you and your sales people.

- **Contract/legal review:** Again, if you need to do something out of the ordinary, you may have certain processes required to get approval.

- **Customer service/delivery:** If you have products or services that require implementation and ongoing support, you'll want to make sure you understand how those work.

- **Order management:** There may be special processes, procedures for accepting and processing orders.

- **Problem management/resolution:** What happens when customers have problems? What's the problem management and resolution process at your company?

These are probably the things that impact you and your people every day, but there are others, like hiring/firing and performance management, that impact your work and how you get things done.

There can be any number of processes and procedures in your organization. It is critical that you deeply understand them because you are going to have to help your people navigate them as efficiently as possible.

SYSTEMS AND TOOLS

As with processes, there are undoubtedly a lot of systems oriented to improve your productivity or critical to coordinating activities across the organization. There are probably some that seem to be more oriented to "Sales Prevention."

You have to understand and master these systems for a couple of reasons.

First, you need to know how you can leverage these systems to help you do your job more effectively and efficiently.

Second, you need to understand how your sales people should be leveraging the systems to increase their own effectiveness and efficiency. Your job will be coaching them on how to leverage these systems for greatest impact.

One of the most critical systems is CRM. I can't imagine any high performance salesperson not leveraging CRM systems to the most effective level possible. The problem is, most of the time, CRM systems are implemented more as a management tool than as a personal sales productivity tool.

Pay attention to how your people are using CRM as a tool to improve their personal effectiveness and efficiency.

Now that you are a manager, the CRM system is your most powerful tool. Leveraging CRM will help you understand what's going in your team. Through CRM you can track deals, pipelines and other items. You can leverage the system to see how people are meeting their commitments, how they are spending their time.

Take the time to understand how you can leverage the CRM system to help you manage your time and your team most effectively. Develop some standard reports that enable you to quickly get snapshots of activities—pipeline health, critical deal activity, stalled deals, prospecting activities, and other information that will help you better manage your team and its productivity.

When you are meeting with your people, doing deal, pipeline, account, territory, or call reviews, use the CRM system. Your example will get your people using the system more themselves, plus it will eliminate a whole bunch of redundant work.

Another critical set of systems and tools are the learning/training systems. You will constantly want to develop the skills and capabilities of the people on your team, as well as for yourself. Many companies have rich eLearning systems or training programs/resources available in eLearning, or classroom based training. These will be critical to understand and leverage as a coach. Make sure you understand what's available, or how you can get other types of training.

There are, undoubtedly a lot of other systems and tools you will have to become familiar with. You may have marketing automation, lead gen, content management platforms, or other enablement platforms. You may have proposal generation/pricing tools, forecasting, budget reporting and management tools, performance management, order entry/management, customer service, and others.

Learn these tools. Look at them from two points of view: How do you leverage them for your own personal effectiveness and productivity? How can your people leverage them to improve their effectiveness and productivity? As you figure this out, share this knowledge with your team, help them understand which tools they should leverage and how to do it most effectively.

METRICS

Every sales organization seems to be run with endless metrics and reporting. By this time you should understand the key metrics and associated goals by which your performance will be evaluated. You should understand the key metrics and goals by which you will measure and evaluate your people.

Make sure you understand the most important metrics; they probably aren't what you think. When I pose the question to sales people and managers, usually the answer is, Quota Performance—sales, revenue, orders, or margin. While that's really important, and, possibly one which drives your performance evaluation and bonuses, it's not terribly helpful. Quota performance, sales/revenue/orders are all trailing metrics. You know what you've achieved after the fact.

It's not too useful to know after the fact that you really missed your goals. You can't do a hell of a lot about it. They are not too useful in diagnosing why your people may not be making their numbers.

The most important metrics for you and your team are the leading metrics. It's understanding: Are you doing enough (quantity) of the right things (quality) to achieve the outcomes and goals you have (quota performance).

Leading metrics can be a variety of things—pipeline metrics are very important. Are your people working enough deals? Do they have good flow or velocity to make your numbers? Prospecting metrics are another great leading metric. Are your people prospecting enough people to find enough deals to fill their pipelines or funnels? There may be other critical activity metrics that help you understand whether your people are on track to making their numbers.

As an example, I have only two sets of sales metrics I track myself and my people on: The number of first customer "meetings" (virtually all are phone calls) they make each week and their pipeline health. I know if their performance is matching the goals in each area, they will have a high probability of making their numbers.

Beyond having good leading metrics, having the right number of metrics is very important. Here's where too many sales organizations go wrong: They have so many metrics the sales people are confused. They don't know what's important, which they should focus on. Usually, they give up, doing what they need to do to get by, or just ignoring the metrics and goals.

Great managers keep it simple. They know the critical few leading metrics that enable their people and them to know whether they are on target to making their numbers. In our company's case, it's only two fundamental metrics.

With your team, figure out the metrics most important to them—the ones that tell them whether they are on track or not. Generally, these will be the most important to you, or at least the roll up of these metrics.

There may be some that are important to your manager. Make sure you understand and pay attention to these.

Metrics are important, but they are only useful if you have chosen the few most critical to understanding the state of your business and you've established the right goals for each metric.

SOME FINAL THOUGHTS

Make sure you understand the processes, systems, tools, and metrics critical to your organization and your people. It's a major part of how things get done in your organization and with your customers.

Make sure you understand how both you and your team can exploit them to the greatest benefit. Effectively used, they don't create more work; they create *focus*, which lets you and your team get more work done, more effectively and efficiently.

6

WARNING!
DO YOU ALSO HAVE A PERSONAL TERRITORY?

In smaller organizations, managers sometimes have both a people management responsibility and their own personal sales territory.

I'd be less than honest with you if I didn't say that this is too often a "no-win" situation.

Think about it.

To be a really high performing salesperson, you have to commit 200% of your time, energy, thinking, and focus to selling. Likewise, to be a great manager and leader, you have to commit yourself fully to coaching and developing your people, getting things done through them.

So as a manager with your own sales territory, you are caught in an untenable position, struggling to do the right things, but being pulled in opposite directions.

Do everything you can to avoid this. If you have to spread your quota across the rest of the team, and can do so without killing them, that would be great. If you can afford to hire an additional salesperson, perhaps committing to a slightly higher quota, that is also a great solution.

If, however, you find yourself caught in the middle, do everything you can to structure your responsibilities in a way that gives you and your people a chance for success.

Here are a few ideas:

1. **Make sure the team you manage is small.** The average span of control for front line sales managers is 8-12 people. If you have to carry your own quota, keep the team small—no more than 4-5, plus yourself. Any larger and you run the risk of not being able to spend enough time with your people, or not spending the time you need in your own personal territory.

2. **Keep your own personal territory quota much smaller than your people's quotas.** Again, it takes full time focus for your people to achieve their quotas. There's nothing magic about the time required to be successful. So if you are carrying a "full territory quota," and trying to manage both a team and achieving your quota, one thing is for certain: You will fail at both, miserably.

   Make sure your personal territory quota is much lower than the quotas your people carry. Ideally, it is less than half of what they carry. Anything more, is simply unrealistic.

3. **Make sure you block your calendar and stick to it rigorously, no exceptions, under any circumstance!** Block time that is dedicated to working with your people. Make sure it is at least 50% of your time. Block time that you are using to manage your own personal territory, make sure it is less than 50% of your time.

   Keep both absolutely sacred. The more you start "borrowing time" you will spend in managing your people to chase your own deals, the more your people will struggle.

5. **As the going gets tough, default to managing your people.** You will face huge conflicts in managing your own time in the territory and spending the right amount of time with your people. At some point, things will break down, and you will be overwhelmed trying to do both.

   At this point, just to survive, you have to start sacrificing something. The only right choice is sacrificing the time you spend in your territory. I'm not offering this guidance to be "people sensitive," though we should be. It's based purely on a pragmatic approach to achieving your goals.

   If you stop spending time with your people, they will start stumbling and missing their goals. In most cases, the "math" of this challenge always says your exposure in not having your people meet their goals is far greater (number wise) than you not meeting your personal goals.

   Try running the numbers in your head. Let's say you have 4 people, each with a $2M quota and you have a $1M quota. Imagine they hit some rough spots, their performance isn't where it should be. Let's say, each of them are struggling to hit 75% of their goal, or $1.5M. Across four people, that's a $2M exposure, compared to your own territory which is a $1M exposure.

   In the real world, the math never works out that cleanly, so it's just an example to get you to start thinking where you have the greatest leverage in driving the total performance of your team. In virtually every case the answer is always working with your team.

5. **Finally, do everything you can to justify hiring another salesperson, so that you can spend full time doing your job**—leading your people and helping them achieve the highest levels of performance.

I've never seen a manager or a business succeed, over a long period of time, with the split responsibility. It's fundamentally untenable, so do everything you can do to avoid it in the first place. If you find yourself in this position, do everything you can do to get yourself into a position where you don't have to carry a personal quota or territory.

This may mean having some very direct conversations with your manager, but remember you both have a shared interest—making sure your team achieves its goals!

7

60-90 DAYS:
THE HONEYMOON IS OVER.
WHAT HAVE YOU DONE FOR ME LATELY?

You're now 60-90 days into your new job as front line sales manager. No matter how you feel, you are no longer a newbie. The honeymoon is over, and you will be expected to be performing as though you've been in the job all your life.

You've applied yourself and used the first 30-60-90 days well. You've learned about your people, your organization, your peers, your manager's expectations, your customers, and how things get done.

You've formulated some ideas about what you need to be doing, where you should be spending your time, things you may need to change, and actions you should be taking. Inevitably, you've already started doing some things and working with your people.

During the process, hopefully, your people and the organization have gotten to know you.

By now, at least two "constituencies" are asking the same question, "What have you done for me lately?"

The two constituencies that are definitely raising the question are your manager and each member of your team. Some of your peers and support organizations may also be beginning to think about asking the question.

If you've been patient and learning, you are probably itching to make your own imprint on the job and organization.

You need to start setting your agenda, priorities, and calendar. You have to establish a regular cadence of critical activities.

Already, you may be getting pulled in a lot of directions and feel your time isn't your own. Before things spin too far out of control, you need to start locking things down.

YOUR SINGLE HIGHEST PRIORITY, 50% OF YOUR TIME

Despite what anyone might tell you, including your manager, your single highest priority is your people. If you're not getting them to perform at the highest levels possible, it will be impossible to achieve your goals (which are probably a roll up of theirs.)

Because of this, your time allocation has to be biased to your team. You need to be spending an absolute minimum of 50% of your time with your people. This includes going out into the field, visiting customers. If you manage inside sales, there is a functional equivalent of field work. You need to see how your people actually work, you need to help them move deals forward, work on tough issues, make sure they have the right pipeline and other activities.

Spend time in high impact reviews, where you both learn what's going on (so you can inform your own manager that you have things under control,) but most importantly so you can coach and develop your people.

You need to keep your hand on the pulse of what's going on with customers. Scheduling travel time and calls with your people helps you achieve this goal at the same time you're working with a team member.

Find the toughest situations or deals, help your people in strategizing and dealing with them. Roll your sleeves up and work on the most difficult stuff; this is where you create the greatest value.

Again, resist the temptation to jump in and do the work for them, but instead leverage this time to help them learn, figure things out, and develop their own skills and capabilities. If your people are performing at the highest level, your job becomes incredibly easy and a hell of a lot of fun!

If you spend a minimum of 50% of your time with your people, you will avoid the biggest danger facing managers: becoming a desk jockey or irrelevant.

YOUR JOB IS NOT TO HIDE BEHIND REPORTS AND A DESK

Computers and systems give you all the reports you need. There are tremendous analytical tools to help you analyze these reports. You shouldn't have any reason to be chained to your desk.

Yes, you will have to do some analysis, sitting and figuring things out, but guess when you do this—in the evenings, at night, and on the weekends. During the business day, your job is either to be with your people or getting things done for them.

As a side note, I hope you didn't think being a sales manager is a 40 hour a week job! And if you did, I'm sure you learned the truth during your first weeks on the job.

THE NEXT 25% OF YOUR TIME

The next 25% of your time will be spent getting things done for your people, promoting their accomplishments, removing barriers, and protecting them.

In terms of getting things done for your people, this may involve obtaining support, gathering critical information, helping them get approvals or resources. Their time is best spent in the field.

As you set about these tasks, you'll immediately see why I suggested you wander around the organization to figure out how to get things done.

If your people are spending their time correctly, they aren't spending much of it "inside" the organization. As a result, people within the organization don't know them or what they are doing. Part of your job is promoting your team internally, making sure key people know who they are, what they're doing, and how they can best help and support your team.

One of the biggest jobs you have is to protect your people. A lot of the time this involves protecting your people from other well-intended people who are just doing their jobs. There are endless numbers of people—marketers, product managers, designers, and others trying to better understand customers, what makes them tick, what they need, and so forth. All these people are well-intended and just doing their jobs. But they can, inadvertently become huge time drains on your people.

I worked with a very large (Fortune 100) organization. I started noticing the sales people weren't spending as much time in the field with customers as they should. We measured their field time. They were only spending 17% of their time (across approximately 2500 sales people,) on sales-related activities (preparing/researching, making customer calls/meetings, following up on those meetings.)

When we looked at what was keeping the sales team from working with customers, we discovered the cause was a lot of well-intended people doing their jobs. Marketing people reviewing programs, content, strategies, and asking for sales feedback. Product Managers (147 product lines with many product managers in each product line,) asking for customer information and feedback. Customer service people looking to address customer experience issues….and the list went on.

Each of these people was trying to be helpful. Each was just trying to do their job, but their efforts were having an adverse impact on the sales people.

This is some of what you have to protect your people from. There are a lot of instances when people will be absolutely insensitive to how your people spend their time.can

There's one other area you've got to protect your people from. When things get tough, the very first finger-pointing is always aimed toward sales. After all, sales is responsible for producing revenue, and if sufficient revenue isn't being produced, the decline must be a sales problem.

Sometimes it is. And if that's the case, own up to it and fix it—that's your job.

But sometimes it's not. And most of the time things are rarely so simple.

Don't make excuses, but never let your team take the blame for things they aren't responsible for, or that are completely out of their control.

THE NEXT 25% OF YOUR TIME

This quarter of your time is for yourself and your manager. Hopefully, your manager isn't a micromanager, and hopefully she doesn't require a lot of your time. But it's your job to keep your manager informed about what's going on.

If there are problems, be straightforward about them. Ask for help where you need it. Make sure your manager knows what you are doing to address the issues, what your action plan is, and keep her informed.

Your manager will need you to do things for her. They may be matters involving your team, or they may be other issues or needs within the organization. Inevitably, there are a lot of other projects and meetings you need to be involved in. Protect yourself, you can spend 150% of your time in these meetings—accomplishing very little for your people and yourself.

Part of the time spent with your manager should involve her coaching you. Don't cheat yourself of this opportunity, and make sure she knows you expect her to be coaching you. After all, you want to be able to perform at the top of your abilities, and you need your manager's coaching and developing you to do this.

Set aside regular time to meet with your manager to review what's happening. Both of you should try to keep this meeting sacred and never move it. The right timing will vary. For some people/organizations, such a meeting may take place once a week. For others, once every two weeks. Don't let the time period between two meetings be too long. You never want to be "out of sight, out of mind."

Some of this 25% of your time is set aside for you to think. Sales professionals tend to be very action oriented: we tend to be Ready, Fire, Aim (then fix) types of people. Understanding this about ourselves and our nature, it's critical we schedule a pretty good amount of think time.

This is time to reflect on what's going on, to think of what's working, what's not. Time to try to sort through things, figuring out if you are focusing on the right issues and challenges. Balance your think time between tactical—what we should be doing right now, what we should be doing in three, six, nine, twelve months. Keep a notebook for your ideas. Where some items need action, take care of them.

THE FIFTH 25% OF YOUR TIME

Yes, I know you are thinking, "We've already gone through the whole 100% of my time and you are talking about another 25%!!!"

I told you this isn't a 40 hour a week job!

In reality, I don't know what percent of your time it is. I hope it's the lowest percent of your time, and it should certainly be your lowest priority.

Every management job has a certain amount of administrivia. You just can't avoid it. There are reports, forms, other things you have to do. If you're like most sales managers, you hate them and want to minimize them. If you revel in them and use them to hide out, you end up being a desk jockey, not a manager.

As much as I may trivialize these administrative responsibilities, they are critical to do. Just get them done quickly and get them off your plate.

There's a reason I put this after allocating 100% of your time. Do this after business hours! Do this in the early mornings, evenings, on weekends. Viciously protect your time during the business day to work with your people.

THE FINAL 25% OF YOUR TIME

By now you are getting really pissed off with me! I have the audacity to schedule 150% of your time. Suck it up; you have to do what it takes! If you want to punch a clock for a 40-hour week, sales management isn't for you.

Other than the 50% of your time you spend with your people, this is probably the second most important time block. It's time to think and reflect. If you look at the very best leaders, they schedule huge blocks of time to think and reflect.

It's hugely valuable to sit down and consider how you are spending your time, what you are doing, the impact you are having. Are you focusing on the urgent—ignoring the critically important? Are you learning and developing? Are your people learning and developing? What are you and they doing well? Where can you improve? What should you be doing that you aren't doing? What are you doing that you should be stopping? Are there changes happening with your customers and competition that impact your success in selling?

What books, blogs, journals are you reading? How are you investing in developing your own skills and capabilities?

Too many managers never take the time to do this. They measure their worth by their activities, how filled their calendars are, and how many balls they are juggling. In the end, these managers end up being the least effective.

HAVE YOU KEPT TRACK OF THE MATH?

Yeah, I know, you think I haven't been keeping track of the math, but I have (remember I'm an engineer/physicist). I've had the audacity to schedule 150% of your time—that' roughly 60 hours. Suck it up, that's probably realistic.

But let's get to my real point, I said 50% of your time needs to be spent working with your people—think about it, run the numbers again. This means you need to be spending at least 30 hours a week working side by side with your people! Yes, those of you who are math majors will say I'm playing games with numbers, and I am.

I just can't overemphasize where the real leverage is in how you spend your time. It's always with your people!

OTHER ISSUES YOU WILL FACE
NOW THAT YOU ARE ESTABLISHED IN YOUR JOB

THE SEDUCTION

Often people who are non-managers or brand new managers are curious about the "Management Meetings." You know what I'm talking about, those are meetings that managers seem to gather together for, spend endless hours around a conference table, looking at presentation after presentation, talking about "important," or "strategic" things, and consuming endless quantities of coffee and Danish.

Sometimes, these meetings cross all sorts of functions in the company, people high up the food chain participate, and consultants come in to lead "thoughtful" discussions.

As a new manager, you will start participating in many of these meetings. In some of them, really interesting stuff goes on. These meetings are fun. You may get to rub shoulders with the top execs of the company and talk about all sorts of wonderful things.

The meeting cycle can be very seductive. Sometimes, you think, "This is where the really cool stuff gets talked about," or "This is where the cool kids hang out."

In some companies, these meetings become all-consuming. So much so, that when you look at your time you find yourself spending the majority of it in meetings getting very little accomplished.

Guess what's happening to your team. You've become an absentee manager! You aren't doing your job. Your team is justifiably upset, asking, "What have you done for me lately."

Some of these meetings are valuable, some you can't avoid, but most aren't necessary and take you away from where you really need to be spending your time.

AVOID KNEE JERKS

Unless, you are in the gym exercising, avoid knee jerk reactions. This sort of reaction is usually wrong, and the amount of time it takes to unwind a bad decision is always at least several times more than it took for you to make the bad decision in the first place.

By our nature, we tend to be interrupt-driven and reaction oriented. We tend to be people of action. We should be doing Ready, Aim, Fire, but for most us it is Ready, Fire, Aim that prevails. We take the action and then clean up the mess.

There is nothing in selling or sales management that ever requires a knee jerk reaction. There is *always* time to think, consider, evaluate—not endlessly, but appropriately.

The biggest red flag, is someone saying, "It's critical to do something NOW."

The more urgent they make their statement, the more confident you can be about how truly un-urgent it is.

Recently, I had the experience of being in an emergency room, not by choice. I was frustrated by the methodical, seemingly slow process. I was sitting there with blood gushing out of my arm, my ear hanging, not completely connected. I wanted to shout, "Do Something!"

But the ER team kept to their pace. And that pace wasn't slow: it was disciplined, methodical.

I watched others, some in greater need than me, come into the emergency room. The ER team acted in a disciplined, methodical manner, at the appropriate speed.

If doctors, nurses and medical technicians know this is the right thing to do in emergencies, when lives may hang in the balance, then maybe there's something we can learn from them.

STAY THE COURSE

This is actually related to the previous topic. Too often, I see management adopting a *strategy or program du jour* approach. They constantly shift priorities and strategies. This is absolutely debilitating to the organization.

First, in constantly shifting, you never give an approach enough time for you to see whether it's working or not. You never have the chance to fine tune a strategy for better results. You never learn, so you forego any opportunity to improve.

Second, you lose time, money, opportunity. It costs you time and money to develop and roll out a program. Then there's the training, coaching and ramp-time for sales people. They are never successful initially, so it takes time to dial it in and produce results on a predictable basis. By cutting the process short, all we've done is spend a lot of time and money. We've lost opportunity because we have diverted attention from something else the people could have been doing which would actually produce results.

Third, you confuse the sales people; they check out. If programs and priorities are constantly changing, your sales people get confused. They don't know what they should be doing or where they should be spending their time. Ultimately, they stop paying attention. They know it's senseless to invest in learning and executing a specific program, because they know the program won't last. So they just don't do it. They know they won't get into trouble, because they know that tomorrow will bring something different for them to ignore.

Fourth, the sales people lose confidence in you: They know you don't know what you are doing. And they're right, if you are constantly changing, you *don't* know what you are doing. People want to be led. They want leaders who are certain of what needs to be done, who have the courage to stick to something, learning, tuning, and improving.

I'm not advocating sticking to something that just isn't going to work. But you have to give your program a chance, and while you're giving it that chance, you have to learn, adjust, tune. If after a fair chance and doing the appropriate things to make it work, then by all means, stop it.

Until then, don't stop.

Not that you're the kind of person who *would* stop. Great managers are great students, interested in learning, growing, adjusting, and adapting.

Your first 90 days are done, and you're no longer a Newbie. Congratulations on a great start! You probably won't hear it from anyone else, but if you've paid attention, you've made a great start.

I'm proud of you!

8

LEADING YOUR FORMER PEERS

If you were promoted into your sales management role, you may now have your former peers and buddies reporting to you.

This creates an awkward position for everyone. You used to get together and gripe about management (I think it's sometimes the moral obligation of sales people to do this—more out of form than reason.) Now *you* are the man/woman! You're the target.

I'm only partly serious. The professional relationship changes; you are no longer a peer, you are responsible for them and their performance. Some of them will try to take advantage of it, trading on the relationship to get what they want. Some people will feel distanced because of the new role.

Whatever the circumstances, things have changed. It's happened a number of times in my career, I've ended up leading teams of people who were my peers, many were (and still are) very close friends.

I've always favored talking it out with people. Some of them won't know how to deal with the new relationship.

Confront it head on, as much as you can, separating the personal friendship from the business relationship. Make sure you address these matters directly with your people. The situation isn't that uncommon: I've had great personal friendships with people much higher than me in the organization, as well as friendships with people several levels below me. There is no reason you can't maintain those close friendships.

Talk about your professional relationship. You are in a new role; you are responsible for coaching and developing them. Your job is to help them achieve the highest levels of performance. Make sure everyone is clear about your new role, your responsibilities, and the new working relationship.

Things about your professional relationship will change. You now have to set the example, you have to be a role model. Some of the things you and your former peers used to do may no longer be appropriate now. There are things you will learn in your role as manager that may not be appropriate to share with your former buddies.

There may be times when there is tension in your relationship. If one of your former peers is struggling, you will be trying to help them, but you may have to have tough conversations. As with conversations with any of your people, it's important to separate the person from the performance.

Nothing we ever do as leaders should be directed at the person, who sales people are as human beings. The only thing we can and should focus on is their performance in the job.

With friends and former peers, you will have to be careful that you separate the personal relationship from the business relationship. Set the example yourself, most of your former peers will "get it" and understand.

One big challenge I faced in my career was terminating a very close friend. He was a great person and could be a great contributor. It was really my fault for putting him in a job he wasn't qualified to do. As you would expect, despite both of us trying really hard, it didn't work out. I ultimately terminated him.

He was disappointed, but understood. He knew he wasn't performing in the job and knew he deserved to be terminated. The meeting was actually pretty easy.

After the meeting, I focused on doing everything I could to help my very good friend find the right job. He's gone on to great success and is currently CEO of a very large company. We remained very close friends during and after that process.

Not everyone has that level or maturity—but you have to. You may find some of your former peers aren't able to separate the personal and professional relationships—it's their problem, not yours.

Some people will try to trade on that relationship; you can't permit that to happen. If you do, you aren't fulfilling your responsibilities as a leader/manager. You might also think, are the people that try to exploit relationships really your friends?

You still have your responsibility as manager. You have to do your job, despite the relationships with people in your organization. If you aren't, you become a problem your manager has to solve. I think you can guess the outcome.

Be straight with all your people. Make sure they understand your new role and the shifts in your professional relationships. If they are any good, they will understand and appreciate what you are doing.

MANAGING PEOPLE OLDER THAN YOU

Through most of my career, I was always one of the youngest people in the role I had. In my first job, I was one of the younger sales people in a team of very seasoned sales professionals. In my first management job, I managed a very seasoned team of specialists. I was five years younger than the youngest, and one was almost old enough to be my father.

I was very worried stepping into that job. Would they respect me? They had many more years of experience than I. How would I lead them?

It took me a little time to gain my confidence. But slowly, I realized a few things. First, management selected me as the leader of this team. They had great confidence I could do the job, which is why they chose me and not one of the more "seasoned" people. So I earned my job and the right to be their manager.

Second, my job wasn't to do their jobs. They were much more senior, much more experienced. They could do their jobs better than I could. But that wasn't my job. My job was to develop each of them to achieve the highest levels of performance possible. And I was in the job because I could do that better than they or any other candidates considered.

The thing I learned in that, and subsequent roles, was I was in the role because I was the best person for that job. No one in my organization could do the job better. At the same time, you always have to earn the respect of all your people—regardless of their age.

You do this by coaching and developing them.

You do this by helping them achieve the highest levels of performance possible.

You do this by challenging them, getting them to do more than they thought they could do.

You do this by recognizing them when they have done something outstanding.

You do this by caring about them!

PART TWO

COACHING IS YOUR JOB

9

WHAT'S ALL THIS TALK ABOUT COACHING? I'M A MANAGER!!

If I haven't made it clear yet, by the time you have finished this book, you will learn coaching is the highest leverage activity a manager can take to drive the performance of his people.

In the very first chapter, you learned your job was to get things done through your people. Without that, it is absolutely impossible for you to deliver the results you are expected to deliver—you can't do it by yourself. We went through the math: this is an equation that doesn't close.

So if that's your job, how do you do it? The major part of the answer is that you do it by *coaching* your people.

But we toss around the term coaching very lightly, as if everyone understands what it is.

- **Coaching is a way we develop people's skills and capabilities to drive their performance in their current job.**

- **Coaching is also a very powerful method for addressing behavioral and attitudinal issues that impact their ability to perform in their job.**

- **The most effective coaching takes the form of helping your people think, not solving their problems for them.**

It's also very important to address one thing that coaching isn't.

Coaching isn't about fixing people!

We aren't shrinks; we don't have the training or skills to do that. We are solely focused on maximizing our people's performance in the job.

I've been very specific here, focusing on performance in the current job. Other people may define coaching a little more broadly, looking at preparing people for future roles in the company. We will talk about this later, but I call that approach development planning. This is important for us to do, but I've always thought it useful and least confusing to separate the issues, focusing coaching on maximizing performance in the current job.

Coaching is not the same as training, although they are perfect complements, as I'll show later in this section.

SOME BACKGROUND DATA

If coaching is the highest leverage activity sales managers have in driving the performance of their team, why do we spend so much time talking about it? In other words, if it's so important and so central to your job, haven't you heard all of this before being given the position? Or even, why did your manager never do this?

The brutal fact is coaching isn't done.

Several years ago, in a study of several hundred sales managers, we asked the question, "How frequently do you coach each person on your team?" We were shocked, when **over 60% of the participants responded "Once a quarter or less."**

As we looked more deeply at coaching, we discovered:

- **Many managers don't know coaching is a key responsibility. Their managers never told them this explicitly.**

- **Most managers don't know how to coach. They've never had any formal training in coaching.**

- **Many are uncomfortable with coaching, thinking it is either too "touchy-feely," or "confrontational."**

- **Many confuse coaching with the performance plan review.**

- **Most managers are not well coached by their own managers.**

There are books dedicated to coaching, so I won't be providing a comprehensive discussion, but I hope to give you a great start in understanding coaching, how to be effective in coaching, and how to integrate coaching into your daily business routines.

As you have already seen, the coaching theme is interwoven through this entire book. So we will keep coming back to it in other sections and chapters. But this section and the following chapters are intended to provide a strong base for the rest of the book.

If you want to be a leader—not just a manager or an administrator—coaching is the single most important skill for your future.

10

COACHING AND BEING COACHED

Coaching is one of the highest leverage activities a manager or leader can perform. Developing the capabilities of people to perform at the highest levels possible, to execute the strategies and priorities of the organization, is the core of any manager's job.

Being coachable is one of the most important characteristics of any individual seeking to be a high performer. Actively seeking coaching, actively engaging with you, as their manager, will be critical to the performance and development of each person on your team.

It takes two to tangle. Active engagement of both you as the coach and the salesperson as the "coachee" is critical. Without that engagement on both parts, you might as well not do it.

Coaching is a two-way exchange, it is a dialogue, a conversation focused on shared discovery and learning. Each person must take responsibility for challenging and engaging the other.

If a salesperson expects to be told what to do and how to do it, the coaching will have little sustainable impact. They will constantly require too much attention and direction. If the coach enters the dialogue expecting to tell people what to do and how to do it, the impact will not be sustainable.

At its core, coaching is about both the coach and the person being coached thinking about what's being done, challenging what's being done, questioning things and each other. At the end, each person has discovered something new, learned, and has a clear course of action.

Effective coaching requires both the coach and the person being coached to be thoughtful. I don't mean "politeness," (though that's important). Rather, both parties need to be engaged in *thinking*. Effective coaching may require both the coach and the person being coached to challenge their own positions, what they think, their preconceived notions, their biases, their previous experiences. It may require each person to change their positions or their points of view.

> *As much as coaching is viewed as a developmental or learning activity for the person being coached, it is also a developmental and learning activity for you, the coach.*

In each session, effective coaches realize that they are learning as much as the person they are coaching. As coaches, we are constantly learning how to listen better, how to probe for greater and deeper understanding, how to engage, how to appreciate a different point of view, how to give up some of our own biases or preconceived notions, how to improve our abilities to help people learn and grow.

As coaches, if we aren't prepared to listen, learn, and develop ourselves, we will never be as effective as we might be.

Coaching and being coached is an ongoing process of discovery—self-discovery on the parts of the coach and the person being coached. Learning from each other, working together to develop ideas and approaches we might not have developed individually. Does this happen in every coaching session? Probably not, but we should always challenge ourselves to learn and discover in each session.

Coaching and being coached is a journey for both parties. We start at a point, marking different events as opportunities or milestones in the journey we are taking together. These events happen every day—after a sales call, in a pipeline review, as a part of a meeting.

> *Coaching is an ongoing process, not an event.*

Between the coach and the person being coached, there is a history or experiences that each builds upon—or, when done improperly, is torn down. Trust is at the core of coaching. We have to trust each other and what we are achieving together.

> *Coaching is a contact sport! You can't fake it.*

11

COACHING AND TRAINING: WHAT'S THE DIFFERENCE?

Training is a key part of any person's development. We need training to develop new skills, to acquire knowledge, and to build our capabilities. Whether it's on new products, new sales skills, or new tools, training is a vital part of everyone's development (sales professionals and managers alike.)

But, training is not a substitute for coaching. I often encounter managers who "don't have the time to coach." Actually, I think the reality is they don't *want* to coach. Instead of coaching, this variety of manager is glad to invest in training, thinking that a few hours or days of training will correct all bad behaviors and skills deficiencies.

In some sense, they are trying to delegate their responsibility to a trainer. A trainer isn't a manager. Trainers don't see people in action in the real world. Trainers focus on specific skills development, not on everything a person needs to do to maximize performance.

Let's take an easy example. All of us make sales calls. Improving our abilities to plan and execute calls, improving the results we get from each call, and reducing the number of calls to close are all critical to improving sales performance. We can take people through training programs on how to plan and execute high impact sales calls. Many of these training programs offer great role-plays, tools and materials the salesperson can use to improve their impact in each call.

But training isn't a substitute for talking to Bill about that last sales call we went on together. Training can't pose questions like: "Did you accomplish everything you planned to achieve?" "Could you have accomplished more?" "What would you have done differently that might have improved the impact of the call?..." and many other questions a manager might ask in coaching the call. Training won't provide that one on one, interactive development that happens between Bill and you.

Coaching is about personal and professional development, but real coaching deals with real situations and behaviors, things that are actually happening, in real time. Training focuses on simulations, coaching lives in the real world.

Training develops the same skills and capabilities for everyone on the team. But each person is different and the circumstances they face every day vary. Coaching is one on one, addressing the specific issues confronting each person. Finally, coaching deals with the observable, with the behaviors and attitudes displayed by the person you're coaching.

Training can never (and should never be expected to,) achieve this.

Training focuses on simulations. Coaching lives in the real world with real situations.

Training and coaching do have a very tight relationship. Too many organizations don't achieve the results they should from the training programs they implement. Little of this is a problem with the training itself, but more a result of the way training has been implemented, and the role—or lack of it—management exerted in reinforcing the training. Training can have a great impact in developing the capabilities of the team—but management has to be engaged, not only in determining what is being taught, but by participating in the classes, and doing ongoing coaching reinforcement afterwards.

Having done a lot of training, it's amazing the number of classes I've been involved with where management doesn't attend or participate. Or those with managers sitting in the back of the room, doing email or working on their smartphones, not participating in any of the workshop exercises (other than perhaps introducing the trainer.) These managers are not participating—they are attending. Managers need to be involved. Likewise, much is done through distance or eLearning. If managers expect their people to take the courses, they need to take the course as well—setting a powerful leadership example.

Most important, however, is what happens after training is completed. This is where managers most need to coach and continually reinforce what's been done in the workshop. Using our sales call skills example, managers need to coach and reinforce the planning process introduced in the class; they need to talk to sales people as they are planning calls, using what they've learned and reinforcing it in their coaching the sales call plan. That's difficult, to say the least, if the manager didn't participate in the class or workshop.

No training program should be implemented without a plan and a commitment on the part of management to coach and reinforce the training afterwards.

Without that commitment, you are just throwing money away and wasting your people's time.

Recently, I got involved in with an organization that invested a lot of time and money in training on major accounts. They used one of the "name" vendors to provide the training, and rightly so—they provided a great program. But the management team asked me, "Why aren't we making the progress in the major accounts that we should?" (It was surprising to me they didn't ask the vendor this, or get the vendor involved in the solution—but that's a different topic.)

In turn, I asked, "What are you, as managers, doing to coach the people in developing and executing the major account strategies?"

They looked at me as if I had two heads. "Don't you understand, we had training on this?"

I asked my question again, with more clarification. "What are *you* doing to coach your people in developing and executing the major account strategy? Your vendor provides great tools for developing major account plans. Do you regularly review those plans and use the tools when you talk to your people?"

They started looking at each other; no one wanted to answer, but it was clear: none of them incorporated any of the training into the way they reviewed the major account plans and progress in executing them. They didn't even know what the tools were and how to use them. It's no wonder they weren't making any progress. Their people weren't using what they learned, and managers weren't continually reinforcing it.

Training and coaching are important. One does not replace the other; both are needed. And each needs to reinforce the other.

12

HOW DO YOU COACH?

I know you've been waiting for me to get to the nuts and bolts of coaching There are enough volumes of books on coaching to fill many libraries, so my goal here is to provide enough for you to understand the concepts and make sure you get the right start.

Of all the matters we discuss in this book, coaching is one area where I definitely recommend formal, workshop-based training (as well as coaching from your manager). One of the things that helped make me a much better coach was formal training. In my very first management jobs, the company I worked for had a huge commitment to developing managers' abilities to coach. Over my first year as a new manager, I spent close to 20 days in training. In roles as a senior manager, I spent a minimum of ten days in training. And my managers viewed their jobs to coach me in coaching and developing my people. As a result, I got some of the best training in the world.

I recommend classroom-based training—with lots of role plays. Yeah—no one likes doing role plays, but role playing really does help you develop your comfort with coaching. In addition, I recommend you take advantage of your manager's coaching.

Remember, our objective as coaches is to help close gaps in performance, attitudes, and behaviors, maximizing the performance of each person in their current roles.

Too many people think coaching consists of telling people what to do. This isn't coaching, it's lecturing, and is probably the least effective method of improving performance.

Think about your own reaction when someone tells you what to do:

- **You don't like it**

- **You don't own it**

- **You probably won't do it.**

- **And you learn nothing in the process.**

And if you do what you are told to do, and it doesn't work, who do you blame? That's right, the person who told you to do it.

Some people think coaching is solving problems for our people. Sometimes we have to, but this is a little like telling them what to do. If we are constantly solving the problems, then our people never develop the capabilities to solve problems themselves.

They become dependent on us. That may be a little ego gratifying. If you are a control freak, it's what you want. But it's unsustainable. At some point the problem solving for them approach breaks down. You become the bottleneck because every problem they face becomes your problem to solve. You simply get crushed under the load.

Add to that the fact that your people won't like it—particularly sales people. We hire them to help customers solve problems. Naturally, they want to be able to solve problems themselves, not be told the solution.

So the most effective coaching focuses on helping your people think. Helping them analyze, consider alternatives, and develop courses of action.

NON-DIRECTIVE AND DIRECTIVE COACHING

The literature on coaching uses these terms quite a bit. You can guess what they mean:

Non-directive coaching focuses on helping your people think, analyze, and figure things out for themselves.

Directive coaching involves telling your people what they should be doing.

Some of you are probably thinking: "Dave, you're speaking out of both sides of your mouth. You just told us *not* to tell our people what to do."

Actually, I told you it was the least effective means of coaching. When you have the option, you should almost always choose non-directive coaching. It's the most powerful and sustainable way of improving performance.

However, there will be some instances, where directive coaching is the best, or possibly the only alternative.

NON-DIRECTIVE COACHING

As I've mentioned, non-directive coaching focuses on getting the salesperson to think about something, to analyze and evaluate what's going on, determine alternative courses of action, and decide what they will do.

It focuses on getting the salesperson to identify and solve their problems.

The beauty of this is that they start getting very good at solving their own problems, reducing the amount of time we have to spend with them tremendously. They have the skills and tools to figure things out for themselves, and not continue to rely on you for help. It also enables us to grow their capabilities very quickly.

Typically, when we are using a non-directive approach to coaching, we do so by asking questions. But they are very special types of questions. The following lists of questions are adapted from "The Thinker's Guide To The Art Of Socratic Questioning," Copyright 2007, Foundation for Critical Thinking Press, www.criticalthinking.org.

QUESTIONS FOR CLARIFICATION

What do you mean by....?
What is your main point?
How does _____ relate to _____?
Could you put that another way?
What do you think is the main issue here?
Can you give me an example?
Could you explain that further?
Why do you say that?
Let me see if I understand you; do you mean _____ or _____?
What do you think _____ meant by his remark? What do you take him to mean?
How would you summarize what _____ said in your own words?

QUESTIONS PROBING PURPOSE

What is the purpose of _____?
What was your purpose when you said _____?
How do the purposes of these two people/groups vary?
Is this purpose justifiable?
What is the purpose of addressing this question/issue at this time?
Questions Probing Assumptions
What are you assuming? What is _____ assuming?
How did you choose those assumptions?
What might you assume instead?
All of your reasoning seems to be based on _____. Why have you based your reasoning on these, rather than _____?
Is this always the case? Why do you think the assumption holds here?

QUESTIONS PROBING REASONS AND EVIDENCE

What would be an example?
How do you know?
What are your reasons for saying that?

What other information do we need to know before we can address this question?
Why do you think that is true?
What led you to that belief?
Is there good evidence for supporting that?
Are those reasons adequate?
How does that information apply to this case?
Is there any reason to doubt that evidence?
What difference does that make?
Who is in a position to know if that is the case?
What would convince you otherwise?
What would change your mind?
What would you say to someone who said _____?
What accounts for _____?
What do you think is the cause?
How did this come about?
How could we go about finding if that is true?
Can someone else give evidence to support that response?

QUESTIONS PROBING VIEWPOINT AND PERSPECTIVES

What are you implying about that?
What effect would that have?
What is an alternative?
You seem to be approaching this issue from _____ perspective. Why have you chosen this rather than another perspective?
How would others respond? What would influence them?
How could you answer the objection that _____ might make?
Does anyone see this differently?
What would you say to someone who disagrees?
How are _____ and _____ ideas different? Where do they agree?

QUESTIONS PROBING IMPLICATIONS AND CONSEQUENCES

How can we find out?
Why is this issue important?
What generalizations can you make?
What are you implying by that?
But if that happened, what else would happen as a result? Why?
What effect would that have?
What is the likelihood of that happening?
What is an alternative?
If _____ is the case, what else might be true?

QUESTIONS ABOUT QUESTIONS

What does that mean?
What was the point of this question?
Why do you think I asked this question?
How can we find out?
Is this the same issue as _____?
How could someone settle this question?
Can we break this question down at all?
How would _____ describe the issue?
Is this question easy or difficult to answer, why?
What does this assume? Why is this important?
Do we need facts to answer this?
Does everyone agree this is the question/issue?
To answer this question, what other questions do we have to answer first?

QUESTIONS THAT PROBE CONCEPTS

What is the main idea we are dealing with?
Why is this important?
Do these two ideas conflict? Why?
What is the main issue guiding the thinking behind this idea?
How is this idea guiding our thinking about this issue? Is it causing us problems?
What do we need to consider in figuring this out?
What main distinctions should we draw in reasoning through this problem?
What issues are guiding their thinking about this? Are there any problems with those?

QUESTIONS THAT PROBE INFERENCE AND INTERPRETATIONS

What conclusions are we coming to about _____?
What information are we basing these conclusions on?
Is there a more logical conclusion we might make in this situation?
How are you interpreting _____'s behavior? Is there another possible interpretation?
What do you think of _____?
How did you reach that conclusion?
Given all the facts, what is the best possible conclusion?
How shall we interpret the data?

Did you notice anything familiar about these questions?

They're not dissimilar to the great probing questions a salesperson might ask a customer—both to get them to think differently, and to really understand what's going on.

Some of you, who've read Neil Rackham's work or been through SPIN Selling, will recognize elements of SPIN in this approach.

Based on your experience selling, you already know a lot about non-directive coaching and the types of questions you might ask. You've probably been using them for years with customers.

The trick now is to use these skills you honed with customers, along with your finely tuned listening skills, but applying them in coaching your sales people and getting them to think differently and to learn how to solve their own problems.

I imagine you can see how doing this dramatically increases the salesperson's ownership and commitment to the course of action they determine. Just like these questions helped increase the ownership and commitment of your customers, they will achieve the same results with your people.

Non directive coaching looks a little easier for you to achieve, doesn't it?

DIRECTIVE COACHING

Every once in a while the circumstances are such that directive coaching is necessary. Directive coaching is basically instructing, telling, and sometimes may involve disciplining.

Sometimes when we are training, we have to be in *tell* mode. There are certain things that are best learned by telling people. They might never discover it through a non-directive manner.

Likewise, when we need to discipline someone, we need to tell them. No amount of non-directive questioning is likely to help them discover they have been very wrong, inappropriate, or have created a serious problem.

Recognizing the challenges in using directive coaching, as well as the impact, may be difficult to sustain. But as I said, sometimes it's the most appropriate approach for the specific situation and individual.

WHICH APPROACH DO YOU USE, WHEN?

Your default mode should be toward non-directive coaching. But there are some times when directive coaching is more appropriate or, in fact, necessary. These include:

- **When there is a real need for speed in addressing a specific issue.** For example, if you are in a car with the salesperson driving and they are about to hit another vehicle, you don't want to go through a non-directive process to have them figure out they should hit the brake. You need to scream, "Hit the brake!" If the situation requires immediate action, you may have to be in tell mode.

- **When there can be no chance of risk or failure.** In non-directive coaching, sometimes the salesperson chooses the wrong alternative and fails. They learn, improve, correct things, and go on. But sometimes the risks are too high and you cannot afford to fail. In this case you have to tell them what to do. As much as possible, help them understand the "why." They will be better executing if they have a context better than, "I'm doing it because my boss told me to do it."

- **When there's no debate, all the decisions have been made.** Sometimes, you and the salesperson may have gone through an arduous problem solving process. Together, you've addressed all the issues, made all the decisions, and it's the point where we need to take action. Ideally, the salesperson has determined and committed to the next actions, but there may be cases where they just can't. At this point, it's appropriate to be directive, e.g. "Go get these 3 things done with these people. Make sure you win the deal!" (My tongue is lightly planted in my cheek.)

- **When an issue is so critical it's necessary for you to maintain full control and responsibility.** The people simply have to follow the instructions. Typically, this might be where the risks are so high or the consequences resulting from a failure are very high. This is not license to be a control freak! The more you need to maintain control and responsibility, the more you limit the salesperson, both in the situation, and in their growth.

- **When the person has neither the capability nor the willingness to solve the problem themselves.** This is probably the worst one, from a people management perspective. While they will do what you tell them to do, it will be done grudgingly. The person is likely to complain, inappropriately. The person will be unlikely to be able to explain if challenged, or may even indicate disagreement, but say, "I was told to do this." We know this is ineffective, and that we can't drive great performance with these types of people. These people become problematic; you can't have them in the organization. So if you find yourself in this situation, you probably need to get on a path to terminating or moving the individual.

As a side note, the risk of winning or losing a deal is, 99.99% of the time, never a good reason to have to take over full control or say the risk is too high. Think about it, if you believe this, ultimately, you have to take over managing all the deals.

The directive approach creates problems or challenges that you should carefully consider before using this mode of coaching.

- **It virtually eliminates all possibilities of collaboration, creativity or innovation.**

- **Playing the directive card assumes you are right. And if you aren't the responsibility for the failure is 100% yours—not your people's.**

- **It adds huge potential for error. If the person you are directing doesn't understand and does something wrong, the mistake could have a huge impact. But again, it's not their fault.**

- It completely takes all ownership and responsibility off the salesperson and put it squarely on your shoulders. They just become the "automatons" executing your will.

- It's impossible to develop people to take responsibility, to learn, to grow, to learn how to handle these situations themselves.

- It has the potential of adding an element of fear and mistrust. What they may have running through their minds is, "Doesn't my manager trust me to be able to do this?" Additionally, there is a real fear about what might happen if they make an error.

None of these is good for individual or organizational growth. Ultimately, organizations run through directive approaches fail. They might perform in the very short term, but they can never sustain it. Or they drive people away; they don't like working where they are treated like idiots.

Think how you would feel. You probably resent people telling you what to do, so will your people.

"STRUCTURING" YOUR COACHING

As you will discover in the following chapters, it is important that you take every opportunity you can to coach your people. A lot of this coaching will be informal—find somebody doing something right, let them know, "You did a great job in that presentation, Anne! What could you do to create a higher sense of urgency with the customers next time?" or "You really nailed the value proposition in that proposal, John! The way you engaged the customer in understanding and quantifying their problems was very powerful—what would happen if you did this with all your deals?"

You will, also, be integrating coaching into your reviews (deal, pipeline, calls, and others,) and your one-on-ones. In these more structured meetings, you want to be very clear about your coaching objectives. The objectives need to be relevant to the discussion topic. For instance, when you integrate coaching into your deal reviews, your objectives should be to help them build and execute stronger deal strategies. Even within that, you may want to have a couple of specific coaching objectives you want to focus on—for example qualifying or understanding the decision-making process.

It's also important not to have too many coaching objectives in these sessions. People can only remember and act on two to three things at one time. If you try to cover everything in one session, you will confuse them. They won't remember everything; they may end up doing nothing. While you may be tempted to fire hose them with a lot of different things, if your objective is to get them to change and improve, you won't accomplish anything by overwhelming them.

If you are trying to get them to change something about what they are doing, give them examples of what "good" looks like. It's hard for a person to improve their deal qualification if they don't know what a well-qualified deal looks like.

Finally, agree on specific next steps for them to "try" some of the things you are suggesting they do. Ideally, they should say, "I'm going to try this in my next call." Alternatively, you might suggest they try something in their next call. Make sure both you and the salesperson take note of it, then follow up. "How did it work out? What did you discover? Did you feel comfortable doing it? Could you have improved it at all? Where are you going to try this again?"

SETTING AN EXAMPLE

There's a final important element in How To Coach. It's the personal example you set for the team, your peers, and the organization.

My father used to jokingly say, "Do as I say, not as I do." But the example you set every day is one of the most powerful ways to drive behavior in your organization.

You can use your behavior to drive huge performance gains, or to take an organization down the tubes.

Think about it:

- **If you want your sales people to use the CRM system and keep it current, but you don't use it at all, what will happen?**

- **If you want your people to use the sales process, but you don't use it when you are doing deal or pipeline reviews, they won't use it.**

- **If you want people to show up on time for meetings, but you are always late, guess what?**

- **If you want people to question, probe, and listen, but you don't…**

As a manager, you are always on. You can't turn off, your people are always watching you, looking at the example you set.

One of the most tragic things I've ever seen took place in Japan a few years ago. The manager spent a lot of time trying to develop his team's professionalism. I joined them at a celebration dinner one evening. The manager got drunk, became loud, offensive, and lewd. That single evening, everything the manager worked toward was destroyed. People lost all respect for him.

So unless you are at home, closeted in a dark room with no one, no phone, no computer, you are *always* "on stage." (If you are always alone, you probably are neither a manager or salesperson.) Make sure you set the example you want your people to emulate.

13

HOW DO WE FIND TIME TO COACH OUR SALESPEOPLE?

Why doesn't coaching get done? I talk to hundreds of managers, they say they know they should be coaching, but it doesn't get done. Remember that survey where we found sales managers "coached" their sales people one time per quarter or less? Based on this, a salesperson is lucky if they get four coaching sessions per year.

Part of the problem with finding the time to coach is we tend to think of "coaching" as a different activity, separate from the other activities that occupy a manager's time. There are meetings we have to understand the status of things, to get information about what's going on. There are deal reviews, pipeline/forecast reviews, call reviews, territory, one-on-ones, and any other sort of meeting. But we tend to think of coaching as something separate.

It may come from confusing training and coaching. We treat training as a separate activity, and so we think of coaching as a separate activity.

When I talk to managers, I see this confusion. They talk about scheduling "coaching sessions." These are meetings solely focused on coaching.

Guess what happens in our normal time pressured days? We focus on understanding the status of things and getting the information needed to make sure business is on track. As we run out of time, training and coaching gets deferred. Many managers know they are doing this, thinking, "I can catch up on coaching later."

If you are uncomfortable with coaching, it's even easier to let coaching get lost in the normal pressure of getting things done.

Clearly, this is a problem. Coaching needs to happen every day, but everyone is busy and time-poor. How do busy managers and sales people find the time for coaching and development?

THE PROBLEM WITH THE "COACHING SESSION"

As I've discussed, too many managers think coaching is a different and separate activity from all the other activities that consume their time. They think there are sessions specifically focused on coaching. There are a couple of things wrong with this approach.

The first is that coaching tends to lose its immediacy, consequently losing impact. I'm sure you've had a manager who thought this way, and recall "coaching" sessions where she began, "Remember that call you made on John Smith at the beginning of the month? How did you feel about how you opened the calls? Could it have been a little stronger?" It's the end of the month, a lot has happened and you may not even remember the call. So the impact of the coaching is seriously diminished.

This "coaching session" mentality creates a huge burden on you as manager. Thinking to the example of the John Smith call, you have to remember all the things you want to talk to each person about—or keep really great notes so you can cover it in the "coaching session."

Obviously, this approach has some real challenges in terms of creating really impactful coaching discussions.

The second challenge—more likely reality—is scheduled coaching sessions are the first things cancelled when you and your people are pressed for time. You won't cancel the pipeline or forecast review, you won't cancel the deal reviews. After all, those are critical to making your number.

So when push comes to shove and the reality of everything you and your people do every day weighs on your schedules, it's the coaching session that's always rescheduled, then rescheduled, then….

It's no wonder so little coaching gets done.

INTEGRATING COACHING INTO EVERYDAY BUSINESS

Effective sales leaders incorporate coaching into their daily business activities. In each meeting, they get the most leverage out of their time, in effect killing two birds with one stone.

High performing sales managers make coaching a permanent part of the everyday conversations and discussions they have with their people. Each meeting has two purposes: a business management purpose (status update, information exchange, etc.,) and a coaching purpose.

When talking about opportunities or deal strategies, strong leaders focus on both understanding the business situation and using the opportunity to coach the salesperson in strengthening and improving what they are doing.

In preparing for a call or debriefing the call, the sales manager will also coach the salesperson by asking things like, "What are your goals for the call?" "If things go right, what are some stretch goals?" "What is the worst thing that might happen in the call, and what are ways to avoid it?" "What value will the customer will get from this call?"

After the call, they might ask, "Did you accomplish all your objectives?" "What went really well?" "Is there anything more that you might have accomplished?" "Is there anything you would do differently?"

As sales managers, we spend our days talking to sales people about prospecting, sales calls, deals, pipelines, forecasts, territory and account plans. In each discussion, the best managers use these as opportunities both to understand what's happening, but also to coach and develop their people.

Coaching doesn't have to be limited to these reviews.

A great way of coaching is "catching someone doing something right," and letting them know immediately.

Or it could be a "Starbucks conversation." (I think standing in line at Starbucks has replaced the proverbial water cooler.) Or it could be "windshield time," as you go on calls with your people. Coaching opportunities are everywhere—and effective sales managers take advantage of those opportunities constantly.

There are several huge advantages to integrating coaching into your everyday routine. The first is that it gets done.

The second is the "immediacy." Imagine walking out of a sales call or hanging up the phone and immediately spending a few minutes debriefing and coaching. This is where coaching is most impactful.

The third is we and our sales people get huge leverage in our time. "Killing two birds with one stone" gives a huge impact on our time.

When coaching becomes part of the everyday business discussions managers have with their people, it is no longer an "unnatural act." Coaching is no longer the meeting we schedule, then postpone, then postpone again.

When coaching becomes part of the everyday business rhythm, the performance of sales people skyrockets—they are getting help when they need it and can use it, not months later, after everything has been forgotten.

14

ARE YOU COACHABLE?
IF YOU AREN'T, YOU WON'T MAKE IT!

You're probably thinking to yourself: "Hold on Dave, *I'm* the manager. Aren't I supposed to be the one to do the coaching? What's this about needing to be coachable myself?"

You will never be effective as a coach or a leader if you aren't coachable yourself. Each of us needs to continue to learn and improve. If you aren't coachable, you will shut yourself off from those opportunities. As a result, you won't have much of a future as a leader.

This is vital issue. You must examine your own coachability.

The best coaching is a dialogue or conversation between you and the person you are coaching.

In great conversations, each party learns.

To achieve this goal, each person must be open to changing their views or positions. Each person must be open to the potential they may be wrong or have a misunderstanding.

Some of the best "coaching" I've ever gotten has been from my people—when I was coaching them. They may not realize it, but if you listen well, you can learn a huge amount.

It's interesting how this kind of "coaching" happens. It's never one of your people sitting down saying, "Dave, I've been observing how you handle these things, have you ever considered…"

It can arrive in the form of the slightest comment, maybe the body language or an expression.

Many years ago, I was the top sales executive for a technology company. My VP of Sales Operations and I were having a review—like every review, my objective was to cover key business management issues, but also to coach and develop her. She was very talented, so the coaching focus was really to get her to stretch even further and to challenge her people more.

But in that meeting, she said something that has impacted me every day since. We were winding up the meeting and joking a little with each other. As she stood, she laughed, and said:

"Dave, you know, I've learned that I have to communicate with you in bullet points."

We each chuckled, and went about our days, but that sentence kept rolling around my mind. Suddenly, I realized, "I really suck at listening! I'm too impatient and focused on my agenda to hear what my people are really telling me. I rush them through things, always telling them to net it out."

Here I was, a senior sales executive, responsible for hundreds of millions in revenue and a very large organization. I prided myself on my leadership skills, particularly my openness and ability to listen. But I was missing a huge amount, much of it critical to the development of the organization and my own development as a leader.

Coaching is a two-way street. We get the privilege of learning and developing—a great ancillary benefit—if we are paying attention.

It's important for us to spend a few minutes on the idea of "being coachable."

Every once in a while we encounter people who aren't coachable.

They may not be overtly hostile or confrontational. They may appear to be paying attention to the coaching, but nothing changes. Despite all efforts, they are unwilling or unable to learn or change. They will overtly or covertly reject every attempt to help them improve or change.

A year ago, I was involved in coaching a regional VP of sales for a large company. We would have very good meetings. We'd talk about things that needed to be done or changed, and how to do it. He was very engaged in the conversations, there was a good give and take, and clear action plans at the end.

Yet the moment he walked out of the meeting, he went on doing the things he wanted to do in the first place. He refused to change; he was totally uncoachable.

Being coachable is essential to everyone's success. The world, particularly our world of selling is constantly changing, we have to learn, adapt, continually improve.

The uncoachable person has stopped learning. They are no longer paying attention. They are on a path to being totally irrelevant.

You may disagree, but the uncoachable person ultimately has no place in your organization. They may be great contributors now, but because they reject learning and change, they will not only become poor performers, but can have very negative impacts on customers and peers.

Be cautious in your assessment. But if you have a person who's genuinely uncoachable, that individual needs to be terminated. The only issue is when.

The coachable person knows they can't stand still. They need to improve, learn, and change. Some will try and fail, but they will learn from that failure and grow as a result. Some may not have the abilities or can't acquire the skills necessary. That doesn't mean they are uncoachable. It may mean they are in the wrong job.

Being coachable is not about blind acceptance. Actually the opposite is true. The highest performers will challenge; they will push back. But all in the spirit of understanding and learning.

Coachable people are:

- **Open to having their assumptions and beliefs challenged.**

- **Willing to challenge your assumptions and beliefs**

- **Willing to take new actions, to try new things.**

- **Willing to take the time to see the outcomes of those actions, tune and adjust them.**

- **Eager to take responsibility and want to be held accountable.**

- **Constantly learning and improving.**

- **Unwilling to give up on themselves or others.**

- **Growth oriented in their mindsets.**

As a manager and coach, you have to be open to these things if you hope to be effective, learn and grow in your role.

Everyone in the organization has to be coachable. Individuals who aren't, regardless of their level, create weakness and dysfunction in the organization.

15

COACHING TO CLOSE PERFORMANCE GAPS, COACHING FOR CONTINUED IMPROVEMENT

Coaching is about helping the salesperson understand and recognize gaps in their performance, behaviors and attitudes, getting them to recognize the need to change to close the gaps, and getting them committed to taking action. It's also about finding opportunities to continue to improve, not just to meet performance expectations, but to get even better. (That's one of the reasons we need to coach high performers as well as those that aren't performing.)

In closing performance gaps, we may have to work on skill development, so the people have the ability to actually correct the situation.

The biggest challenge is the salesperson may be completely unaware there is a gap, deficiency, or opportunity to improve, or may be unaware they are not meeting expectations.

Before you can start coaching to close the gaps, you have to know a few things:

1. **What are the expected levels of performance?** What are the expected attitudes or behaviors? How will we measure those? How will we know whether people are performing to expectation? What is the best practice? Let's take a very simple example. How do you know if the salesperson is doing a good job in executing their deal strategy if you have no sales process, or incomplete/ bad process metrics? Without these, you and they have no basis for knowing what great execution of a deal strategy is, so you have no basis for assessing an individual performance or coaching them.

We see the same thing with competencies, attitudes, behaviors, and so forth. Unless we know what we are looking for, we have no ability to assess how well or how poorly a salesperson is doing.

2. **Your sales people should understand what their expected levels of performance are.** "We know you are developing and executing great deal strategies when you are doing these types of things…." "You must keep a healthy funnel/pipeline. Healthy funnels have high integrity, should have this volume and should have this flow/velocity…" For example, if they don't know the sales process, if they don't know they are expected to use the sales process, then they won't have any idea what they are doing right or wrong.

We often hear of sales people feeling "blindsided," surprised. Often it's legitimate because they haven't clearly understood the expectations, how they will be measured, or have never been trained in them.

I'm not one for any bureaucracy, but documenting some of this information is really critical. The process of writing something down causes us to think and really understand what we're trying to achieve. Things like the performance expectations might be very powerful if you and the salesperson arrive at them jointly and document them.

Having a documented sales process provides your team a guide to refer to when they don't understand the process. Documented expectations around prospecting, clearly defined Ideal Customer Profiles, Documented pipeline metrics, and so forth.

Having documented competency models. Something that describes expectations for various skills, attitudes, or behaviors. (We'll cover much of this in later sections, Refer to the appendix or web site for more information on Sales Competency models.)

3. **Observing the actual performance.** You don't know what they are doing well or where they can improve unless you are actually watching, listening, and observing them as they work. It's impossible to be a great coach unless we are out working with our sales people, seeing what they are really doing, watching them in action, listening.

We don't have to be side-by-side with them for everything. Sometimes we can use surrogates to help assess how they are doing. For example, as you'll see when we talk about deal reviews, how we can look at how they are utilizing the sales process to assess how well they are executing developing and executing their deal strategies, subsequently coaching them to improve.

Likewise, pipeline metrics help us assess and coach them on improving the quality of the pipeline.

There's an important caution about observing actual performance. If you've been a manager for some time, you might have encountered the following situation.

Someone in the organization (your boss, your boss's boss, some manager in another function,) comes to you, saying, "Keith is terrible in sales calls, he doesn't accomplish anything, is all over the place, and not in control."

You have nothing you can do in coaching Keith on this feedback. You didn't observe it yourself, you can't discuss what happened, explore what Keith was thinking, discuss alternative ways Keith may have improved the sales call, or anything else important to helping Keith plan and execute better calls.

The input from others may be important, it's important to probe and understand what the others observed, but then you have to see it yourself before you can effectively coach people on improving. (By the way, if they have an incorrect assessment, be sure to correct their mis-impressions.)

4. **Now that we know where we'd like people to be and where they are, we've identified the gap and we can now start coaching them on closing the gap.**
How you close a performance gap is affected, sometimes powerfully, by the performance level of the salesperson being coached.

CLOSING THE GAP WITH TOP PERFORMERS

Some of you may be thinking: "What about top performers, does that mean I don't have to coach them?"

Absolutely, not! In fact, you'll find most of your top performers are hungry for coaching because they are driven to get better.

With top performers, as with everyone else, there are some areas in which they excel, and some where they can still improve performance. We may not have to spend much time coaching someone on prospecting if they are really outstanding at prospecting. But we may have to coach them on how to create, present, and defend value if they are always discounting.

We have to recognize where the gaps are and focus our coaching on those gaps. Everyone has areas in which they can improve their performance. Your job as manager is to lead your people in discovering those gaps and thinking about how to improve performance.

With top performers there's one other area you should be aware of. Top performers are always looking to improve. Even in areas where their performance is already outstanding. These are actually some of the most fun coaching conversations. They are the conversations where you will learn a huge amount yourself. Often, these are great brainstorming conversations. They are creative conversations where both of you start exploring new ideas, methods, approaches.

For example, one of the people on my team has a very high close rate. It's about 85%. Clearly, trying to get him to 100% is probably neither realistic nor a good use of our time. Instead, our coaching discussions focus on compressing the buying/selling cycle—so he can close more business in the same amount of time. It drives more revenue growth—and certainly impacts his earnings.

CLOSING THE GAP WITH BOTTOM PERFORMERS

Bottom performers are completely different from top performers. We can't ignore them—they drag overall performance of the organization down.

But when we look at them, we may be overwhelmed with the number of gaps, or the how deficient they really are.

It's impossible to coach problem performers in all areas at once. There are too many, you'll confuse them and set them up for failure. You'll confuse yourself as well.

The reality is you can only focus your coaching on one or two things at a time. Get them to improve their performance in those areas, then move to the next, then the next…

With bottom performers, you have to choose the right areas in which to focus. Which two may not be intuitively obvious. For example, problem performers will never be able to improve the quality of their pipeline unless they really understand and execute the sales process. And within that, probably the most important part is qualification, and within that, the most important element is chasing the right deals in the first place.

So if you focus on improving pipeline management skills, you are probably wasting time. The team member may be able to bring more volume into the pipeline, but it may not improve the quality or integrity of the pipeline. You'll likely have just more bad deals they can't close.

In this case, it's better to focus on qualification and sales process. Building their capabilities in these areas will automatically improve their deal strategies, pipeline management, and other areas. After they demonstrate improved performance in sales process and qualification, you can focus on closing the gap in the next areas.

Like everything else, prioritization and focusing on one to two items at a time is most critical.

CLOSING THE GAP WITH MIDDLE PERFORMERS

Most of our people will fall into this category. As a result, we have to use some combination of the approaches we use for top and bottom performers. There are some areas where they are really good, so we want to sharpen their performance there. There are other areas where they are not as good as they should be, and we need to help them improve.

Again, don't overwhelm them with everything at once. Prioritize those areas that drive the highest levels of improvement, focusing on those, and moving later to those that have lesser priority.

In the next chapter I'll look more closely at the different challenges and opportunities presented by each level of performer.

16

COACHING A, B, C PLAYERS

Each of your people is different. You may have one or two top performers, one or two poor performers, and a number of folks somewhere in the middle. But even within this, each individual is different.

There lots of different opinions about who you coach and how much time you spend coaching them.

Some say focus on your A players—a little bit of performance improvement has a huge magnifying effect. For example, a 10% performance improvement with an A player has a greater impact than a 10% performance improvement in a C player.

Others recommend focusing on the middle players, often for a similar reason, thinking that a 10% improvement on half a dozen B Players has a greater impact than a 10% improvement of a single A player.

I think all of this is misguided. For the most part, all that is proved with those arguments is that math works.

The other reality is you aren't directly managing hundreds of people—or even dozens. If you were, I might suggest you be selective. But you are probably managing a team of 8-12 people. There is no excuse for not investing time in each one. It's why you were put into the job!

Let's be pragmatic:

You have to coach everyone!

You are responsible for the performance of everyone on your team. You have to do everything you can to maximize each individual's performance.

How you coach, and where you allocate your time, will be different for each individual. It's senseless to have some sort of rule that you should "spend a minimum of 37 minutes with each person each week." There is no "optimal" amount of coaching time, just what enables us to achieve our goals with each individual.

I think the reason thoughtful experts make these mistakes is that they treat coaching as a separate self-contained activity, rather than integrating it into what you do every day in every interaction with your people.

As I've said in previous chapters, we're doing one-on-ones, deal reviews, pipeline reviews, and all sorts of other reviews every day. A critical reason for these reviews is simply in managing the business; we need to understand what's going on. Every one of these business management activities present great coaching opportunities.

We have informal moments, whether it's conversations waiting at Starbucks, quick hallway conversations, or other opportunities to coach.

Take every moment you can to coach everyone on your team.

You'll have to invest time differently in each person. There is no "ideal" amount of coaching time, despite what some gurus might claim. Some people will require more time than others. Some will *want* more time than others—beware of those that say they don't need any coaching—they probably need it the most.

The content of each discussion will vary depending on the person, their needs, their abilities, and the gaps in their performance.

A PLAYERS

A Players are the most fun to coach. Coaching an A Player is like sitting down with a peer and having a great discussion. They may not appear to need coaching, but it's a mistake not to coach them.

Challenge their thinking. Help them stretch even further than they are currently. They tend to be big thinkers, but push them even further. Test them on their deal strategies—are they thinking things through as completely as possible? They probably have winning deal strategies, but maybe there's an opportunity to really compress the sales cycle, or to increase the average value of the deal.

Sometimes, A Players can get careless—because they are very good, they may not be focusing on the details as much as they should, they may be taking shortcuts, or skipping things.

Challenge them to think bigger about their role overall—how they manage their time, how they are developing their accounts, how they are growing the business in their territory. They are probably over achievers, so they are unlikely to "coast" when they hit their number. They probably want to be the top performer in the company. They probably want to learn and do more.

In your coaching, think about their long term development. How they can contribute more, in ways that are meaningful to them? Perhaps give them some collateral assignments to broaden their perspectives on business. It may be working with product management in developing the launch plan for a new product. It may be working with marketing to develop a new marketing program. For those that aspire to move into management, consider having them "mentor" and help onboard new hires.

A Players don't require a lot of time, but you can't and shouldn't ignore them. Even top performers can improve. It's your job to help them discover how.

B PLAYERS

It is likely the bulk of your team are B Players. They are probably solid players, not superstars. They are probably struggling to achieve their goals. Very few are likely to overachieve, at least consistently. Most likely achieve their goals at the end of the month, quarter, year—barely scraping through, creating a few anxious moments for each of you.

They have their moments of brilliance, and those where they screw up. Since they may represent the majority of your team, they exert a tremendous impact on your ability to make your goals. This is where your coaching investment will have great impact.

Each person will have different specific needs. Some will be stronger in some areas than others. As we've discussed before, you'll have to identify and prioritize the things you want to focus on now. Don't try to do everything; focus on one or two areas at a time, and when they master that, move on to the next priorities.

One of the biggest challenges B players face is consistency of execution. That's a big part of what separates the A Players from the B Players. The A Players have figured out what works, and they do it time after time.

B Players struggle with consistency of execution. The better they get at this, the more their performance improves.

As you coach them, focus on a specific thing. Don't overwhelm them with all sorts of disparate items, they'll get confused. For example, in deal reviews reinforce the sales process and the importance of thinking several steps ahead on the deal strategy. If you are looking at a call plan, focus on the objectives of the call, the outcomes they want to achieve, how they will lead the meeting to achieve those. Reinforce best practices in whatever it is you are coaching. It may be best practices in preparing for and executing a call, prospecting, developing their territory, keeping deals from getting stuck in the pipeline, managing their time effectively, developing strong deal strategies, prospecting, or improving their ability to connect and communicate effectively with people.

Get them to reflect on past successes. For example, a deal strategy that was very good. Help them think about what they did and how they might apply the same things to current deals. "Remember the deal with Ginormous Inc last quarter? What if you tried applying some of the things you did, for instance, A, B, C? Would that help you strengthen your strategy in this deal? What about some of your other deals?"

Over time, improving the consistency of what they do will drive huge improvements in performance. Those who play sports may be familiar with the concept of 'muscle memory,' or 'motor learning.' Muscle memory is developed through repetition, performing a task so often the body responds automatically. As your B players repeat successful tasks, those tasks become automatic responses and their sales performance improves.

As they get better, some of the B Players will turn into A Players, some won't, but they will become increasingly more consistent in the way they do things. The trick is getting them doing the right things more consistently and getting them to stop doing the ineffective things.

C PLAYERS

C Players are your problem children. They are your lowest performers. They probably aren't doing much right, and probably for various reasons.

Poor performers may be resistant to coaching. Too often, they are trying to "hide out." They want to keep a low profile. They know they aren't performing as they should and they are worried about keeping their jobs.

You may be tempted to let them hide out. It's never fun coaching poor performers, but they can drag down the performance of your overall team if you don't address them.

Each coaching session with them is likely to be a struggle. Sometimes, in coaching C Players, I've gotten so frustrated that I've wanted to rip my hair out.

C Players need lots of coaching—consequently, they can become a huge time drain. You have to be very careful about this. Soon you might find yourself spending all your time with them, and not enough time with your B and A Players.

There are several important things to bear in mind when working with C Players.

Is their challenge skills or inexperience? Is it attitudinal or motivational? Is it behavioral? Are they in the wrong job?

SKILLS/INEXPERIENCE

Skills and inexperience problems are pretty easy to address. It may take some time, but you can identify and prioritize specific skills development. Maybe some formal training will help. Maybe pairing them with a high performer as a mentor will help. You can develop a plan to help them.

The most important thing with these types of performance problems is not to try to improve everything at once. Too often, they may have many challenges, for example bad deal strategies, poor call planning habits, inability to compete effectively, and on and on.

We're tempted to try to address all of these skills deficiencies at the same time. It just doesn't work. As hard as they may try, the person will get confused. They'll get discouraged and their performance will suffer further.

It's important to prioritize the skills issues with the individual, then focus on only one or two. For example, build up their skills in understanding and executing the sales process. Do nothing else. Once they start improving on that, then add another area, then another.

Sometimes it might be useful to team them with an A player to let them see what they should be doing. Plus this gives your A players a developmental opportunity. Be careful, however, that they don't become a time drain to the A player.

Sometimes, you'll want to go on calls with them, to demonstrate what they should be doing. Don't take over the call, but help them see how they should be conducting effective meetings by the way you engage the customer.

ATTITUDINAL ISSUES

Attitudinal or motivational problems may be very difficult to change. You want to identify what's driving the attitudinal problem. It may be they want to be successful, but due to lack of skills, they have become discouraged. It could be they don't care, or they can't take personal responsibility, "It's always someone else's fault."

I just got off the phone with a senior salesperson who had just this problem. He's hopelessly behind in reaching his goals. We know he has the skills and capabilities. In fact, when he chooses to apply himself, he's quite good.

But he has a huge attitudinal/mindset problem. He won't take ownership, he has an excuse for everything—and it's never his fault. It's always his manager, the company, or the customer. Even the simplest thing—he had a number of critical phone appointments set, he missed all of them. When I probed him on this, his response was, my mobile shut off, it didn't have power. I'm almost expecting him to say in our next call, "The dog ate my homework."

If the attitudinal problem is something other than skills, such as refusing to take personal responsibility, you face a large challenge. At least in my experience, those are virtually impossible to change. You may have to look at moving the person out of the business In these situations, sometimes they will improve their performance when they see their job may be threatened. Be careful, watch them. Too often, they slip into bad habits and their performance degrades again. Also be careful about how much of a time drain they create for you. You can get them to perform, but you have to be very directive and constantly follow up.

BEHAVIORAL ISSUES

Behavioral problems are very similar to attitudinal problems. They can be very difficult to change. Behavioral problems are where people aren't doing things wrong, but where they are doing the wrong things. Things like not showing up for work at the right time, not keeping CRM updated, causing problems with other people in the office, misreporting expenses, leaking confidential information.

In addressing behavioral problems, you have to first determine if the person knows the right behaviors. While the right behaviors might be obvious to you, we can't assume everyone knows what the right behaviors are.

If the person doesn't know the right behaviors, you have to explain them to that individual. You have to give them specific examples of things they have done that are the wrong behaviors and what the correct behaviors might have been.

You may be tempted to refer to some of your top performers, "See what Joe does..." In my experience, that's not effective. They've seen what Joe has been doing, and they still aren't exhibiting the right behaviors. You have to focus on the specific individual's specific behavior and their willingness to change it.

If the behavioral problem is an issue of not knowing the right behaviors, you should see a change very quickly. If the behavior doesn't change, there are other issues at play.

I alluded to a problem of my own behavior earlier. I was recruited as the top sales executive for a large company. The company I came from had a very aggressive, direct, sometimes confrontational management style. We had a name for it, "Contention Management." It worked brilliantly in my former company because no one took it personally, it was all focused on coming up with the right solution.

My new company was very collegial and collaborative. They tended to avoid conflict, perhaps to a fault. But I didn't change my behavior and was creating a huge amount of tension and resentment among my colleagues, senior management, and my people.

Fortunately, one of my people had the courage to sit down and coach me. He started, "Dave, your behaviors are causing real problems. I'm sure you don't mean to be that way, but...."

Sometimes people just don't see the impact of their behaviors on others. When this is the case, they can be addressed very quickly. I immediately changed my behaviors. I didn't defocus on our strategies and goals, I just behaved in a way that engaged everyone else more effectively. (I also would keep looking at Richard in meetings and he would give me a subtle Thumbs Up—or Down when I slipped.)

Behavioral problems have to be addressed with urgency. They don't only impact the performance of the individual, but they are also likely to impact others on your team, in your company, or customers.

If a behavioral problem cannot be corrected, the person will have to be moved, or terminated.

FINDING THE RIGHT BALANCE

There's no magic formula for the right amount of coaching time for each person. If you are using reviews as coaching opportunities, you are working with everyone in a natural manner, integrated with the day to day activities.

- **Each person has different needs, each person will require a different investment in time.**

- **Beware of those poor performers who can become time drains.**

- **Don't let bad performance linger: address it quickly and effectively.**

17

WHAT DOES THE HEISENBERG UNCERTAINTY PRINCIPLE HAVE TO DO WITH SALES LEADERSHIP?

Those of you who have followed my blog, or have followed me socially, know I was actually trained as an Applied Physicist, but somehow found myself going to the Dark Side—Sales. But, I keep going back to my roots in physics, and it sometimes helps me understand phenomena we encounter in sales.

One of the more well-known areas of physics is the Uncertainty Principle, originated by Werner Heisenberg in 1927. Basically, it dealt with quantum mechanics and the difficulty of simultaneously measuring speed and momentum of particles. We often confuse the Uncertainty Principle with the Observer Effect—which is really what I want to talk about, but thought you'd enjoy the history of physics observations.

The Observer Effect is very important. It states the very act of Observing or Measuring impacts the thing that we are Observing or Measuring and changes its behaviors in some ways.

This is important to physicists as they try to measure the properties and behaviors of atomic and subatomic particles. They have to be able to account for the impact of their observations and measurements on the behaviors of the particles in order to have a good understanding of the real properties and behaviors of the particles they are trying to measure. (This work, by the way, is very important to each of us because it is the foundation for developing new materials and components used to make all the cool toys and gadgets we can't live without, as well as a lot of the really cool stuff Elon Musk does.)

End of the physics lesson.

Our own filters and biases cloud our abilities to understand and to communicate effectively.

It turns out the Heisenberg Uncertainty Principle and the Observer Effect are really important in our effectiveness as sales people and managers.

Naturally, we'd like to think what we do has an impact on the behaviors and actions of our customers or people. We'd like to think what we do, say, and how we engage them changes their behaviors.

But there are some important subtleties to this process. It means what we hear or observe with our people may not be what really what is happening with them. That somehow, we project our own filters, experience, and behavioral biases onto the other person. We may not be accurately understanding what they really are doing or what they intend. As a result, we may respond incorrectly or inappropriately.

The easiest way to think of it is like this: There's a person I used to deal with whom I really didn't like or respect. He felt the same about me. (Don't worry, it's none of you—he wouldn't be caught dead reading this book.) Whenever he said something, "Black," for example, I could only hear and see "Red." My own biases, attitudes, and experiences were so severely affecting me, to the extent I wasn't hearing him or what he was saying—even though, I suspect, much of the time he was saying something important. Likewise, he was doing the same thing. So while he was a very smart, capable person, we never could agree on things and move forward—and our failure was largely driven, not by what each of us was saying, but by how each of us heard and responded to the other.

This is a personally painful example, but dramatically shows how the Observer Effect impacts our effectiveness and ability to get things done with our customers or colleagues.

Like physicists, unless we understand and account for the filters (or blinders) we apply in engaging with our people, we can never have the impact we hope to have with each person on our team.

The Effect flows both ways—our people have their own Observer Effect, which colors how they hear and respond to us.

Now that we understand the impact of the Observer Effect, what do we do about it?

The simplest thing is simply to be aware of the Effect, understand that we each have biases, filters, and experiences that color what we hear, observe, and how we may act or react. As much as we can understand what those are, and "account for them" in the situation, we can more effectively connect and engage our people. (This is great for connecting with and understanding customers, as well.)

Likewise, understanding the biases, filters, and experiences our people have and "accounting for them" helps improve our ability to truly hear our people, understand them, and engage them.

BEHAVIORAL STYLES

"Behavioral Styles" is the name for this phenomenon according to researchers who study the way people communicate and interact with each other. Each of us has a Behavioral Style. We're "wired" with it. Without getting into the science, our behavioral style is partially inherited or genetic, and partially a result of our environments or upbringing.

It turns out that our behavioral styles don't change much over time, with one important exception. When we are under extreme stress, our behavioral style tends to shift. With some people it's a small shift, with others it's pretty big.

But both our normal style and our stress style are very consistent.

There's no good or bad behavioral style. Our individual style is just who we are and how we tend to interpret and react to things.

It's this individual behavioral style that colors how we interact with people, and how they interact with us.

This is a large part of what causes communications to break down and can adversely impact our effectiveness as leaders—or even as sales people communicating with our customers.

But because there's a lot of interesting work on behavioral styles, if we learn a little about them we can start to understand where miscommunication happens, and be more attentive to potential break downs.

LEVERAGING BEHAVIORAL STYLES

There are a lot of "assessments" or tools we can use to understand our behavioral style and those of others.

Many sales and professional people go through something called a "DISC" Assessment. It looks at behavior across a few dimensions (Dominance, Influence, Steadiness, and Conscientiousness)

When you take an assessment like DISC, you get a rich profile of your style. I encourage you to take some sort of assessment; they are available online and aren't too expensive. You really learn a lot about how you present yourself and the filters that influence how you see or hear things and how you react.

But without getting into behavioral styles, let me give you an example of what happens. This will be very simplistic, so take it in that spirit. Also, to avoid confusing you with labels of particular styles, I'll just call them Types A, B, C, and D. The labels are absolutely meaningless.

Type A	Type B
Type C	Type D

Each of us is positioned somewhere in this grid. It turns out, people who are diagonally opposed to each other often have great difficulty in communicating.

So a very strong Type A and a very strong Type D are "wired" to have difficulties in communicating. Likewise, Type B and Type C will have difficulties.

Regardless of how well intended each type is, or how badly we want to communicate effectively, if Type A says Black, Type D is likely to hear Red. You can see how this is a huge problem.

What we say may be heard completely differently than how we intended it to be heard. Likewise, what we hear may be completely different than what the person intended for us to hear.

But if you have a little training in Behavioral Styles, you can start to decode this potential for miscommunication pretty easily. You can begin to think, "Dave has this particular style, so when I say something this way, he's likely to hear it that way and react. But if I adjust what and how I say something, Dave will better understand what I really mean."

The process also works in reverse. If Dave is saying something to you, because of your behavioral style and filters, you will hear it a certain way. But if you understand both Dave's style and your own, you can "translate" what Dave is saying and truly hear him.

Once you understand these, your sense of behavioral styles and their effect can be quite powerful in improving your own ability to connect with and communicate with each other.

By the way, this works with everyone. If you and your people understood the styles of each of your customers, you could connect with them in far more impactful ways.

Behavioral styles are very powerful. But even if you haven't had any training, just recognizing that there are differences and they impact our ability to connect should help you be more conscious of your communications with your people and their communications with you.

18

GUIDELINES FOR
GIVING AND RECEIVING FEEDBACK

Probably the single most important skill anyone can have is the ability to receive feedback. Some of the most important data we can receive from others (or give to others) consists of feedback.

Feedback provides great learning opportunities. Receiving feedback enables us to understand how others see us. It allows us to understand how others react, and to witness the consequences of our own behaviors.

Feedback helps to make us more aware of what we do and how we do it. It helps us to improve our abilities to modify and change our behavior and to become more effective in our interactions with others. The inability to receive feedback ultimately cripples your ability to learn and progress in your career.

As leaders, the most important gift you can provide your people is powerful feedback. Feedback provides valuable insight to help our people understand their behaviors, giving them the chance to think, analyze, and adjust their behaviors to improve their effectiveness.

Feedback is a two-way street. We should actively seek feedback from our people, peers, managers, and others we work with. This feedback helps improve our own effectiveness and grow as leaders.

Early in my career I struggled with feedback. Too often, I took it as an attack on me and who I was. I became very defensive, either rejecting it outright, or going into attack mode to prove the person providing the feedback wrong.

This inability to accept feedback seriously hurt me. I was not as effective as I could have been as a salesperson. While I was very good, I could have, in hindsight, been so much better. I remember one particular incident. My manager was telling me what my annual performance bonus was. It was much lower than I expected, when he provided me the feedback on why it was so low, I totally rejected everything he said.

Part of the reason was he was a pretty bad manager; I didn't respect him very much. Because of that "preconceived notion," and my inability to accept feedback, I took some actions that were not great. This manager and his manager valued me; they ended up moving me to another unit so I could "start fresh."

It was only several years later, with more experience and some maturing, I discovered, his feedback was right on target. My lack of respect for him and my inability to accept feedback so blinded me I lost about two years in my development as a salesperson. I sometimes wonder how things might have turned out, where I might have been, what I might have learned if I had the courage and maturity to listen to him.

It's something all of us struggle with. Accepting feedback, particularly on something that doesn't fit our own self-perception, is difficult. It's difficult when it comes from a friend, and even more difficult when it comes from someone you don't like very much.

The inability to accept feedback is probably the most limiting thing we face in our personal and professional development.

As managers and leaders, providing feedback is one of the most important things we can do. Helping our people learn how to "receive" feedback is a gift that pays off for the rest of their lives.

We tend to treat feedback lightly. We are often bad at both giving and receiving feedback. Your personal growth as a leader will be directly tied to your ability to give and receive feedback.

The growth and development of your people will be tied both to their abilities to receive feedback and your ability to provide it in a deep and meaningful manner.

Dr. George Lehner[1] was a colleague and mentor of mine. He was a world leader in leadership, interpersonal communications, and behaviors. Leaders in government and business sought his counsel. Dr. Lehner taught at some of the world's leading universities. I remember him calling one time, asking, "Dave, I'm meeting with the UN Secretary General and his staff tomorrow afternoon—want to tag along?"

I was privileged to have him as a mentor and colleague in my company for a number of years before he passed away.

At various points in our relationship, we had discussions about giving and receiving feedback.

I've never found clearer or more concise guidelines on giving and receiving feedback. The words that follow on the next two pages are his:

---

1 Dr. George Lehner passed away in February 2007. George was a good friend and tremendous mentor. He provided simple and clear lessons everyone he touched valued. I find his lessons very important and still relevant. So many of the problems leaders, managers, team mates create is by providing ineffective feedback which reduces trust and adversely impacts relationships.

To help us develop and use the techniques of feedback for personal growth, it is necessary to understand certain characteristics of the process. The following is a brief outline of some guidelines that may assist us in making better use of feedback, both as the giver and receiver of feedback. You may wish to add further guidelines.

- **Focus feedback on behavior rather than the person.** It is important that we refer to what a person does rather than comment on what we imagine the person is. This focus on behavior further requires that we use adverbs (which relate to actions) rather than adjectives (which relate to qualities) when referring to a person. Thus we might say a person "talked considerably during this meeting," rather than that this person "is a loudmouth." Talking in terms of "personality traits" implies inherited qualities which are difficult, if not impossible, to change. Focusing on behavior implies that it is something related to a specific situation that might be changed. It is less threatening to hear comments about behavior than about "traits."

- **Focus feedback on observations rather than inferences.** Observations refer to what we actually see or hear in the behavior of another person, while inferences refer to interpretations or conclusions that we make from what we see or hear. In a sense, inferences or conclusions about a person contaminate our observations, thus clouding the feedback for another person. When inferences or conclusions are shared, and it may be valuable to have such data, it is important that they be so identified.

- **Focus feedback on description rather than judgment.** The effort to describe represents a process for reporting what occurred, while judgment entails a subjective evaluation in terms of good or bad, right or wrong, nice or not nice. Judgments arise out of a personal frame of reference or values, whereas description represents objective, neutral (as far as possible) reporting.

- **Focus feedback on descriptions of behavior which are in terms of "more or less" rather than in terms of "either/or."** The "more or less" terminology implies a continuum on which any behavior may fall, stressing quantity, which is objective and measureable, rather than quality, which is subjective and judgmental. Thus, participation of a person may fall on a continuum from low participation to high participation, rather than "good" or "bad" participation. Not to think in terms of "more or less" and the use of continua is to trap ourselves into thinking in categories, which may then represent serious distortions of reality.

- **Focus feedback on behavior related to a specific situation, preferably to the "here and now" rather than to behavior in the abstract which places it in the "there and then."** What you and I do is always tied in some way to time and place, and we increase our understanding of behavior by keeping it tied to time and place. Feedback is generally more meaningful if given as soon as appropriate after the observation or reactions occur, thus keeping it concrete and relatively free of distortions that come from the lapse of time.

- **Focus feedback on the sharing of ideas and information rather than on giving advice.** By sharing ideas and information, we leave the individual free to make decisions—based upon personal goals—as to how to use the ideas and information in a particular situation at a particular time. When we give advice, we take away the individual's freedom to choose the most appropriate course of action.

- **Focus feedback on exploration of alternatives rather than answers or solutions.** The more we can focus on a variety of procedures and means for the attainment of a particular goal, the less likely we are to accept prematurely a particular answer or solution—which may or may not fit our particular problem.

- **Focus feedback on the value it may provide for the recipient, rather than the value or "release" it provides the person giving the feedback.** Feedback should serve the needs of the recipient rather than the needs of the giver. Help and feedback need to be given and heard as an offer, not an imposition.

- **Focus feedback on the amount of information that the person receiving it can use, rather than on the amount that you have which you might like to give.** The person who receives too much feedback may be unable to react effectively. When we give more than can be used, we may be satisfying our own needs rather than helping the other person.

- **Focus feedback on time and place so that personal data can be shared at appropriate times.** Because the reception and use of personal feedback involves many possible emotional reactions, it is important to be sensitive to when it is appropriate to provide feedback. Excellent feedback presented at an inappropriate time may do more harm than good.

- **Focus feedback on what is said rather than why it is said. The aspects of feedback which are related to the what, how, when, and where of what is said are observable characteristics.** The why of what is said takes us from the observable to the inferred, and brings up questions of "motive" or "intent" unless the why explicitly refers to goals. To make assumptions about the motives of the person giving feedback may prevent us from hearing, or cause us to distort what is said. In short, if I question "why" a person gives me feedback, I may not hear what is being said.

In short, the giving (and receiving) of feedback requires courage, skill, understanding, and respect for self and others.

I've provided these in downloadable form at the website. If all you learn from this book is how to give and receive feedback, you will improve your abilities as a coach and leader profoundly!

19

THE SECRET TO EFFECTIVE COACHING

We've had a very quick, focused journey, covering a lot of ideas and advice about coaching. But honestly, none of it means anything until you know the secret to coaching.

Actually, it's two secrets. Without knowing these, too often, coaching is just going through the motions.

Ready? Here they are:

- **You have to care!**

- **You have to believe in your people more than they believe in themselves!**

That's it. If you don't believe totally in these two things, you will never be as effective as a coach or leader as you should be—or as your people deserve.

While I hesitate to use these words, caring is that "tough love" thing. Yeah, I know it's really hokey, but I don't have a better way of expressing it.

Part of this comes from real empathy for the people and the things they face in doing their jobs. You've been there, you've done it. You know the reality of what they face, you also know the BS or the games they might play (all well intended).

But empathy differs from sympathy. Empathy is recognizing those realities, but having the courage or caring to believe they can be and want to be better. Most people want to be successful, they want to improve and grow.

If you don't believe more strongly than they do, you will never be able to maximize their performance or fulfill their potential. At most, you'll get some improvement, but it is unlikely to be sustainable improvement.

Our jobs as leaders are to get our people to perform at the highest levels possible, fulfilling both their short and long term potential.

Sometimes, I think it's this absence of belief that most directly impacts our effectiveness as leaders and coaches. If we are asking our people to change, to step up what they are doing, but we don't believe in their ability to do it, then they never will. We've created a self-fulfilling prophecy, and it's not our people's faults, it's ours. We become the weak link in driving performance improvement.

Coaching and developing our people is a "contact sport." (Figuratively, that is.)

We must dedicate our full commitment and engagement to the work of seeing our people succeed and believing they can!

Improving performance, whether it's taking someone who isn't performing well and getting them to improve, or taking strong performers and challenging them to stretch, is about change. We are asking our people to change what they are doing. Perhaps, they are doing something wrong. Perhaps they can do something better. Perhaps they need to do something differently. But to be effective in getting our people to change and improve, we have to help them discover the path forward. We have to get them engaged in understanding, as well as believing and owning the change.

To get them to see this, to give them the courage to step up to the change, we have to believe they *can* do it. Otherwise we set them up for failure—wasting their time and ours.

This is particularly important with poor performers. If we have given up on them, if we don't believe they can fix their performance problems, then they never will. And we may be cheating them because of our own beliefs. If we can't get our heads wrapped around believing they can improve, we might as well stop. We are best having a heart to heart with them, moving them into a role where both we and they believe they can achieve success.

Coaching and developing our people is the single highest leverage activity we can undertake as managers and leaders:

- **Regardless of how well we know how to coach**

- **Regardless of how skilled we might be in asking non-directive questions,**

- **Regardless of how disciplined we are in investing the time in coaching,**

- **Regardless of how well we execute the "mechanics" of coaching…**

We never achieve sustained success unless we believe in the ability and willingness of our people to do achieve the goals, sometimes more than they do.

If we don't believe in our people, if we don't believe *more strongly* than they do, we will never help them change and achieve extraordinary goals. We—our people and ourselves—end up just going through the motions. Our lack of belief holds them back from achieving what they could.

We can't do this casually. We have to be fully engaged. Belief is not about cheerleading (though some amount of cheerleading helps,) it's about helping our people learn about themselves, helping them see a path to improving and growing. It's challenging them, getting them to think, and figure things out. It's about getting them to believe in it, visualize, and take action.

Think back to the good managers and inspirational leaders you have had. They probably had one thing in common: They believed in what you could do or what you could achieve more strongly than you believed it yourself. They challenged you, and they inspired you. They were disappointed when you didn't challenge yourself to achieve your full potential.

As I reflect on my career, a number of key people—my parents, my wife, my family, some close friends, a few teachers, some inspirational managers, a few peers or colleagues—stand out in their belief in me. All of these people knew I could achieve more. They believed in me. They challenged me — not to meet *their* expectations, but to fulfill *my* potential. They continue to do this, because they know I can do more—and because they believe that, I know I can do more.

Do you care about your people and their potential as team members and individuals? Do you believe in your people? Do you believe more strongly than they do? Are you committed to their success?

If you are, both you and they will accomplish tremendous things. If you aren't, then you will never be an effective leader.

You may be getting tired of these words by now, but your job is to get things done through your people. If you don't care enough about each of them, if you aren't trying to get the highest levels of performance from each, then you aren't doing your job.

Everything I've written in the previous chapters helps you execute more effectively as a coach. I am confident you are developing your coaching skills. But even if all you have at the moment is an intense belief and commitment in your people, you are 80% of the way there.

PART THREE

REVIEWS: ACCELERATE YOUR COACHING IMPACT!

20

THE REVIEW PROCESS:
KILLING TWO BIRDS WITH ONE STONE

Managers spend a lot of time doing reviews. We do deal reviews, pipeline, forecast, territory, account, call, prospecting, one-on-ones, QBR's, and the list goes on! Our weeks are consumed with trying to understand what's going on and whether we are on track to make our goals. Each month, and quarter, we hit reset and start all over again.

My experience is that we don't use our time and that of our people as effectively as we could. The reasons are:

1. **We mix or confuse what we are reviewing.** For example, virtually every pipeline review I've participated in becomes a deal review. We forget the objectives of pipeline reviews and deal reviews are very different. It's difficult to achieve our goals in any review when we keep shifting them up.

2. **Too often, we don't really know why we are doing the review in the first place.** We do reviews because we think we should do them. We do them because our managers ask us to do them. We do them because we were subjected to these when we were sales people. We may get some good information or data, but we don't have a great sense of why we are doing it. Often, we are just going through the motions.

3. **We don't get the most impact out of the review process.** Too often, reviews seem to look like us interrogating our sales people. We focus on getting information and status updates from them in order to understand the state

of the business. We're using the review only for our business management purposes, or to keep our own managers off our backs.

But the review process is one of the greatest and most natural opportunities to coach our people. Most of the time, managers tend to separate coaching from the review process, scheduling reviews, then separate coaching sessions. We've talked about this before: What gets sacrificed when you get pressed for time? You guessed right, the coaching session is always the one that's pushed off.

THE PURPOSE OF THE REVIEW PROCESS

The review process has two key purposes: a business management objective and a coaching/learning/development objective.

The business management part of the process is where most people focus. We want to know what's going on, whether it's about a specific deal, account, territory, a sales call, how people are using their time, or any number of other things.

As managers, we need information and we need to understand what's happening. We need the information to be able to determine whether we will hit our goals, whether people are doing the right things with the right people at the right time, and to assess risk or problem areas. We need to be aware of what's going on and, to the degree possible, make sure everything's under control.

We also can't forget our managers and others in the corporation. They have expectations of us. They want to know what's going on. They need information to do *their* jobs, and so we use reviews as one method of getting and sharing that information.

The second part of the review process is coaching. This is the part I don't see many managers doing. Usually, in their quest to keep informed and stay "in control," they seek information above all else.

And they forget it's a great opportunity to coach.

Some managers think they may be coaching, because in the review they get the status information, then tell people what to do. "Go do this, this, and this, then come back and tell me what happened!" Alternatively, "Your pipeline/funnel looks terrible, you need to get more deals and spend more time prospecting."

Remember: Telling is not coaching. Look back at the chapters on coaching to help you become a more effective coach.

Great reviews accomplish both these things at the same time:

- **We achieve our business management objectives**

- **We get to do awesome coaching.**

Combining these two is so powerful, not only from a time management point of view, but also from an immediacy and impact point of view. Imagine doing a deal review, brainstorming (coaching) with the salesperson on strategies and next steps. It's fresh in their minds; it's timely, and immediately actionable. Or in reviewing a call, understanding the business objectives that were achieved, and then spending a few minutes discussing how we might have done something differently or better or anything else, has impact because the information is still fresh.

We are maximizing our impact and productivity when we combine business management and effective coaching into each review we conduct.

REVIEW CADENCE

It's important to discuss the cadence or frequency of reviews. We have the greatest impact in developing our people, as well as in keeping up on what's going on when we have a disciplined approach to performing reviews.

The right cadence depends on a number of things, including: the number of people on your team, the activity levels, the sales cycle, and what's going on in your business. It's up to you to figure out the most appropriate review cadence.

But, here are some things to think about, or biases that I have:

1. **Sales people, regardless of being inside, field, B2B, or B2C spend most of their time doing deals and making sales calls.** So that's what we should be reviewing most frequently. If you have win rate, sales cycle, discounting, deal slippage problems in your pipelines—where you fix it is in sharpening their ability to develop and execute winning call and deal strategies. If your pipeline shows prospecting problems, you don't fix it in the pipeline review, you fix it in the prospecting review.

I like to advise managers in complex B2B sales to conduct at least one deal review and one call review every week with each of their people.

Do the math. If you have ten people and it takes half an hour for each review, that's ten hours a week focused on their most important deals and calls. On the surface that seems like a lot of time, but think about it. This time has the biggest impact on your people's and your abilities to achieve your goals—deals and sales calls! That's a lot of time—but it's worth the investment.

You'll have to figure out what is realistic for your circumstances, but don't let two weeks pass without doing at least one of each with each of your people.

2. **Managers seem obsessed with pipeline and forecast reviews.** It seems the higher you go in the food chain; the more obsessed managers are with the funnel or pipeline.

But most people tend to conduct pipeline reviews far too frequently.

As an example, I have a client whose top management was obsessed with the funnel—particularly in their last quarter of the fiscal year. The CEO and CFO insisted on daily updates of the funnel and forecast.

Here's the problem: their sales cycle was about 18-24 months. So the pipeline didn't change that often. Yesterday's pipeline/forecast report looked the same as today's, and would look the same tomorrow and even the following week. Increasing the frequency of the reviews, doesn't change the pipeline dynamics—it just wasted a lot of time with people asking the same things over and over.

A daily pipeline/forecast review might be good if you are in a very short sales cycle, possibly a B2C, a retail type of environment, or certain types of SaaS businesses. But daily reviews and updates for very long/complex sales cycles are a waste of everyone's time.

In the case I mentioned, the poor SVP of Sales had me sit down with the CEO and CFO to explain how they were taking valuable time away from selling.

You have to look at the dynamics of your sales cycle and activity in your pipeline to determine the right frequency for pipeline/forecast reviews. In this client's case, a monthly review was very appropriate. (I also set some reports up for the CEO and CFO in the CRM system for those times when they felt insecure—at least they could see the information.)

3. **As for account or territory reviews,** unless there is a lot of change going on in the accounts or territories, the frequency of these needs to be even less. Generally, a quarterly or sometimes even a semiannual cadence is sufficient

There are other reviews you'll be conducting. Some may be focused around prospecting, others around time management, and so forth. Figure out what the right cadence for each is. If it's a very big issue, prospecting reviews should be conducted weekly. You can look at their activity levels, conversions, emails, listen to calls and coach them—probably not all of this in one review. You can look at their calendar blocking and time management in their weekly one-on-ones.

Each of these types of review is very powerful, and each will have a different cadence and objective. Make the reviews too frequent and you will be wasting everyone's time. You will also be, justifiably, accused of micromanagement.

Make them too infrequent or irregular and you run huge risks from both a business management and coaching perspective. You won't be spending sufficient time coaching and developing your people. You will not know what's going on with the business and what actions need to be taken to keep things on target! (Not knowing what's going on in the business will not make your manager very happy with your performance!)

Create great habits for yourself and your people. Develop a regular schedule and cadence. Do as much as you can to stick to it; avoid cancelling and rescheduling. Cancelled and rescheduled reviews generally don't get done.

CONDUCTING EFFECTIVE, HIGH-IMPACT REVIEWS

We know each review has different objectives. How we prepare, conduct, and follow up each review will vary depending on the type of review. The next few chapters will go through the major types of reviews we need to conduct:

- **Deal/Opportunity**

- **Pipeline/Forecast**

- **Sales Call**

- **Account/Territory.**

- **One-on-ones**

One thing you will discover in this process is all these reviews are closely interrelated. The pipeline review will identify challenges your people may be having with their prospecting, deals, or call strategies. Account/Territory plans tie very closely to prospecting, call, and deal plans; which, in turn, drive the deal strategies. Deal strategies drive call plans.

As you start to see how these are interrelated, how they work together, you will discover a very powerful platform to understand what's going on, as well as to drive the performance of your people.

As I've mentioned, there are other types of reviews, but once you start seeing the process outlined for those just mentioned, you'll find it easy do figure out how to do the others.

The review process is the single most powerful tool for managers to use both in business management and developing the capabilities of their people. Be sure to use every review for its real power!

21

THE BASICS:
FUNDAMENTALS OF THE REVIEW

As I discussed in the introduction to this section, managers tend to spend their lives in reviews. We have all types of reviews: deal reviews, pipeline, call, account, territory, performance, activity, one-on-ones and any number of others.

Despite the amount of time we spend in reviews, much of that time is wasted. We don't learn as much as we should from a business management point of view, and we don't leverage the review as a powerful opportunity to coach and develop our people.

Regardless of the type of review, there is a common underlying process that maximizes the impact of each review. Understanding this process, and executing it sharply has a profound impact on both the time invested in the review process and the outcomes achieved.

Before diving into that, let's review some of the problems with how most reviews are conducted.

FUZZY OBJECTIVES, MIXING APPLES AND ORANGES

One of the biggest problems in reviews is that our objectives for each review are ill defined, or even unknown. Too often, I see managers, particularly new managers doing reviews, and emulating bad practices they learned in reviews with previous managers. Sometimes managers are simply doing what they *think* they should be doing when conducting a review, or just inventing it on the fly.

Or we inappropriately combine different types of reviews. For example, about 95% of all the pipeline reviews I ever participated in have become deal reviews.

You've seen what happens. You start looking at the pipeline, then you ask about a key deal, all of a sudden you shift to talking about that deal, spending your time on that, forgetting what you were trying to accomplish was to understand the health of the pipeline.

The underlying problem is that the objectives of deal reviews and those of pipeline review are completely different. You have to separate these reviews.

Don't get me wrong, we can conduct both a pipeline review and a deal review in the same meeting, we just can't mix them. We might spend the first 15-20 minutes just focusing on the pipeline. Then we might spend the next 30 or so minutes on a deal review. We could also spend the final 10-15 minutes in an activity review. In an hour, if we conduct the reviews properly, we can accomplish a huge amount.

LACK OF PREPARATION

Once we are clear about the objectives of the review, the next time waster is lack of preparation on both the parts of the salesperson and the sales manager.

For example, perhaps we schedule 30 minutes to conduct a deal review. Most often, because either the salesperson or the sales manager is poorly prepared, 20 minutes are spent catching each other up on the deal background, what has happened to date, or even just figuring out what we should talk about. In the end, we are left with about 10 minutes to talk about the really critical issues and the actions we need to take.

We use our time more effectively if both the salesperson and the manager spend a few minutes before the meeting reviewing the status and background of the deal in CRM (or whatever tool you use to capture this information.)

Because the manager and salesperson are prepared, we can spend our time in the meeting focusing on the most important part of the review: What are the risks? What are the things we should be doing next? What do we need to do to maximize our ability to win? How can we compress the sales cycle? What do we need to be doing to position our value in order to protect our pricing or deal margin?

Yes, we'll probably need about 5-10 minutes doing a quick recap of where we are with the deal, but we spend most of the review time on what we need to be doing.

While I've used a deal review as an example, having pre-established objectives, and spending a few minutes preparing before any review will produce far better results.

ONE-SIDED REVIEWS

Too often, the review is very one-sided. It may be the salesperson doing a data dump with the manager—primarily to let the manager know what's going on, fulfilling the manager's business management needs.

Often it's one-sided in another way. Typically, it's the manager in *tell* mode.

They've gotten some information and immediately start dictating what to do (even though the salesperson is closest to the situation). No one learns anything from these and the salesperson grows to resent the manager.

Or sometimes the review looks a little like a ping pong game. The manager asks something, the salesperson replies, back and forth, asked and answered, but nothing other than information sharing happens.

The review should be a dialogue or conversation. Managers leveraging the coaching opportunity will be asking a lot of questions to get the salesperson to think about what they are doing, to analyze the situation, to assess different alternatives. Typically there a lot of why, what, and how questions. Thing like, "Why is the customer…".: "What if you tried this…" "Have you considered this…" "Why do you believe this…" "What would happen if…" "How might you get this done…" (Go back and review some of the non-directive coaching questions for clues about questions you might ask.)

At certain points, it may be useful to drill down a little deeper in exploring the issues and what we might do about them.

Through this dialogue, the manager will always achieve their business objective, and the salesperson will be challenged to think, evaluate, and learn through the coaching conversation.

Both the manager and the salesperson have learned and have a shared perspective on how to move thing forward.

CONCLUDING WITH A WHIMPER

The fourth biggest problem with reviews, is that we fail to establish and agree on action plan. We don't identify: What do we do next? By what date? What is the anticipated outcome? Who is responsible?

We want to make reviews more than just sharing of information. If that's all we use reviews for, then we should just read reports or look at CRM.

We want to end each review with actions we will take. With a deal review, it might be next steps on the deal. A pipeline review might end with actions to improve the pipeline integrity, volume, or velocity.

Some of the actions might be things a manager needs to do to help move something along, or remove a barrier.

Some of the actions might be things to help improve the salesperson's ability to do things—perhaps some training, reading, or something else.

Some of the actions might involve putting some of the coaching recommendations in place, testing, practicing.

A key outcome of reviews is to make progress, identifying how to move things forward and improve. Without agreed upon follow-up actions, we lose this phenomenal opportunity.

Without agreeing on action plans, it's kind of like running in place—there's a whole lot of effort, a lot of sweating, but you don't get anywhere!

FAILING TO FOLLOW UP

Once we and the salesperson have agreed upon an action plan, it is crucial to follow up to see what was done and what outcomes were achieved (or failed to be achieved).

This is just good management discipline. It also makes sure that we are consistently moving forward and making progress.

Following up reinforces the accountability of everyone involved in the review.

Consistent failure to follow up ends up with too many people failing to follow through, and the time spent in the review was just wasted.

SUMMARY AND QUICK TIPS

There is a common process that maximizes the value of *every* review:

1. **Kill two birds with one stone in every review.** You have business management (informational) and coaching objectives. Leverage each review to achieve both.

2. **Be clear about the objectives of the review and stick to them.** We don't have to reestablish the objectives for every review we conduct. Every deal review will always have the same objectives/.Likewise, every pipeline, call, account, territory, one-on-one, or whatever review has specific objectives. Know them; don't deviate from them.

3. **It's a learning/problem solving conversation:** It's not just an information dump or a lecture; it's you and your salesperson collaborating, figuring out what needs to be done next, how you can improve, how each of you get better.

4. **Execute all four elements of the review in every review:**
   a. **Preparation.**
   b. **The meeting is a dialogue/conversation.**
   c. **Agreed upon actions and next steps.**
   d. **Follow-up.**

As a final thought, there is a multiplier effect in this approach to doing reviews. Since we've converted them from status reporting to powerful coaching sessions, what the person learns in a single review will be applied in everything else they do.

For example, in deal reviews, as we get them to think about developing and sharpening their strategies—and as they see the great results—they will start doing the same thing with every other deal they work on.

Alternatively, if we help them think about how they improve the results of a specific prospecting program, they will start thinking about the same things in every other prospecting effort they have.

106 I David A. Brock

The magic in this is we don't have to review every deal, every sales call, every prospecting program. Because of the multiplier effect, we only have to spend time on a small percentage of the things they are doing, but know they will apply the same thinking to everything they do.

22

DEAL REVIEWS

Reviewing where people are with their deals or opportunities and coaching them on developing winning strategies is where managers spend a lot of time. It's time well spent.

We want to assure they are doing the right things in the deal. We want to help them develop and execute winning strategies, as well as develop their skills to improve their execution on future deals. We want to maximize their ability to be successful.

THE PROBLEM WITH MOST DEAL REVIEWS

Most deal reviews I sit in accomplish very little.

Usually, the objectives of the meeting are unclear, the sales manager is ill-prepared, and perhaps the salesperson is not prepared.

Most of the time is spent reviewing background information and talking about what's already happened. By the time all that information is shared, there is not a whole lot of time to brainstorm the steps the salesperson should be taking to maximize her ability to win the deal.

And that's in the *best* of circumstances. I've seen it a lot worse.

Sometimes, the review goes on and on and on. Most deal reviews can be accomplished in about 20-30 minutes. Admittedly, there will be some very complex deals, some that are very large, and some that are very important, all of which merit more time. But most reviews, if conducted effectively, should be completed in about 20-30 minutes.

THE OBJECTIVES OF THE DEAL REVIEW

First, we need to be clear about the objectives of the deal review:

1. **From a business management perspective, we want to understand the deal and understand what it takes to win. Are there risks? Is a winning strategy in place and ready to be executed? What are the next actions the salesperson needs to take in executing that strategy?**

2. **We probably want to understand the compelling business problem for the buyer, where the buyer is in their buying process, their decision-making process, the competition, and things that impact our success.**

3. **Naturally, we want to understand the projected deal value and whether the target close date is reasonable or achievable.**

4. **Finally, the review represents a great coaching opportunity. We want to help them improve their abilities to develop and execute winning deal strategies.**

A NOTE ON THE SALES PROCESS

The sales process is the most important tool you have to help with the review process. (Yes, I'm going to keep repeating this through the whole book!)

If you don't have a sales process, or people aren't using it, you will find it virtually impossible to manage performance. Research shows organizations consistently using the sales process have higher quota performance than those who don't—the performance difference is over 20%!

While a pipeline review is not the same as a deal review, without a sales process, we have no idea of where we are, and consequently we have no ability to accurately position the deal in a pipeline.

The sales process is a fantastic "cheat-sheet" for the manager in conducting the deal review. It tells you the questions you should be asking in order to understand where the opportunity is positioned in the buying/sales cycle. The sales process provides you the questions that enable you to understand if the things that should have been done to this point are actually done. It also provides you with the questions that enable you to start discussing, "what should we be doing next?"

I lead hundreds of deal reviews every year. Most of the time, I don't have to know much more than the sales process and a little of the background information in order to conduct a high impact deal review.

PREPARATION, BEFORE THE REVIEW

Spend 2-3 minutes reviewing the deal in your CRM system. If you don't have a CRM system, you should require the salesperson to provide no more than a half-page write-up on the deal.

(Really, if you don't have a CRM system to track opportunities, put together the business case to implement one. I can't imagine a high productivity sales organization not leveraging CRM to the utmost level possible.)

In your preparation look at:

1. **Who the customer is and what are they trying to achieve? What is causing them to want to buy right now? Who is involved from their side, who should be involved? That information should be captured in the notes on the deal. Get some idea of the company and who from the company is involved.**

2. **Where we are in the sales process, what the projected close date is, what is the projected deal value?**

3. **Think of two or three questions you might ask to ascertain which stage the deal is in.**

4. **What are the risks, threats, challenges the customer faces on this deal? What are those we face?**

5. **What are the big two-three questions we should be asking ourselves about the deal or the next steps? (Again, the sales process should give you clues).**

This whole thing should take you no more than a few minutes if the salesperson is keeping things updated in CRM. If they aren't then that's another discussion.

CONDUCTING THE REVIEW

I recommend both you and the salesperson look at the deal in CRM. Ideally, you are looking at the same screen at the same time. If you are in the same conference room or office, you can sit next to each other as you study at the screen. The salesperson can keep notes or updates in the opportunity record, updating it in real time.

If the salesperson is remote, try using some screen-sharing software so you can both look at the same thing.

Deal Background: Ask the salesperson to spend just a couple of minutes providing some "color" on the deal. The CRM notes won't have a whole lot (and probably shouldn't). The salesperson should provide a little background about the deal, what's driving the customer decision, why they want to change, who's currently involved, and the key things we (and the competition) have been doing with the customer. This should just cover the highpoints. It should take only a few minutes.

Leveraging the Sales Process: As the salesperson is talking, ask questions to ascertain where they are in the sales process, and that they are actually where they think they are.

CRM will tell you the basic stage they are in, for example Qualifying, Discovery, Proposing, Closing. Every sales process contains a number of activities, information we need to know, commitments the customer should make, and other issues that must be addressed at that stage of the sales process.

If the salesperson is leveraging the sales process effectively, they should be able to respond well to your questions probing these activities or issues.

Think of the front end part of the process, where the salesperson has a qualified opportunity, and they are now in the discovery (needs identification, understanding decision-making, competition, buying criteria etc.).

In this case, if they have leveraged the sales process well, they should be able to answer the following without hesitation:

1. **What is the compelling need causing the customer to make a change?**

2. **What are the consequences of doing nothing?**

3. **Why are they interested in considering our solution?**

4. **What are they committed to do get the funding, if they haven't already?**

Those are fundamental issues in qualification, so if they don't have clear responses, they may not have done the best job of qualifying. To understand this, drill down a level or two. For example, on number (1) above, ask them things like:

1. **What's happened that has caused them to decide to change?**

2. **Why do they want to change now?**

Again, if the salesperson struggles in responding to these or doesn't have good customer based data, they may not have done as good a job at qualifying as they should have. This should be a big red flag to you. You may want to spend some time just on this issue.

In the Discovery phase of the sales process, there are usually key items like:

1. **We understand all their business and technical needs and requirements for a solution.**

2. **We understand who is involved in the decision-making process, their roles, and their priorities. How will they make a decision?**

3. **How will they justify the solution to their management? What does the business case need to be? Do we have the information we need to create a business case?**

4. **We understand the alternatives they are considering, making sure we are developing strategies to position ourselves against those alternatives.**

5. **What are their attitudes toward us and the alternatives?**

There are undoubtedly other activities at this stage of the process, but take one or two of the most important and ask the salesperson about them. For example, using (1) immediately above, they should be able to tell you the top priorities in needs and requirements for a solution. They should be able to explain why these are important.

Drill down one or two levels to test their understanding—again making sure they demonstrate they really know and are not guessing.

In each of these make sure they are expressing things in terms the customer has told them, not assumptions or guesses they are making.

Too often, sales people make major errors by making assumptions and guessing, rather than asking the customer directly.

I like to say, "Until it comes directly from the customer's mouth, it's not fact."

Don't ask questions about every activity in your sales process. Just test their knowledge of four to five key activities, based on where they are in the sales process. If they are leveraging it well, they will have very good responses based on facts from their engagement with the customers.

They will respond to your questions without hesitation, and be able to give you deeper insight about the issues.

If they don't know, or hesitate, or seem to be guessing, you should be concerned about whether they are using the sales process, and if they have the level of understanding about what the customer wants to do, or if they have an understanding of what it takes for you to win.

If they are at all uncertain, probe more, ask more questions about where they are in the sales process.

You may discover they have skipped important steps. In your coaching, you may want to help them understand why these are critical and why they need that data to move successfully toward closure. In your action planning, you may suggest they back up a little and go get that information, after all it's critical to executing a winning strategy.

If the person is executing the sales process well, this whole background, the entire *"where we are"* part of the review process should take no more than ten minutes for typical deals. For very large, complex deals, you will want to take a little more time on this part of the review.

MOVING FORWARD: WHAT DO WE DO NEXT?

This is where we want to spend most of the time in the review. This is the part of the review where you create the greatest value in helping the salesperson think about what they should be doing to move the deal forward and to be improving the ability to win.

Here, again, the sales process provides clues about questions you might be asking the salesperson to think about.

For example, in many sales processes, as you are completing the Discovery

Stage and moving to the Proposing Stage, there are a series of validation activities, for example:

1. **Reconfirming priorities and needs.**

2. **Testing aspects of our solution to get their reaction on how well it meets their needs.**

3. **Demonstrating potential solutions both to show how we meet needs and to confirm their views about the solution.**

4. **Making specific value based solution recommendations.**

5. **Validating the business case, our value proposition, and differentiation.**

6. **Understanding their attitudes about our solution versus the alternatives they may be considering.**

Use these sales process activities to get the salesperson to think about why these are important to their strategy, and the actions they need to take to get these things done. Pose them as questions:

1. **How will you be reconfirming the priorities with each person involved in the decision making process?**

2. **What can you do to assess the attitudes each person has regarding our solutions and those of the competition?**

3. **What can we do to align the differing agendas and priorities among the decision-making group?**

4. **How will we get the customer to validate our value proposition and differentiation?**

Use these to get the salesperson to think about the issues, and why and how they might most effectively engage the customer. Probe, question further, each time, getting them to think more about the issues they and the customer must address in moving toward a decision.

Get them to consider alternative approaches by using questions that start with, "What if you…." Or, "Have you considered…."

If they are stuck, if they don't know what to do, ask them to think about their past experiences: "How have you done this in other deals?" Alternatively, "Remember when you faced this in the XYZ deal, you tried…." Or share some other experiences with them, "Nancy was facing the same issues with her customer. She tried these things… Could you adapt them to your situation?"

The whole point of this part of the discussion is to get your salesperson to think about what's next, to get them to figure out the answers themselves.

The very worst thing you can do is to tell them what to do. This has several problems, the biggest of which is that they won't know *why* they should be doing what you're telling them to do. As a result, their execution of the action will probably be very poor.

TAKING GIANT STEPS FORWARD

If you've done your coaching well, the salesperson will have identified a number of activities to move the deal forward in the sales process.

Sometimes you want to challenge the salesperson with ideas for giant steps forward in the process or giant improvements in your competitive positioning.

Look for opportunities in the review to test some of these ideas:

- **How do we maximize our probability of winning?**

- **Is there anything we can do to compress the sales cycle?**

- **What can we do to maximize the deal value or margin?**

You won't want to do this with every review or with everyone. But sometimes, looking at for these opportunities, brainstorming these issues with the salesperson, enables them to change their thinking and make giant leaps in both the deal strategy and in their personal development.

AGREEING ON NEXT STEPS

As they start to develop these ideas of what to do next, they need to be thinking of very specific actions:

"I need to meet with _____ by this date _____, to accomplish these things _____"

"I need to do this _____ with _____, by this date _____ with these outcomes _____"

For the salesperson who hasn't been executing the sales process well, and may have skipped important steps, your discussion should focus on going back getting that information, completing those activities. If they haven't done those well, then they will have missed things critical to a successful outcome.

As you complete this discussion, make sure the salesperson documents the next steps and actions. Ideally, since you are both looking at your CRM system, they will do it in the CRM system itself.

However you do it, don't finish the discussion until they have documented the next steps.

Whether it is in CRM or some other form, (make sure you have a copy). If they leave the meeting without documentation of the agreed-upon next steps, you know what will happen—They will move on to the next *thing*, completely forgetting the next *steps*.

The whole value of the review will be completely lost.

FOLLOW-UP

This is critical, and too often forgotten. It's important to follow up with the salesperson as they execute the next steps. Follow-up is powerful in a couple of ways:

- **Assuring they are actually executing what they agreed to, moving the deal forward in the process. This focuses on improving accountability.**

- **Discussing what happened, leveraging the discussion as another opportunity to reinforce the deal strategy, change strategies, and continue to develop the salesperson's skills in developing and executing the deal strategy.**

You don't need to follow up on every action item, just the one or two most important items.

The beauty of recording these actions in CRM is it gives you the ability to easily monitor the status of these activities, making sure people are doing what they committed.

If you don't have a CRM system, one trick I use, so that I don't have to remember the follow-up is:

Immediately after the meeting, I write an email to the person about a specific activity asking "How did it go?" I use my email system to schedule it for future delivery—generally I schedule it for the day after the specific activity is to be accomplished.

So if the salesperson has committed to complete something by a certain date, I schedule the email for that date + 1 day. I blind copy myself on the email, so I also see it as a reminder to talk to the salesperson.

Most email systems have a capability for scheduling emails for future delivery.

OTHER IMPORTANT DEAL REVIEW ISSUES

There are a number of other things to think about in doing deal reviews:

1. **Each week choose a different deal to review with the salesperson.** That way you get to see what's going on with more deals, better addressing your business management needs, and you continue to reinforce your coaching.

2. **Make sure you choose deals in different stages of the sales process.** Too often, managers make the mistake of only reviewing deals in proposal or closing stages of the sales process. It's a huge mistake. By that time, the options you have in helping develop winning deal strategies are very narrow. Often, it's so late in the process there is virtually nothing you can do. Doing

deal reviews for deals in the qualifying and discovery stages give you the most flexibility in brainstorming alternatives and developing strong deal strategies.

3. **Inspection, leverage the sales process!** You will never have the time to review every deal your sales people are working on. But if you see your people effectively leveraging the sales process and developing strong deal strategies in the deals you do review, then you can expect they are applying the same principles in all their other deals. So you don't actually have to review every deal they are working on (that could be hundreds of deals every month across your team!)

CONCLUDING THOUGHTS

The deal review is, in my view, the single most powerful tool for understanding what's really going on in your people's territories, and for coaching them. Most managers spend too little time and get too little value out of deal reviews.

But think about it. Where your sales people spend most of their time—or should be spending most of their time is doing deals—finding and pursuing great opportunities.

If this is where they are spending most of their time, isn't this where you should be spending most of your time as you conduct reviews and coach them?

23

PIPELINE REVIEWS

95% of the companies I work with waste too much time on pipeline or funnel reviews. The time is wasted in two ways:

- **Most pipeline reviews turn into deal reviews:** It happens every time. The salesperson starts reviewing the pipeline and the managers asks about a certain deal. All of a sudden, the pipeline review is abandoned, and it becomes a deep dive into the deal. The manager may return to the pipeline, only to ask about another deal, going through the same cycle again.

  As a result, the manager and the salesperson never really complete a pipeline review and the manager has no idea about the health and vitality of the pipeline.

- **Pipeline reviews are conducted too frequently:** Managers obsess about pipelines; they want to see, "Are we going to make our numbers this week, this month, this quarter, this year?" As a result, they are always asking about the pipeline, sometimes conducting daily or weekly pipeline reviews.

It's important to have the right "cadence" in your review process. Too frequently and there are too few changes in the pipeline, so it's a massive waste of time. Too infrequently, you have no idea of what's happening and whether your people and you are on target for making your numbers.

You want to find the cadence that is just right.

We spend way too much time on pipeline reviews.

Because of the items I've listed above, and because we have unclear objectives for pipeline reviews, the time we spend in each pipeline review is usually far too long.

In most cases, reviewing individual pipelines with each salesperson should take no more than 15 minutes.

THE OBJECTIVES OF THE PIPELINE REVIEW

We have only 3 key objectives in pipeline reviews:

- **Assure we have high pipeline integrity.**

- **Assure we have the right pipeline shape/volume.**

- **Assure we have the right velocity/flow.**

PIPELINE INTEGRITY

A strong sales process that your people are actually using is the cornerstone of a high integrity pipeline. Without this, it is impossible to know where deals should be positioned in the pipeline.

We want to make sure opportunities are positioned correctly in the pipeline. Part of this is actually accomplished in our deal reviews. If, during the deal review, we see people are using the sales process and have an accurate view of where they are in the sales process, the deal will be correctly positioned in the pipeline.

Pipeline integrity issues can usually be seen though some sort of stage/closing date misalignment, deals that have been in cycle too long or too little, deals that haven't moved. We want to look at where they are in the sales process and the target close date. They should be aligned.

Here's an example of what I mean. Just yesterday, I was reviewing the pipeline for a large organization. They had a huge pipeline integrity problem:

- **20% of the deals in the pipeline had target close dates 3-15 months in the past.** Were those real deals? Were they abandoned? Had the salesperson forgotten them?

- **30% of the deals had serious stage/closing alignment problems.** For example, they had a 120 day sales cycle. There were a large number of deals in the Qualifying Stage of the pipeline projected to close within 45 days. Is it reasonable to expect these to go through the entire sales cycles on 45 days, when the norm was 120 days? The target close date was probably way off.

- **5% of the deals were in the pipeline for longer than 365 days.** This is three times their typical sales cycle. Sometime deals are slow, but when you see a large number, you should suspect that something is off in terms of pipeline integrity.

- **The aggregate team win rate was in the 20-25% range, yet the pipeline only had 2.5 times coverage. (Forgive me, I don't like aggregate coverage numbers, these should be individualized, but I'm using this just as an example.)**

You can see that this company had major pipeline integrity, velocity, and volume problems. It simply wasn't accurate, you couldn't tell what was going on, and had no ability to predict whether you could reach your numbers. (You could also see they clearly weren't leveraging the sales process, so their deal strategies were probably pretty weak.)

It's important to note, this doesn't mean the deals these people were pursuing were bad deals. It just means they were inaccurately positioned in the pipeline.

PIPELINE SHAPE/VOLUME

It's important to know your salesperson is pursuing enough deals to make their numbers. Here, it's critical to know the healthy pipeline metrics for each salesperson.

At the most basic level, it's taking the total volume needed for the salesperson to make his number, divided by the win rate.

For example, if a salesperson has a $1 million quota, with an average deal size of $100K, he will need to close ten deals to make his quota. If his win rate is 25%, on an annualized basis, his healthy pipeline needs to have $4M worth of deals, roughly a total of 40 deals. Anything less and it is very unlikely he will make his number.

Some people call this shape, or volume number, the amount of "coverage" needed in the pipeline. Using the example, they would say the salesperson needs four times coverage.

A mistake many organizations make is having an overall coverage rule. They declare, "Everyone has to have four times coverage in their pipelines." The problem with that is it penalizes top performers. If a top performer has a 50% win rate, they only need two times coverage to make their number.

The rule also creates a problem for low performers. If a low performer has a 20% win rate, they need five times coverage. Measuring them on four times coverage assures they won't make their numbers.

It's critical that each salesperson knows their healthy pipeline metrics.

PIPELINE FLOW/VELOCITY

It doesn't help to have the right volume of opportunities in the pipeline if they aren't moving. So it's important to look at pipeline flow or velocity.

There are lots of ways to look at this, but the most basic is sales cycle time. Opportunities in the pipeline that have sales cycle times that are significantly longer than the normal sales cycle are opportunities that are stuck.

In the example at the beginning of this chapter, the company had 5% of their opportunities in the pipeline longer than 365 days—on an average sales cycle of 120 days. This reveals a pretty significant velocity problem that impacts overall pipeline health. You need to figure out how to "unstick" these deals. (These might be deals you review with the salesperson in a deal review session.)

Don't just pay attention to deals that are stuck. Look at deals that seem to be going too fast. Yes, every once in a while, you get a bluebird and a deal rockets through the process, but most should be clustered around your average sales cycle (to that point in the process). If deals are going through way too fast, it may be an indicator of deal strategy problems (for example, they may be discounting way too much to drive deal velocity).

I like looking at average time in each sales process stage, and the flow from stage-to-stage. This gives a more refined view of deal velocity or flow. This is a standard report in most CRM systems, so it's very easy to track.

YOU DON'T FIX PIPELINE PROBLEMS IN THE PIPELINE

This may be a little counterintuitive. The pipeline is a great monitoring and diagnostic tool. But when you have pipeline problems, you can't fix them by focusing on the pipeline.

Let me explain myself. There are only five problems you will ever have with the pipeline: Integrity, Volume, Velocity, Win Rate, Average Deal Size.

Integrity, Velocity, Win Rate, Average Deal Size problems are deal strategy problems. Perhaps we are qualifying poorly, perhaps we have bad strategies, perhaps we are being outsold. You don't address these problems in the pipeline review—the pipeline review just shines a light on these issues. But you address these problems in the deal and call reviews—improving people's abilities in these will show great results in the pipeline.

Likewise Volume problems are likely some combination of deal strategy (I require very high volume because my win rates are low, because my deal strategy/ execution is bad.) Alternatively, it's a prospecting problem. Your people aren't spending enough time hunting for new opportunities or they are very ineffective in their efforts.

The power of the pipeline is that it helps you identify trends and issues your people may be having in developing and executing their call, deal, territory, account, and prospecting plans.

PREPARING FOR THE REVIEW

It should only take a few minutes to prepare for the review. The salesperson must make sure they have provided you their most updated pipeline.

You'll want to skim the pipeline to see if there are any glaring integrity issues. You'll want to look at the volume—do they have the right number/value of deals in the pipeline. You'll want to look at the flow, seeing if there are any deals significantly outside the norm in sales cycle (or sales stage cycle) time. (All this means you have to know what each person's healthy pipeline numbers are, in the first place.)

CONDUCTING THE REVIEW

Generally, I want the salesperson to present their pipeline to me. You both should be looking at the pipeline report in the CRM system.

If they are managing their pipeline well, there should be no, or very minor, integrity issues. So the discussion becomes more about volume and velocity.

If there are integrity issues, probe the salesperson about the deal. For example, if they are in the qualifying stage of a deal (120 day sales cycle) and they are projecting a close date within 45 days, ask them if it's realistic. For example, you might ask, "You haven't even qualified this deal yet, but are projecting it will close in 45 days. Typically it takes about three months for us to close deals after they are qualified. What's different about this deal? What makes you think you can close it in about 40% of the time it normally takes?"

The salesperson should be able to answer in a sentence or two. They may have a good reason—sometimes deals fly through the process. Or they may realize they were over optimistic and have to push out the target close date. If it needs a longer discussion, you should schedule a specific deal review.

If there are a lot of integrity issues (your early pipeline reviews are likely to have these,) you will want to highlight them and ask them to go back, review their deal strategies, and correct them.

If they don't have enough volume in their pipeline, ask them what they are doing to fill the pipeline. Generally, this involves doing more prospecting. You'll want to understand at a high level that they recognize the problem and are taking actions to resolve it. But you will want to look at their prospecting plans and goals in a prospecting review session.

The big "red flag" is if they start complaining about not having enough leads, blaming marketing or someone else. It's *their* responsibility to make sure they have enough pipeline volume, and to have an action plan to resolve it.

If they are struggling with developing the action plan, talk about things they might be doing to find new opportunities, prospecting programs they should be undertaking, or other actions they might be taking.

They should be identifying velocity or flow problems. If they aren't, ask them about deals that seem to be stuck or taking too long. Again, they should be able to answer in a sentence or two. If a longer discussion is needed, you should probably schedule a deal review.

Beware of the following:

- **Target close dates that are too optimistic based on where the salesperson is in the sales process**

- **Target close dates that are constantly slipping, qualified deals with no deal value**

- **Deals that seem to be stuck in a certain stage**

- **Deals that have had no activity for some period of time**

- **Deals that have no next steps.**

Do your pipeline reviews properly, and all this should be apparent very quickly.

AGREEING ON ACTIONS AND NEXT STEPS

During the meeting, make sure the salesperson has updated information on any pipeline integrity issues. Generally, this involves changing a sales stage, target close date, or both. Sometimes, there may be dead deals that need to be closed out,(which may create pipeline volume issues.)

If there are volume or flow problems, the salesperson should identify the actions they are taking to resolve them. Make sure the actions are specific and time bound. Some of the actions might include more detailed deal reviews and strategy meetings.

Have them record the actions in the CRM system so you can follow up on them.

FOLLOW UP

Track the actions your people have committed to, making sure they are doing what they agreed.

Very often, some of the actions may involve you sitting down to help them develop ideas to address a specific problem.

For example, they may need to do more prospecting. It may be helpful for you to work with them on how to prospect, how to improve the effectiveness of their prospecting, and other things. Maybe they need some training, maybe they need marketing to help them develop some prospecting programs.

Many of the follow up sessions are best conducted as deal reviews, where you can go deeply into the deal, helping them improve their strategy.

OTHER PIPELINE REVIEW ISSUES

- **Improving conversion and win rates:** Since issues like the conversion and win rates are critical pipeline metrics, some managers try to coach improving win rates as part of the pipeline review. This is a mistake. The pipeline, by definition is an aggregation of deals. Improving win rates is really about sharpening deal strategies and improving execution.

  Consequently, while the pipeline metrics indicate a win rate problem, you only address this problem at the individual deal level, strengthening sales people's abilities to develop and execute winning sales strategies.

  When you see win rates declining in your pipeline reviews, it's a good indicator your people have problems in executing the sales process and developing winning strategies.

- **Improving velocity:** Like improving win rates, some managers try to coach sales cycle reduction in the pipeline. Again, this is really a deal strategy and execution issue. We should always be coaching our people on reducing sales cycles when we are coaching deal strategies.

- **Forecast:** This is probably the biggest confusion managers have about the pipeline. Developing the forecast is very different from the pipeline.

  The pipeline provides the "input" for developing the forecast. Deals that are moving into the closing stage of the sales process should be considered for the forecast. But each deal should be reviewed individually with the salesperson when committing something to the forecast.

  Committing opportunities to the forecast is really a variant of the deal review process. With the salesperson, you want to assess where the customer is in their buying cycle, their propensity to buy, their attitudes to you and the competition, their required commit date, and other factors, assessing whether to commit a deal to the forecast or not.

  Management may put a lot of pressure on you to increase the forecast. Don't do this blindly, it always comes back to bite you. Sit down with your sales people, identify deals you might be able to move into the forecast, make sure the sales people have strong action plans in place to make this happen.

- **Pipeline Integrity:** If your team or organization has had bad pipeline discipline, you are likely to have lots of pipeline integrity issues. It's important to deal with these head on—if you have poor pipeline integrity, you will never be able to have good visibility into your ability to achieve your goals. The garbage in the pipeline masks the real pipeline and business challenges.

  You have to be vicious in making sure you have a high integrity pipeline. As bad as it may look, you will at least know the core problems and can start addressing them.

  After you've worked with your people in instituting strong pipeline discipline, the pipeline integrity issues will probably disappear.

- **Advanced pipeline management:** The pipeline is a great diagnostic tool. Having strong pipeline metrics, analyzing them over time—are they improving, are they declining, are the stagnant—all give important clues to performance trends as well as ideas to improve execution.

  For example, while it may be counterintuitive, one of the fastest ways to improve the win rate is to disqualify more deals—focusing more tightly on the sweet spot.

  The pipeline gives you other clues of places to sharpen performance and sales cycle. Increasing average transaction value, or increasing win rates, meaning you don't require as many opportunities (coverage) to make your numbers.

  Spend time analyzing the pipeline and getting under the numbers to identify opportunities to improve the performance of your team.

CONCLUSION

The pipeline is one of the most fundamental tools for sales people and managers to use to make certain goals will be achieved. You cannot have a high integrity pipeline without having a strong sales process that your people are using.

When conducting pipeline reviews, be clear about the right cadence and the objectives of the pipeline review. When done correctly, it seldom takes more than about 15 minutes to do a pipeline review with each of your people.

24

CALL REVIEWS

Call reviews are probably the second most frequent reviews you will conduct, following deal reviews. Call reviews can be very powerful because of the immediacy of the coaching impact.

Before we jump into conducting high impact call reviews, let me clarify some terminology. Sales calls can take any number of forms. They can be face to face meetings. Increasingly, they are phone calls, web or video conferences. We want to maximize our impact in each call.

Usually, call reviews take place either when planning an upcoming call, or during a debriefing after the call has been completed.

Often, the pre-call review is actually a brainstorming session to help the salesperson develop their call plan. Sometimes it's a quick conversation, check-pointing the salesperson's plan before they execute it.

Call reviews may take the form of a quick hallway conversation, or, for very important calls, a scheduled planning meeting. They can be in-person meetings with individuals or groups, or they can be held as telephone or web conferences.

Call planning and execution are very closely related to deal reviews. Probably the majority of actions we agree upon in the deal review are meetings with customers, focused on helping them move through the deal process. These become "calls."

Likewise, call planning and execution are critical to effective prospecting, so the call reviews will be tightly linked to your prospecting reviews.

Good call planning and sharp execution are critical to improving our ability to win and to compressing the sales cycles. If you haven't done so, you should make sure your people have good training in call planning—perhaps in the form of a topic in a sales meeting.

Before we can move into a discussion of call reviews themselves, let me provide some groundwork regarding high-impact calls.

It's important for sales people to be well-prepared for each customer meeting. Preparation enables them to maximize their impact in the meeting, and in doing so create great value for the customer and improve the likelihood of achieving their goals. In planning a call, the salesperson needs to ask: :

- **What are their goals and objectives for the call?** The salesperson's goals and objectives are derived from the deal strategies and the next key actions in the sales process.

- **What are the goals and objectives the customer may have for the call?** The customer's goals and objectives are derived from where they are in their buying process. If we are advising them and facilitating their buying process, we should have a good idea of what they hope to accomplish. Agreeing on agendas for meetings up front facilitates this process.

- **Do we have the right people participating in the call?** Too often, sales people fail to move deals forward because the right people, either from the customer side or from the salesperson's company, aren't participating in the call. I remember participating in a call review for a salesperson making a closing call on a multimillion dollar deal. She had been working on the deal for over a year and had the most favored position. She was planning a final closing meeting with key people at the customer. In reviewing the call, we discovered she failed to invite two of the key decision-makers. If they weren't at the meeting, it would have been impossible to close the deal. Catching this up front enabled her to invite them, so she could accomplish her goals (she got the deal, by the way—I'm still fighting with her for some share of the commission ;-)

- **What commitments or actions do they want to derive from the call?** In each deal the salesperson wants to move the customer through their buying process and move through the sales process. To do this, you need to work with them to identify the commitments or actions needed to keep making progress (and the target dates for those commitments.)

- **What value are we creating for the customer in the call?** If we aren't creating value for the customer in each interaction, we are wasting their time and ours. If the salesperson cannot identify the value of the call to the customer, up front, then she's not ready to make the call.

With this as a framework for planning and executing high impact calls, let's shift to the call review process.

OBJECTIVES FOR PRE-CALL REVIEWS

As managers, our objectives in conducting call reviews include:

- **Are we meeting with the right people?**

- **Assure the salesperson has clearly defined goals or outcomes that are appropriate for where the customer is in the buying process.**

- **Make sure the salesperson is moving the deal through the sales process and enabling the customer to progress through their buying process.**

- **Make sure the salesperson maximizes their impact and value created in the sales call.**

- **Make sure the salesperson will be using the customer's time well.**

- **Explore ideas for compressing the sales cycle by setting more aggressive goals for the call. For example, can they complete more activities from your sales process checklist?**

- **Is the salesperson making sure the customer is prepared for the call by publishing an agenda in advance and gaining the customer's agreement to the objectives?**

PREPARING FOR THE PRE-CALL REVIEW

To prepare for the call review, take a few minutes to look at most current update to the deal or opportunity strategy. (Make sure your sales people are keeping CRM updated.) Look at the notes, review where the salesperson is in the sales process, and check the next steps that have been identified in moving the opportunity forward.

These steps will help you think about how the salesperson can design a call that accomplishes as much as possible.

CONDUCTING THE REVIEW

Usually, I like the salesperson to outline their objectives for the meeting and the outcomes they'd like to see. It's good to test those objectives against where they are in the selling process, as well as the appropriate next steps.

Next, it's important to discuss who's participating in the meeting. Are they the appropriate people for the goals and objectives of the meeting? Should others be invited to make sure the goals can be achieved?

Getting the salesperson to anticipate things that might happen in the meeting helps them better deal with those things if they arise. Probe the salesperson on what the customer expectations are for the meeting. Will the salesperson be prepared to meet them? What objections might the customer have? Does the salesperson have ideas about how to deal with those objections?

One question I always like to ask: "What is the worst possible thing that might happen in the meeting and how will you deal with it?" Oddly enough, sales people always have something they are very worried about. But they seldom think about how they are going to deal with it. Guess what happens, a large percentage of time their biggest worry happens and they aren't prepared to deal with it.

It's always good to get the salesperson to think big. In research we've conducted, we've found that sales people tend to make 50% more calls than needed. Usually it's a result of poor planning, lack of preparation, or poor execution.

As a result, the pre-call review can actually get the salesperson to think, "Can we accomplish *more*?" The next key activities in the sales process might help you and the salesperson identify what more might be achieved in the meeting.

Another way to increase the impact of sales calls and to compress the sales cycle is to make sure the customer is as prepared for the meeting as the salesperson is. Particularly for very important meetings, ask the salesperson if they have shared and agreed upon an agenda with the customer. Doing this in advance, sets the stage for very powerful meetings.

ACTION PLAN

As a result of the review, the salesperson should update their call plan. I strongly believe in written sales call plans, even if it's no more than half a dozen bullets written on a 3x5 card. A written plan both helps the salesperson internalize the call plan, and also serves as a reminder during the call to help keep them on track.

Another thing I find very powerful, and encourage sales people to do as part of pre-call planning reviews, is to prepare a written agenda for distribution to participants in the meeting. A physical agenda helps keep everyone focused and on track in the meeting.

FOLLOW-UP, OR POST CALL REVIEW

After the salesperson completes the call, ideally as soon after they've completed the call as possible, do a quick follow up. Among the questions you might ask are:

- **How did the meeting go? Were the right people there? Was the customer prepared to participate actively in the meeting?**

- **Did they achieve all their goals? Were the expected commitments made? If not, what prevented them from achieving the goals?**

- **What did they do really well in the meeting?**

- **What could they have improved?**

- **Were they blindsided or surprised by anything that came up? How might they avoid that in the future?**

- **Could they have accomplished more in the meeting? This is very powerful** in helping sales people stretch, setting bigger goals, using their and the customer's time more effectively.

- **What are the next steps?** Make sure they have updated their deal strategies with these next steps.

OTHER THOUGHTS ON POST-CALL REVIEWS

You can conduct post call reviews on any call, even those you haven't done a pre-call review. The questions are the same.

For inside sales and SDRs, if your phone system allows for call recording, it's fantastic to record some calls, then listen to them with the salesperson. I'm constantly amazed people don't realize they have certain bad habits, or they think they may have asked great questions or were listening well to the customer. On listening to recorded calls and discussing them with sales people, so often they say, "I can't believe I said that," or "I really missed that, I need to pay more attention next time."

OTHER CALL REVIEW ISSUES

- Sometimes in planning for particularly difficult calls, it's effective to do a role play, helping the salesperson actually practice responding to and dealing with tough issues before the call itself. Or the salesperson may want to dress rehearse a critical presentation.

- With some calls, particularly prospecting calls, it's good to focus on how the salesperson opens the call. What do they say to capture the customer's interest? How can they present themselves most positively? Sometimes you can help the salesperson develop templates for these calls. Again, role plays can be a very powerful tool.

- On every call you make jointly with the salesperson, make sure you sit down and plan the call with the salesperson. Be very clear about the role they expect you to take in the call. It's their call so you need to consider yourself a resource to help them achieve their objectives. Have a written call plan that you both have in the meeting. Don't take over the call from the salesperson! It's *their* call!

CONCLUDING THOUGHTS

As I mentioned at the beginning of this chapter, call reviews are powerful because of their immediacy. You help the salesperson prepare for a high impact meeting, they execute the meeting, and you debrief immediately afterwards.

Because of this immediacy, Call reviews can exert a huge impact on sharpening execution.

25

ONE-ON-ONES

By now, you should be coaching your people at every opportunity you have. You are leveraging reviews to keep you informed about what's going on with the business as well as improving your sales team's performance.

You are leveraging informal opportunities, windshield time, Starbucks time.

You are finding opportunities to reinforce the things your sales people are doing right through "Atta' boys/girls."

You're wondering what else you should be doing with each person on your team, suddenly remembering the one-on-ones you used to have with your manager.

One-on-ones are important. They are regularly scheduled opportunities to talk about a variety of issues you may not cover in the reviews you are conducting or which may be inappropriate for team meetings.

CADENCE

It's important to set a regular schedule with each person on your team. The right cadence for the reviews depends on a number of things. Some managers like having them on a weekly basis. For some people that's too frequent—perhaps every two weeks. Set the time that seems most appropriate for each person. However, make sure that no more than two weeks pass without a one-on-one.

Some things to think about in setting the right schedule:

- **Newer people probably need weekly meetings.** You want to make sure they are getting up to speed as quickly as possible. You want to help them avoid mistakes. You want them to get into a highly productive rhythm. (By new, it may be very experienced people, but new to the organization. Alternatively, it may be people relatively new to selling.)

- **Clearly, people struggling with performance may need weekly meetings or even daily meetings.**

- **If you have remote people, it's probably important to make sure you have regularly scheduled weekly meetings.** When you see people every day in the office, informal hallway chatter and banter is very powerful in helping people feel part of what's happening and keeping them informed. But many people are working remotely. You know the saying, "Out of sight, out of mind." We tend to forget about them. They don't get to participate in the hallway conversations. Over time, they may feel and become disconnected. One-on-ones become very important in keeping them and you informed and keeping them engaged. You don't want any of them to feel like they are orphans or that you don't care.

Keep the schedule sacred. Both you and the salesperson need to do everything possible to avoid skipping scheduled meetings, rescheduling them, or letting other interruptions arise.

If you do let things interrupt or are constantly rescheduling, you are on a death spiral, ultimately, one-on-ones fall by the wayside. Pretty soon you and your people are losing touch.

I like to focus my one-on-ones on two specific things: looking at how your people are planning and spending their time, and "taking their temperature."

One-on-ones should take roughly 30 minutes per individual. Remember, you cover deal, call, pipeline and other reviews in other sessions with your people, so don't waste your time covering these again. Make sure you stick to the objectives of the one-on-one.

PLANNING AND TIME MANAGEMENT

It's very powerful to use some of the time in the one-on-one to look at how your people are planning and spending their time.

Too often, all of us fail to manage our time as effectively as possible. We get distracted, we are interruption or crisis driven. Over time we find these consume us, and we aren't spending our time as effectively as possible.

Helping reinforce good planning and time management habits with your people is critical. Don't micromanage their calendars, but help them develop a structure and make sure they are looking forward and managing their time as effectively as possible.

Make sure they are taking a balanced approach to blocking weekly activities and time. Are they allocating and blocking specific time periods for prospecting? Are they blocking time to research and prepare for key meetings, deals, prospecting?

Look at CRM. You should be able to see their follow-up activities—calls, customer meetings, other activities related to the deal, pipeline, account, call reviews agreed upon in the action plans established for the reviews. You should be able to look at their calendars and how they are blocking their time.

Are they overscheduling themselves? Everyone knows crises pop up, something unanticipated happens, you may have a management imposed "fire drill." We have to make sure we have a certain amount of unscheduled time that enables us to deal with these things when they arise.

If the salesperson overschedules their time, anything unanticipated destroys their calendars. Meetings have to be cancelled and rescheduled. Important things get deferred. And the impact ripples through everything in their calendar—this week gets destroyed, next week gets destroyed, then the following….

Pretty soon things spin completely out of control.

I like to look at people's calendars for the next two weeks. They should have these two weeks relatively well planned and structured—including some unscheduled time.

If there are *huge* unscheduled blocks, something's wrong.

If there isn't prospecting time, something's wrong.

If their meetings/activities in CRM are becoming delinquent, or are continually being pushed, something's wrong.

There's no magic formula. No X% of your time spent on this, Y% of time on that. You just want to look at the structure, and see for yourself how they are thinking about their own productivity, their purposefulness in moving things forward.

You might look three to four weeks out. There will naturally be less structure to their time. There will be some regular things—like prospecting time, but there will also be time that should be filled with customer meetings and other activities resulting from the current and following week.

Finally, make sure your team members are spending time on the right things. Elsewhere in the book, we will be looking at metrics, particularly activity and leading metrics. These help us make sure we are doing enough of the things we need to be doing right now (for example prospecting calls,) to produce the outcomes we need over time.

"TAKING THEIR TEMPERATURE"

While most of your one-on-ones will probably be focused how they are managing their time, you do want to spend some time "taking their temperature."

You want to see how your sales people are feeling, how engaged they are, if they have any concerns, if something's bothering them. Is there something they are really excited about and haven't had a chance to share? Are they having problems that you haven't had the opportunity to discuss before? Are they concerned about anything—in their territory, changes in the company, anything else? Is there anything they are hearing from their customers that is important for them to share with you?

This is a chance for you to share some of the things going on—a little more informally.

There may be some general or administrative matters you need to cover: one-on-ones are great times to do these.

YOUR PLACE OR MINE?

If possible, conduct the one-on-one in their office. You know what your office looks like, you don't learn anything by having people come to your office. Sit with them, whether it's a cubicle, at their desk (as long as you can have a private conversation). You learn a lot about a lot just by looking at their workspace.

Consider getting out of the office, go for a cup of coffee, sit in a park, do something different.

These days, with people working virtually, it's often difficult to get together "physically." Make sure you visit anyone that's remote at least once a quarter. Perhaps combine some customer meetings with the opportunity for a longer one-on-one.

THE ONE-ON-ONE IS NOT

The one-on-one is not a deal, pipeline, or any other kind of review. You might schedule these back to back, for example, a one-on-one and a pipeline review. But be clear, the objectives of each are different, so don't confuse them.

The one-on-one is not a performance review. Performance reviews have entirely separate objectives.

CONDUCTING THE ONE-ON-ONE

Like all the other reviews, we have the same process for conducting effective one-on-ones—preparation, execution, agree on action plans, follow up.

- **Preparing for the review:** Hopefully, you've established a standard agenda for the one-on-one, that helps your preparation. If how they are using their time is a critical element, you may want to quickly look at their calendars in CRM. Don't look at the detail of everything in their calendar, but look at how they are blocking their time, look at how the prospecting activities of this week, lead to the meetings for next week, and so forth.

  There are other things you want to talk about in the one-on-one. Your salesperson will have some things on her mind. You will have one or two things on your mind—know what you want to highlight, keep it to one or two; don't inundate them with a laundry list.

  Remember, in your preparation not to over prepare. That is, part of the one-on-one is purposefully unstructured to let the person talk about whatever's most important to them.

- **Conducting the review:** Unless this is your first one-on-one, you probably are into a rhythm with a standard agenda. For example, you may spend the first ten minutes looking at calendar blocking and time management.

  The next part of the review is the salesperson's. It's their time to talk about what's on their mind, issues, concerns, problems, or things they are excited about. Listen carefully, probe, ask questions. Realize you don't have to immediately react to everything or even anything. You may need to take some time to think about the issues.

  Also realize that sometimes the salesperson needs to vent. They just need to get something off their chests. You don't need to do anything other than to lend an empathetic ear.

  Finally, if you haven't had the opportunity, you have a couple of things you want to share.

- **Next Steps:** Agree on next steps, if any. There may not be action plans for each one-on-one. If there are make sure these are documented so you can follow up. A lot of the next steps may be on your shoulders. If the salesperson has some problems, challenges, or needs some help, you may have the "to-dos" on your list. Make sure you get them done!

  Not living up to your commitments and getting things done is a betrayal of trust and a violation of the relationship you have with your people. There is nothing better to get your people to live up to their commitments than to see the example you set.

- **Follow Up:** As you've seen in the previous chapters, there are things that you may have to do. Make sure you follow up with the salesperson with what you've done. Make sure they know what's happened and what they might be doing. Likewise, make sure you follow up on what they committed to do.

CONCLUSION

One-on-ones are critical in maintaining good communication with each sale person, making sure you stay engaged and connected.

26

ACCOUNT AND TERRITORY PLANNING

In the "old" days, we spent a lot of time and energy on account and territory planning. I don't see much of this anymore. I think there's a good reason for this.

Many of those account and territory planning sessions became top heavy with of methodology or tools. The sessions became more about filling out forms than really thinking about what a salesperson wanted to achieve with an account.

This chapter won't provide comprehensive account or territory planning coverage. I hope to provide ideas you can leverage to help your sales people think about their accounts and territories differently.

There are a lot of purposes for an account or territory plan. But to my mind, the primary reason is to find opportunities to grow the relationship and sell more. Despite its name, the account or territory plan is actually all about creating a structured *prospecting* plan.

I learned this from experience. I'd gone through all sorts of account planning training, participated in, even led numerous account planning sessions. People talked about all sorts of almost noble goals—developing closer relationships, better alignment with customer goals, increasing customer satisfaction and loyalty, getting to know more people, becoming more important to the customer.

All of these are important, but one day it struck me, "The only reason we are doing this is to retain and find more business." All the rest is just nice words.

What we were doing was wrapping a lot of fancy words, methods, and structures around what was really simple: How do we develop a structured approach to prospecting in our accounts and territories? Our goal is to use this approach find more opportunities we can quality and ultimately close.

Before saying any more, I have to confess to a certain mentality about account and territory planning:

It is my God-given right to a 100% share of my customer and my territory. As a sales professional, it's my job to figure out how to achieve that goal!

When I first started selling, I was fortunate to be instilled with this mentality. It changes the way one looks at everything. I suppose it's the "hunter's" mentality. Whether it's a single large account or a multi city territory, the hunter wants to find and get all the business possible.

Part of our job as managers and leaders is to get our sales people to think big. In helping people think about their accounts and territories, we want our people to be thinking about rooting out every opportunity for business and competing for it.

While we can never achieve that 100% goal, having that as a mindset creates relentlessness in continually seeking new opportunities.

THE REVIEW PROCESS

There are a couple of ways to approach the account/territory planning review process. Typically, sales people are given a bunch of forms and told, "Go out and plan, don't come back until you fill out the forms."

They fill out the forms, we glance at them, then they are filed away, forgotten until the next year.

I like to approach the review process differently; I view these particular reviews as huge teaching moments. Opportunities to get the sales people to think about their customers differently. Opportunities to explore new ways of engaging their customers—both the current ones they deal with and new customers they intend to develop in their accounts or territories.

As a result, I tend to divide the process into a few phases. The first might consist of brainstorming sessions about new things we may want to accomplish with our accounts and territories. These sessions can be conducted individually, with account teams, or with the entire team.

You might focus on one strategic initiative—perhaps driven by your company's business strategies, or perhaps one you create. It could be, "How do we maximize the penetration of XYZ product line in our territory?"

Right now, I'm working with a client, we have each of the account teams focused on: "How do we find the opportunity to get the right people in the customer to understand the impact of waste on their business? How do we quantify their specific problem and get them committed to doing something about it?"

Their target customers are in the food industry, and waste is a huge problem. Even small reductions in waste have a huge impact on overall profitability. They decided to find the people who were most concerned with these issues and those that owned the problem and engage them in good discussions about the impact of this problem and how they might solve it.

The managers launched this initiative in team meetings. They provided some basic training about these "personas," for example: Their role in the organization, how they are measured, what typically drives them, and so forth. Managers reinforced their understanding of the basic problems and issues they are leveraging to gain an audience with the customer.

The sales people are coming up with their own approaches within specific accounts and parts of their territories.

With another client, we are having the account teams analyze their customers. They are mapping where they've done business, the relationships they have. More importantly, they are identifying divisions, business units, and functions where they have done little or no business. They are developing plans to get introduced to key people within those organizations, learn more about them, and find opportunities where they might start solving problems.

There are a huge number of ways you can kick off this process with your people—all focused on growing the share they have with their accounts and territories.

As you think about engaging your team in account and territory planning, consider breaking away from the traditional "fill out the forms" exercise, to thinking about specific programs that expand relationships and share of account/territory. Don't do this just once a year, but keep it alive by developing new initiatives throughout the year.

Whatever you do, don't give the sales people a blind challenge such as, "Tell me what you are doing to expand your relationships and grow the business." It's impossible for them to respond in a meaningful way, and it's impossible for you to monitor their execution.

Nothing will get done.

Focus their planning on two to three key initiatives or priorities.

OBJECTIVES FOR ACCOUNT/TERRITORY PLANNING REVIEWS

Our key objective is to make sure our sales people have a structured approach to prospecting in their accounts and territories. We want to see they have a plan to expand relationships, identify new opportunities, and grow the business.

But we need to go a little further. We need to make sure their plans are aligned with our own company's strategies and priorities. This is vital—It is the sales team that executes the company strategy in front of the customers.

If the company has a strategy to grow certain market sectors, grow certain solution or product areas, the salesperson *must* have a plan to execute that strategy in their accounts and territories. Too often, though, they get stuck on their favorite product lines, their favorite customer segments. If that approach is not totally in sync with the company strategy, then they aren't doing their job.

Finally, the objective is expansion and growth. It's our job to make sure our sales team has a specific plan to do this.

PREPARING FOR THE REVIEW

If you're doing your job properly, you've provided the sales people some sort of format and specific objectives for their account and territory plans. These should be completed prior to the meeting. Take some time to review them before the meeting begins.

Since these plans are likely to be pretty comprehensive, make sure you allow yourself time to look at them. Don't just glance at them before the meeting. Study them and know the information and insights they contain. Otherwise, the salesperson will waste too much time telling you what you should have read in the first place.

Identify in advance the few key areas you want to focus on in discussing the plan.

CONDUCTING THE REVIEW

Presumably you've set some specific goals or initiatives, which focus the discussion. As the salesperson reviews their plans to execute within the accounts and territories, focus on the following:

- **Are they thinking big enough? Part of our goal with account and territory planning is to get them out of the rut of what they do every day. Are they thinking big enough, are they trying to get that 100% share?**

- **Are they being very specific and focused? This may sound a little at odds with the previous point, but we don't want them just casting a wide net. We want them to be identifying specific people—or at least roles ("I need to meet the person who has this responsibility at these accounts.")**

- **Do they have a specific plan with which to engage these people? How are they doing this—are they focusing on the customer business perspective, or are they "showing up and throwing up?" Do they have a schedule for accomplishing this?**

Since a lot of this is likely to involve doing new things—focusing on new segments, new roles, new solutions; ask what support and resources they need to be effective in executing their plan.

Look closely at their time allocation. Are they being realistic? Ideally, they have a lot of current activity and opportunities in their pipelines. Are they being realistic in their account and territory plans, given everything else they are doing?

Simultaneously, have they scheduled these activities into how they are managing their time? Too often, they are well intentioned in their planning, but they never get around to executing them because their everyday activities take precedence.

The account and territory review are one set of reviews that are often more powerful to conduct in a group. Since each account or territory manager is trying to do the same thing, it's often very powerful to share ideas and approaches with each other.

TAKING ACTION

At the end of the review the salesperson has identified specific activities and the schedule for accomplishing them. These could include:

- Meeting with the client to discuss goals and progress by a specific date.

- Having three conversations with specific types of people in my territory each week so I can understand their priorities and concerns when addressing issues and problems.

- Scheduling a webinar for all the division controllers in the customer to explore the "waste" challenge and opportunity.

- Inviting compliance managers from every healthcare account to a seminar on changes in the regulatory environment.

Whatever actions are established, make sure the salesperson is identifying them in the CRM system.

FOLLOWING UP

As you would expect, once the salesperson has established the specific action plan, you want to follow up with them.

You want to see how they are doing. Are they making progress? Where are they having difficulties? If they are having challenges, you want to engage them in discussions about how to overcome them?

Since our goals in account and territory planning are often higher-level and longer-term, it's also useful to schedule periodic checkpoint meetings. "Where are we? What have you accomplished? Where are you running into difficulties? How can we overcome them? Should we shift or change our overall plan to more effectively achieve our goals? What do we need to do to update the plan?"

CONCLUDING THOUGHTS

Account and territory planning gives both you and your people the opportunity to step back from the day to day activities and think big about what you want to accomplish.

Challenge your people to stretch, to think big, to break out of the rut of doing the same things. Challenge them to wander around in their accounts, and territories, but make sure it's purposeful wandering, not just aimless meandering.

The execution of the account or territory plan, however, is quite different. Since it's a structured prospecting plan, the execution becomes very tactical.

Every week each salesperson should be executing their plan, prospecting, and reporting on results and next steps.

Frequency of account and territory planning reviews and checkpoints depends. I tend to favor quarterly meetings and updates. The annual review really isn't effective.

Sometimes, you may need to do reviews more frequently. If a large, important account is undergoing massive change, you may want to schedule reviews even more frequently—both to take advantage of new opportunities, as well as to identify potential threats.

Make sure you take the time to do a good review. I've been focused on how to conduct efficient deal, pipeline, and call reviews. Since the account and territory review is our chance to think big with our sales people, take time. Schedule several hours, even an entire day. Consider holding the review off-site so you can get away from disruptions.

Account and Territory Planning is critical. Developing and executing these plans enable your sales people to identify new opportunities to fill their pipelines.

If they aren't doing it, and if you aren't challenging them to think big, their pipelines will dry up.

27

TEAM MEETINGS

So far in this book, I've focused primarily on individuals, that is working one on one with each person on your team. That is by design. Pragmatically, most of your time will be spent working with each person on your team, one on one.

But you can't forget you are managing a *team*, a collection of individuals reporting to you. There is huge power in high impact team meetings.

Notice that I said, "*High Impact* Team Meetings." Too many team meetings I participate in are purely wastes of time—and that's the sales manager's fault.

Team meetings are very powerful for a number of things, including:

- **Sharing the same information across the whole team.**

- **Training and development.**

- **Sharing ideas, experiences among team members.**

- **Collaborative learning and problem solving.**

- **Reinforcing best practices for the team.**

- **Reinforcing alignment of priorities within the team.**

- **Getting collective feedback about the "state of the business," and issues the team faces.**

To complete the thought, team meetings are the *wrong* vehicle for:

- Reviewing individual performance.

- Addressing specific individual performance or related issues.

- Coaching and developing skills for a few rather than everyone in the organization.

- Bitch sessions, dumping and complaining.

- Random get-togethers—go to the bar instead

PURPOSEFULNESS AND AGENDA

Every team meeting must have specific objectives and an agenda. This needs to be published in advance. Ideally, some preparation work is assigned beforehand, so everyone comes into the meeting prepared to accomplish something.

Your team meeting agenda should not try to achieve more than two to three major goals. There may be a need for a general discussion of new policies, tools, processes, or sharing new strategies. There may be a learning/training element, there may be a problem solving work session.

Too many of the bad team meetings I participate in either have no agenda, or too much on the agenda. Keep a simple agenda with two to three key items, ensuring the meeting is on-point, focused and short.

As you think about the agenda, ask yourself: "Is the team meeting the best way to cover a topic?" If you just need to pass information along, without questions or discussion, emailing the team might be more appropriate. If the topic is relevant to a minority of the team, then don't waste the time of other people.

PASS THE "TALKING STICK"

Certain Native American tribes had a fantastic concept for tribal meetings. They had a "talking stick." The only person who could talk was the one in possession of the talking stick. They would pass the talking stick around to those who wanted to contribute to the discussion, not letting any one person dominate.

Too often, team meetings end up being lectures (or tirades,) from the manager. This is just an exercise in gratifying the ego of the manager and wasting the time of the people. The team meeting is a terrific chance to share ideas, learning, and solve problems.

If you don't have a real "talking stick," conduct team meetings as if you had one. Make sure everyone gets a chance to talk, express their ideas and opinions.

You might do this more formally by making a different person responsible for the agenda and leading each meeting. For example, if you want to leverage the meeting for some training, assign one person the responsibility for developing and presenting the training (you may have to support them). Rotate the responsibility for leading the meeting across the entire team.

MAKE THE MEETING INTERACTIVE

Team meetings are great for addressing specific issues, exploring alternative approaches, or solving problems everyone is having. Focus on a single issue, developing an exercise to address the issue.

For example, I've seen teams struggling with how to handle a certain objection. Use the team meeting as an objection-handling clinic. Take the objection, have people role play how they might handle the objection with the customer. Give everyone a chance to role play.

Or use the team meeting as a brainstorming session for solving a problem. Or look at a specific issue, prospecting, for instance, and have each person present what they do that works, guide the discussion, but make sure each person participates.

SET THE EXAMPLE, DISCONNECT, PAY ATTENTION

You've experienced it. You walk into a meeting, everyone has their laptops or tablets in front of them, supposedly to take notes or to follow a presentation. As an outside consultant, sometimes I walk around the table, looking at what's actually on the person's screen. Most often, they are reading email, perhaps tweeting, reading a website, or playing solitaire.

If they don't have a laptop or tablet, it doesn't mean they are paying attention. Are both their hands below the table, is their head bowed, looking down? No they probably aren't praying (unless it's to get out of the meeting). They are looking at their phones, messaging, reading emails.

Some of the worst offenders are managers themselves. They call the meeting, kick it off, turn it over to the team, and spend the rest of the time not paying attention!

If you are having a meeting, practice good etiquette. Shut down all unnecessary devices. Have everyone toss phones into a basket at the center of the table.

Be present, pay attention.

WHAT ABOUT REVIEWS IN TEAM MEETINGS?

I used to think there was some power in sharing deal, account, territory, even pipeline reviews in team meetings.

My thinking was that we could leverage the power of the team in sharpening the strategies and dealing with tough issues a salesperson may be facing. In reality, a large amount of time, the sales people really didn't care.

If someone was presenting a deal strategy, they would listen with one ear, but they would really be thinking about their own upcoming presentation. As a result, the discussion, the shared learning, and the collaborative problem solving I hoped would be accomplished, simply wasn't being achieved.

This wasn't a case of sales people being jerks. It was just a matter of material being related to one deal or account specific to a single salesperson, but may not have been relevant to everyone.

There's another problem with leveraging meetings for reviews. They become unbearably long. Do the math: If each person spends only 20 minutes doing a deal review—presenting where they are, asking for ideas and input, that's a minimum of 3 hours and 10 minutes for a team of 10 people—not counting bathroom and coffee breaks.

As a rule, I generally don't like to include reviews in team meetings. Sometimes, someone is facing an issue that impacts everyone. In that case a single review, treating it as a case study and using it as the cornerstone for a focused conversation among the team, is helpful. But as manager, you need to facilitate that discussion carefully.

SOME CREATIVE IDEAS

Consider bringing in a guest speaker—perhaps an executive in the company or someone from a different function. Make sure they don't dominate the discussion, but provide good give and take that gets everyone actively participating.

Sometimes invite an external speaker—maybe even a consultant. ;-)

Mix it up, don't stick with the same boring format.

FREQUENCY AND TIME

Each organization has to determine how frequently they need to have a team meeting. If there is a lot of change, if there is a lot of training, it may be reasonable to have a team meeting weekly.

In general, however, I tend to favor no more than one team meeting a month. Even then, keep them to 60-90 minutes. Make sure you keep them focused.

Remember, if there is something special, like a product launch training program, or some other thing, you can always call a meeting for that specific purpose.

MAKE THE MEETING OPTIONAL

Imagine holding a meeting and no one showed up! That would tell you something important. Consider making the meeting truly optional. Perhaps not for all of the team members, but optional for some of them. If people stopped showing up, it's probably because there's something wrong with the meeting!

CONCLUDING THOUGHTS

As I talk to business professionals around the world, there seems to be universal agreement: We waste too much time in too many meaningless meetings. These meetings rob the participants of precious time for getting things done. For sales people, meeting-time may be robbing them of critical selling time.

Meetings can be valuable, but only if they are very purposeful, structured with an agenda that's adhered to, and we meet for no longer than necessary.

These are *your* meetings. Don't waste your people's time by having worthless sessions!

WOULD YOU INVEST 45 MINUTES A DAY IN TRAINING YOUR PEOPLE?

I had a fascinating conversation with my friend Tory Hornsby. We got to talking about the performance of his sales team—they've produced great results over the past couple of years. I asked him what his secrets were. One struck me as remarkable—and completely counter to what most executives would do.

Tory said, "Every day, we devote the first 45 minutes to sales training."

I had to stop him there, "Did you say every day? Did you say 45 minutes a day?"

In my head, I was doing the math—assume a 9-hour day, assume 90 minutes lost in lunch, breaks and so forth. That leaves 7.5 "productive hours" in the day (we know those aren't all productive), or 450 minutes—so he is investing 10% of everyone's time in sales training—every day!

Tory knew what I was thinking, he said, "Yes, it's a huge impact on time—but it's the biggest multiplier in sales effectiveness that I've found. I literally could not afford to stop doing this. The adverse impact in sales would be unacceptable!"

He had the data to support this, In the past year his team has grown sales 138% over the prior year. While there are a lot more things Tory has done to drive sales performance, according to him, this is the single biggest impact. Constant training, constant reinforcement, constant learning, all enable his team to continue to grow and improve their performance.

They have a regular cadence of how they conduct each meeting. Each day is the same, but different.

They'd spent some time figuring out the optimum amount of time. They started with 60 minutes a day, reduced it to 30, finally have settled in on 45 minutes—every day. For everyone, all the sales people, sales managers, and even others participate (though not every day).

The meeting starts with the team celebrating their accomplishments of the previous day—maybe landing some big orders, though those don't happen every day. They are things like great sales calls/meetings, reaching their goals for the day, something they have learned. It's followed in scrum-like fashion by each salesperson taking about one minute outlining their goals for the day. The sales people set these goals for themselves and measure their attainment of the goals. This takes the first 10-15 minutes.

The remaining 30 minutes is spent training. They rotate the responsibility. Tory may lead the training, one of the sales managers, or any of the sales people. Tory described one of the sales people using the game "Jeopardy," as a way of training the team on a new product they were launching. Every day, they attack something different. It may be a new sales or marketing program, learning about a new product, building sales skills—yes they do lots of role plays.

An important part of the training is constant reinforcement. Tory says, "We have to reinforce every new thing for 4 weeks until people have internalized what we are trying to get them to learn."

The way it works is they may introduce something new on Monday, on Tuesday, they spend a little more time talking about it. Later in the week, they may spend a few more minutes. The following week they cover it several more times—each time they change things up a little, it may be a presentation, a discussion, role plays. They continue this for 4 weeks. By this time the new skills and capabilities are ingrained in each of the sales people.

They also provide tools to support the sales people. I laughed as Tory described his sales enablement platform—each person has a three ring binder. They keep the latest sales programs, some "cheat sheets," and notes they take from the daily meetings. They use those constantly through the day.

For training to work, it can't be just one class or workshop. It has to be constantly reinforced, exercised, developed, and coached until people have internalized whatever it is you are training them on.

I was still astounded by the commitment Tory and his team make to daily training. Tory had all the math done and all the data. He knew how many person hours it took—both in the daily training meetings and in the time people spent preparing. He knew that at a minimum the daily 45 minute meetings "robbed" them of at least 10% of their selling time. As he reviewed the data about time, investment—then results, he concluded, "I can't afford not to do this! The adverse impact on sales productivity and sales results would be huge!"

Can you afford not to invest in training, reinforcing, and developing the capabilities of your people?

PART FOUR

RECRUITING, INTERVIEWING, HIRING, AND ONBOARDING

28

BUILDING A TEAM

You will only be successful in your role if you have the right team performing at the highest level possible. We've spent time talking about coaching and developing your people, setting performance expectations, making sure they are clear on their expectations. Even dealing with poor performers.

At some point, ideally through growth, but inevitably also through replacing people who've left voluntarily or involuntarily, you will need to hire more people.

While we know how important people are, I've found it very odd the way too many managers go about it. Too often, it's too casual, too informal, too unstructured.

The manager may post a job, skim through some resumes, interview a few candidates, ultimately finding someone that's "sold" them and bonded with them—a likable person that thinks like the manager.

Other times they rush through the process, not finding what they want, but settling on what they get. They are so desperate to fill a hole; they don't take the time to find the right people.

Then there are others who think, "So what if I make a mistake. The first 90 days is probation. If this person doesn't work out, I'll get rid of him and find someone else."

Each of the people decisions a manager makes is a multimillion dollar investment decision!

When your customers are making multimillion dollar investments, they take their time, put in place the right evaluation processes to make sure they are making the right decision.

Just like your customers, you cannot afford to make a mistake because the costs of a bad hire are so high.

In the following chapters, we will step through the entire process. We'll look at:

- **The true cost of a salesperson.** This will provide some detail about the multimillion investment decisions you are making, and why it's so important to have a structured process for hiring.

- **Building a sales competency framework.** As you recruit and interview, you don't know what you are looking for until you've build a "picture of your ideal candidate." Sales competency frameworks are terrific tools for doing this. I've provided a detailed discussion of this, and a "starter template," in the Appendix.

- **The recruiting, interviewing, hiring and onboarding process.** How we find the right people, hire them and get them productive as quickly as possible.

- **Finally, there's the issue of attrition—voluntary or involuntary.** Attrition is a leadership failure. While a certain amount of attrition is unavoidable, we want to be very careful about losing good people—or hiring bad ones.

By now, you won't be surprised to see the underlying theme of this section. It is the same as the overall theme of the book:

Whatever aspect of our job we are doing, our main responsibility as sales managers is to build the strongest teams we possibly can and maximize their short and long term performance.

29

A FRIGHTENING LOOK AT "THE COST OF A SALESPERSON"

I worry, sometimes, that we take the process of recruiting, hiring, onboarding, coaching, developing and managing the performance of sales people too casually. Too often, managers tend to treat sales people as commodities.

There's an attitude of quickly hiring the best person that's available, and if that person doesn't work out, we can always fire them and hire someone new.

Likewise, as business goes through its natural ups and downs, sales organizations are expanded and contracted to fit our budgets, creating, however inadvertently, that commodity perception—some would say callousness, and some of them would be right—toward the people who are, after all, our team members.

It's not just a sales management issue. I see it in the team members themselves. Too many sales people move from job to job, never staying with one company long enough to produce results.

Recently, I heard a great speaker at the Customer Executive Board (CEB) conference. He outlined some frightening statistics, here are some that scared me to death:

- **From their first day on the job to the time they leave, the average salesperson's tenure is less than 2 years (Sales Readiness Group).**

- **The average tenure of a sales manager is 19 months.**

- **47% of companies say it takes 10 or more months for new sales people to become fully productive. 67% say 7 or more months. (CSO Insights).**

- **58% of reps make quota. (CSO Insights).**

Taken together, these figures present a frightening view of selling and of the cost of sales. Basically, we have to make our money from a salesperson in a little more than a year. That is, to get a return on our investment in hiring and onboarding someone-who takes 7-10 months to become fully productive, but who will probably leave within the next 14 months; we have them produce at least two years' worth of business in those 14 months.

It gets even worse. That salesperson who has been around that long is probably on their second manager, who also takes some time to ramp and become effective as a manager. So the salesperson may not be getting the coaching needed to be as productive as possible.

But think further. Many people selling complex B2B solutions have sales cycles longer than 18 months. Coming into a job, a new salesperson may "inherit" great deals started by the previous salesperson—but being new, the likelihood of winning is low.

You remember this from your own days as a new salesperson. The number of high quality deals that we qualify early on in our tenure on a job is probably very low. We're new and don't know the right deals to qualify, or are in a rush to prove ourselves, so we chase lower quality opportunities. As we get to the ten plus month mark, we begin to recognize the nature of a quality opportunity, and the quality of the deals we chase go up. Then, 14 months later…

It's no wonder overall quota performance is so bad. It's no wonder we constantly struggle with the cost of selling, and of actually getting a return from our investments in selling.

And then there are the customers. We talk about the importance of relationships, of establishing their trust and confidence. Yet, the salesperson calling on them can look like a constantly revolving door to our customers. For a buying cycle that may be longer than 12 months, a "trusted" salesperson is seldom involved for more than one cycle. Customers have to constantly invest in "training" the salesperson, and developing relationships with new sales people and sales managers.

It's nor surprising that customers search for ways to minimize sales involvement in their buying process. If they are constantly "training" new sales people, if the salesperson isn't as knowledgeable as she should be, and if there is no long term relationship, the salesperson can become a disruption.

You can see that at a high level, the economics behind a salesperson and sales organization are challenging. The challenges become even larger the more deeply we look at the data on time to productivity, average time spent in a job, churn at a sales and managerial level, and declining performance results.

There is always a danger in dealing with high level data and averages across large numbers of people. But I feel that the data should cause us to rethink the people side of our profession. We can't be casual about this—it's simply costing us to much in money and opportunity.

We have to be purposeful about recruiting. The costs of a bad hire can be millions. Get the wrong person and you lose millions in deals.

We have to be purposeful about onboarding: We need to get people to full productivity as quickly as we can. Customers aren't waiting for us. We stand to lose more deals the longer it takes a person to get fully productive.

We have to be purposeful about performance management, coaching and development. Competing and winning, requires each of our people to be performing at the highest levels.

We have to look to retaining sales people—providing great work environments, and meaningful career development. If we want to maximize our success over time, we have to build a team with deep experience and strong capabilities.

Churning through people as business goes through ups and downs, or as we look at different *strategies du jour* is expensive and wrong for both the business and people. It's a demonstration of bad leadership/management. It costs us millions in lost opportunity.

This isn't just a management issue. Sales people own a large part of this.

Jumping from job to job may seem to be the thing to do, but you are cheating yourselves and your companies. If you want to be a high performing business professional, you need to hang around long enough to learn and to prove you can accomplish something.

I'm amazed when I see resumes of people with ten jobs in as many years. That employment history causes me to question the individual's real capabilities and experience, particularly, since it's unlikely that whatever success they attained was primarily due to their efforts. Even as you wonder about "loyalty," your real concern should be whether they can produce? Have they stayed in a position long enough to fairly claim the results of their work, or do those results rightly belong to someone who preceded them? People may be able to fool hiring managers through a sequence of a few jobs, but ultimately, hopping jobs catches up with everyone.

Both managers and sales people seem to demonstrate a very short-term attitude toward longevity and experience in their role.

This is a costly attitude, both from an organizational and individual point of view.

The impact on organizations is measured in millions.

The impact to individuals can amount to hundreds of thousands to millions because the individual never developed the deep experience they need, and that can only be developed by staying in a role long enough to master it.

It's time to understand the true business and personal costs of the short-term perspectives both sales managers and many of their team members take.

30

RECRUITING:
FINDING THE BEST AND BRIGHTEST

Finding people for any job openings you might have is easy. Just put a job posting on your company's website, on LinkedIn, or any of the dozens of job posting boards out there, and you will be inundated with candidates within hours.

Finding the *right* candidates takes time! And that's the problem. When you have an open position, you are usually in a huge hurry to fill it. You are either backfilling for someone you lost, or you are trying to fill a new position. In either case, you have to have someone in place to start achieving your business goals.

So you are in a rush!

You are tempted to take shortcuts, perhaps not taking the time to find the right candidate. But, as we've already seen, you are probably in the process of making a multi-million-dollar investment.

That's right, multi-millions of dollars. At the very least hundreds of thousands of dollars for the most junior of sales roles. Re-read the previous chapter if you don't believe me,

In looking at the economics of hiring, the mistake too many people make is focusing on the recruiting costs, the onboarding costs, and the salary/overhead of the salesperson. No way that amounts to millions. You have to look at *all the costs.* In other words:

Make a bad hire and you stand to lose millions of dollars in business to your competition or in opportunity costs.

More personally, your performance is judged by the quality of people you hire and bring on board. Making bad hires can cause you to lose your job.

You and I both know making the right hire takes time. But that raises another quandary. The longer you have the territory open, the more customer business you are not competing for and losing.

So there is huge pressure to fill the job fast.

There's a ticking clock. It can take months to find the right person. How do you compress that?

There are two key components to recruiting the right candidates to fill your open jobs:

1. **Having a clear picture of your ideal candidate.** Without knowing very specifically what you are looking for, what skills, behaviors, attitudes, values, experiences are required for top performance, any and every candidate can look good.

2. **Reducing the time required to identify ideal candidates.** It can take months to find the right salesperson. Time you can't afford. How do you compress this time?

KNOWING WHAT YOU ARE LOOKING FOR

Any salesperson worth her or his salt is going to be able to present themselves in a way that makes them attractive. If they can't sell themselves, how can they possibly sell your products and services?

But unless *you* have a "picture" of your ideal candidate, you have nothing to compare even the most attractive of candidates with. You need this picture, both for your recruiting and interviewing efforts.

This ideal candidate profile has a couple of elements:

- **A clear description of the role, and the responsibilities a person in that role must fulfill.**

    This can be a job description. Most organizations do a pretty bad job of describing jobs, they are pretty generic, like: "Achieve quota, represent the company well, leap over tall buildings without tripping." So often these are pretty weak or very outdated.

    But think a minute. You already have a team in place. Unless this is a completely different role, you can look at your current team. They have performance plans in place which describe at some detail their role, responsibilities, the behaviors and attitudes expected.

    These performance plans provide the starting point for developing a rich description of what you are looking for. Naturally, there are some elements of the performance plans that are specific to an individual or a territory, but look at the common elements across your team. This is the foundation of the job description.

- **A clear definition of the competencies, experiences, attitudes, behaviors, and values you require.**

This overlaps a little with the role description but has a lot more information. The next chapter introduces the Sales Competency Model. Developing this for each of your key roles is critical to having a complete picture of what you are looking for. (The Sales Competency Model also has lots of other uses in developing the people currently on your team.)

Once you have the ideal candidate profile, and the competency model for this particular job opening developed, quickly take the time to test it against your current team. Look at your very top performers. How well do they match what you've outlined? It should be pretty close. Have you missed anything?

I CAN'T AFFORD THE TIME, I HAVE TO START LOOKING NOW!

Now you're probably a little frustrated. You have an open position you need to fill fast! And here I am, saying you have to take the time to do your homework and develop a job description and a competency model. That adds days and weeks you don't have.

Well, here's the secret: You should already have these developed and in place!

For each different role you have in your team— territory salesperson, account specialist, inside sales specialist, SDR — you should already have job descriptions and competency models.

Job descriptions and sales competency models aren't just used for recruiting. They are also very powerful tools for helping you coach and develop your people. You are already doing this with your team.

Having these existing descriptions and models in place means you have a consistent base from which to start developing each person's performance or development plan. Naturally, each is customized to the individual, but you need these as the starting point.

If you've been doing things the way you should be doing things, and I know you are because you are a top performing sales manager, then you have these in place. When an opening occurs, all that may be required is a quick review, perhaps a little updating. Your job description and competency profile will be ready to be put to work in only a few minutes.

COMPRESSING THE TIME TO FIND THE RIGHT CANDIDATE

You now have a clear picture of the type of person you are looking for. How do you find them as quickly as possible?

There all sorts of things you can do to find acceptable candidates. Recruiters might help compress it a little. Maybe some members of your current sales team know people who might be good candidates. You could reach out to your own network. You could search sites like LinkedIn, and reach out to people you find

And then there are the job boards, but these are usually very low quality.

Each of these has pros and cons. But each of these still take time—probably time you don't want to waste.

Or, you can start recruiting long before you even have a need to hire a person.

ALWAYS BE RECRUITING

Experienced leaders are always looking for talent. Long before they have positions open, they are on the hunt for "A candidates" for each key role in their organizations. When they meet people at conferences, trade shows, or other events, they are looking for people who might be great fits for their organizations sometime in the future.

They are constantly building their networks, finding people they might recruit when the opportunity arises.

They've done their homework upfront. They always have current job descriptions at their fingertips. They have developed a competency or similar model to develop a picture of the ideal candidate for each position in their organization.

So they are on the lookout. They constantly meet people, and as they do so they are always looking for talented individuals that might be a good fit.

They pre-interview. That is, they don't really interview, but they do learn about the person, what drives them, how they think, how they look at things, their values, goals and aspirations.

They build a portfolio of people who could be very good fits for each job in the organization. They keep in touch, continually learning and building relationships.

Experienced leaders are always doing this, knowing that while they have no current opportunity, they will at some point in time. They want to be prepared when that time occurs.

When a vacancy occurs, they have an immediate short list of potential highly qualified candidates they can bring in to recruit. In doing so, they dramatically reduce the potential months in time that it takes to find the right candidates.

There are all sorts of powerful tools to help you with this, including LinkedIn and other online tools. And there are the people you meet at conferences, trade shows, or that you run across in the normal course of a week.

Reflecting on my own career, I've hired hundreds of sales executives, managers, and sales people and interviewed thousands more. I've only had to rely on recruiters a handful of times and for very specific reasons. I've been able to fill the rest of the jobs through my networks, all with candidates that are a cut above those sourced from other channels.

As you grow in your management responsibilities, one of the biggest areas of focus will be talent. Adopting an approach where you are always recruiting is the most powerful way to build a team of "A" players in the shortest time possible.

WHAT ABOUT RECRUITERS?

I start this section with the statement, "I have many close friends who are recruiters."

Having said that, I use recruiters rarely, and only for the most senior, difficult jobs.

I've not had great experiences using recruiters for normal sales jobs. Most of the time, they do little more than pull resumes from their data bases, find potential matches, and forward them to you.

When I talk to first line managers using recruiters for normal sales jobs, I get similar feedback. Usually, they are inundated with resumes from the recruiters; there may be some level of screening, but usually not a whole lot. Inevitably, the quality of candidates is very mixed.

It's not that recruiters are bad people trying to take advantage of you, or don't care. You really have to look at the economics of the situation, and look at it from the recruiter's perspective. For a person you may be recruiting for a base comp of $50-150K, and total comp as much as a few $100K, except for the most senior level jobs. When you look at the income for the recruiter, there isn't a whole lot of money in it for them.

They can't afford to do highly targeted searches, they can't take a lot of time to hunt down candidates, research, screen, and present the most qualified to you. If they do, they simply won't make money.

But I think there is another bigger problem with using recruiters—and it's not the problem with the recruiters, but with sales managers. Too often, we set the recruiter up for failure because we haven't invested the time or done the things that can make the recruiter's search effective.

I've talked to many recruiters expressing high levels of frustration. They say things like, "The only thing I've gotten is a ten year old job description that's no longer relevant." "All I've been told is to get someone who can 'leap over tall buildings with a single bound.'" Or managers that have unrealistic expectations, "Find me someone with 15 years of successful experience, capable of bringing in $10M of new business per year, for $25K in compensation!"

Recruiters can't do a good job finding you candidates if you don't take the time to help them understand exactly what you need or if your expectations are unrealistic.

If you do choose to use recruiters for normal sales jobs, be very clear about what you are looking for. Make sure the recruiters have the *current* job description—but spend a little time talking with them about it, and what it really means. They won't "read between the lines" —you will have to do this for them.

Present them a competency model with your requirements for candidates. Spend time reviewing it with them. Make sure they understand who you consider an ideal candidate and why. Make sure you let them know any "show-stopper issues" that would immediately disqualify a candidate.

Listen to their advice about how to be more successful with your search. If they think your expectations are unrealistic, listen to them. They are more experienced at this than you! You're paying them for their expertise, take advantage of it.

When the recruiter starts presenting you with candidates, review them to see how well the recruiter has followed your guidelines. If the candidates are wrong, sit down with the recruiter again, make sure they have internalized your picture of the ideal candidate. After all, they can't read your mind.

If they won't take the time to do that, if they aren't presenting you the right, high quality candidates, then they aren't doing the job you need them to do.

Don't look for quick wins in finding candidates. If recruiters are doing their job it will take weeks before they are getting you really good candidates, and potentially months before they find the right ones.

Be fair in your expectations. The recruiter has to make money from this project. You can't expect them to invest huge amounts of time in searching and screening candidates if the income they receive is only a few thousand dollars.

Leverage recruiters in the interviewing process. Some may have assessment tools you can leverage to test the candidates. Some can follow up with reference and credential checks, (I always prefer doing the reference checks myself, but that's just me.)

While this book focuses on front line managers, remember, as your career advances, recruiters can be very powerful resources for very senior level jobs. For virtually every executive level job I've filled, I've leveraged recruiters—but that's a topic for the next book.

JOB BOARDS

Job boards are probably the least effective means of identifying candidates. Again, it's not the job board itself, there are some very good job boards, and some that specialize in sales people.

It's the thousands of candidates who scour these boards for opportunities. If you are relying on them, be prepared to search through thousands of submissions, 99% of which are not even a close fit.

In posting a position on a job board, be prepared to be flooded with hundreds to thousands of resumes—most of them terrible quality. The best performers don't need to rely on job boards to find jobs, so you are unlikely to find the best performers there.

If you aren't careful with your use of job boards, they can be a total waste of time!

LINKEDIN

LinkedIn is a very powerful tool with which to research candidates that have been presented to you, or to find candidates that might fit your requirements. But when using LinkedIn, remember a few things.

The most important of these is the size of your LinkedIn network. There are plenty of reasons you should be expanding your network, but I'll just focus on recruiting.

If you haven't invested in developing your own personal network, you will be limited in the volume of candidates you can find. As an example, if you only have 100 contacts, the number of second- and third-degree contacts you might have might be in the thousands. You will be restricted to that population for your recruiting pool.

On the other hand, if you have 1,000 or more connections, you will have a pool of hundreds of thousands to millions (second- and third-degree) of candidates to look at.

Remember, those candidates will also be looking at your LinkedIn profile, as well as that of your company, so make sure you are presenting yourself and your company positively.

USING PEOPLE IN YOUR ORGANIZATION

Your own people may be great sources for high quality candidates. Ideally, they are well-networked, they may have worked for other companies, they have friends at other companies.

Use your own people to help you find candidates.

RECRUITING FROM YOUR COMPETITORS

I have mixed, tending toward negative, feelings about recruiting directly from the competition. The very best sales people in your competitors' organizations are probably happy and very unlikely to be recruited.

Those most interested are likely to be bottom performers. Your competitor would be delighted to have you take their problem performers off their hands, making them *your* problem performers.

Beyond that, you have to be really worried about "fit." While a hire from the competition can pick up your products and services quickly, they may have ways of working that are based on your competition, and not what's most effective for you. Changing those behaviors and habits are very difficult.

If you recruit from your competition, be very careful. Any good salesperson can learn your products, services, and markets relatively quickly, particularly if you have a good onboarding program. But changing culture, value system, and ingrained habits are more difficult.

If you do find good candidates in your competition and end up hiring them, make absolutely certain you assign them to a completely different territory than the one they covered for the competition. If you don't do this, you may face some legal exposures, but more importantly, the salesperson will have real credibility issues with the customers.

Think about it. They were calling on customers talking about how great their products and services were, demonstrating superior value to yours. Now they are calling on the same customers, saying completely the opposite. What's *your* customer going to think?

THE RECRUITING PROCESS

The recruiting process focuses on identifying potential candidates, screening them, conducting preliminary interviews and narrowing to a short list of candidates.

Screening candidates: Don't start calling the very first candidates you identify. Take some time to build a pool of candidates, so you can compare them with your competency model, the job description, and with each other.

Don't restrict yourself to just their resumes or CV's, look at their LinkedIn profiles, Google them, look at their social profiles and activities.

Narrow down to a pool of candidates, perhaps 10-20, that appear to be the best fit.

Never ever delegate screening the candidates. Your recruiter may conduct a screening process, HR may conduct a screening process. They may be helpful in narrowing a pool, but take the time to screen them yourself, narrowing to the top 10-20 candidates. You know better than anyone else what you need, and you will also have to ultimately be dependent on whoever you finally hire. Invest time in this part of the process so you can do some comparison shopping.

Doing so will make you smarter as you start doing phone screens of the final candidate pool.

PHONE SCREEN INTERVIEW

For the pool of candidates you've narrowed your search to, conduct phone interviews. Use the phone interview to get a good initial sense of them. Understand their current role, their background, and their interest in changing jobs.

Before you make the first call, make sure you are clear about what you are screening for and what you are looking for. Think of it as a variant of a sales call. You know you have to plan sales calls to be effective. , You have to prepare for the screening interviews if you are going to be effective.

Write down your objectives, write down your questions, think of the questions they may pose to you. I find it useful to have the competency model in front of me, scoring as many elements of the competency model as you can.

Be consistent in your screening interview with each person. Without this consistency, it's hard to compare and evaluate them.

Be sure the conversation is evenly balanced. Let them ask you questions, and think about the quality of the questions they are asking, think about how they are presenting themselves.

As you evaluate their responses, focus less on the specifics of their answers than on what the answers indicate about their drive, their values, their motivations, and how they think.

Realize they will be trying to sell you; look at their "sales" approach. If they aren't great at selling themselves, why would they be great at selling your products and services?

When you end the screening interview, make no commitments on next steps, but ask the candidate to be patient for a week or two until you get back to them. You will want to have screened your entire pool of candidates, stack-ranking them based on the interviews.

Like screening, never delegate the phone screening interview. Always conduct it yourself. Again, you are the best person to know what you are looking for, so take the time to conduct good screening interviews.

DEVELOPING THE SHORT LIST

After you have completed your screening interviews, you can now evaluate the candidates based on these interviews, stack ranking them based on how closely they fit your ideal candidate profile.

Typically, I'll want to develop a short list of the five top candidates to bring them in for a more extensive interviewing process. Contact them and arrange for them to come in. For those who clearly don't fit, who are at the bottom of your ranking, give them the courtesy of a follow up phone call. Be honest with them, give them some feedback about why they aren't a good match. Be sure to thank them for their time. You want to leave them on a positive note; they may be candidates for a future position.

For those who aren't the top five, but not at the bottom, you may want to hold them as alternatives, if the top five don't work out. Make sure you communicate this to them.

FINAL THOUGHTS

Recruiting is tough and time-consuming. But remember you are trying to build an "A" team, so you have to invest the time in identifying and screening potential candidates.

Too often, when managers have open jobs to fill, they are impatient, setting for lower quality candidates, but wanting to move fast. Remember this is deadly, you are making a multimillion dollar investment. You want to take the time to get the right candidates.

About the only shortcut you can take is to always be recruiting. Build your "short list" of potential candidates over time by constantly looking for the best talent you can find.

31

SALES COMPETENCY MODEL

Several times in this book I refer to a Sales Competency Model. Basically, this model is a tool you can leverage to develop a "picture" of an ideal salesperson—that is, the ideal characteristics of an individual for a specific role, or for a person at a certain point in her development in that role.

It's a tool you can use to help recruit the right people, to make sure they have developed the right skills and capabilities at the conclusion of their onboarding. Its utility doesn't stop there. It can be used to help in the development of your people.

For example, what skills, capabilities, behaviors, and attitudes would you expect after a year in the role? What about a senior person? Perhaps even, what skills, capabilities, and attitudes would you expect of a manager, or a sales specialist.

This approach can be used for every key role you might have on your team or in your organization. The specifics of the Competency Model will vary, so it's important to look at different models for each key role.

A SALES COMPETENCY FRAMEWORK

I'll suggest a framework for developing your first sales competency model. You may have different ideas, so feel free to adopt the approach to best fit your needs and business.

The framework we'll use as a starting point is for a salesperson in a B2B complex selling organization. Even if what you are trying to describe fits in this context, undoubtedly, there are things missing or irrelevant.

If you are in a B2C environment, there may be some common elements, for example industry or market knowledge, or basic selling skills. But there will be some big differences.

Likewise, some roles may be so different you may want to develop completely different models. For example, the competencies for a SDR will be very different from those for a Global Major Account Manager. Though test that thought a little before you start proliferating models. You may find the competencies are similar, but the skill levels in execution may differ. You'll understand a little more as we dive into building this framework or model.

- **Step 1:** The framework starts with identifying the major categories that characterize the ideal salesperson for your organization. Most of these, in fact, will be common across many different types of organizations.

    I've categorized 10 major areas that contribute to sales success. Too often, managers take far too narrow a view of competencies needed. For example, some look only for sales skills. Others may look at market/industry knowledge and sales skills. I think it's critical to look at the competencies in a much richer way.

    1. Behaviors and Attitudes
    2. Industry and Market Knowledge
    3. Customer Intimacy and Knowledge
    4. Understanding of Your Own Products and Solutions
    5. Understanding How to Get Things Done Within the Company
    6. General Business Knowledge
    7. Ability to Provide Insights to Customers
    8. Value Creation, Communication, and Delivery
    9. Sales Process, Planning, and Execution
    10. General Selling Skills

    You may want to combine some of these categories, you may see some that are missing.

- **Step 2:** The next thing you want to do with each category is drill down and describe specific characteristics, skills, experiences, attitudes, behaviors that are important for the role.

    For example, within the Behaviors and Attitudes Category, you may want to consider things like:

• Time focused	• Critical thinking, problem-solving skills
• Growth oriented mindset	• Passion, energy, enthusiasm
• Professional appearance, conduct, demeanor	• Can do, get it done

• Follow through/ability to complete things	• Technical aptitude, comfort with technology discussions
• Takes responsibility, personal accountability	• Cognitive capability
• Curiosity	• Problem solving orientation
• Team orientation	• Interested in other people and their success
• Listening skills	• Strong self-confidence and self-image
• Comfort in talking about money	• Requires minimal management supervision, requires minimal direction
• Able to deal with conflict and confrontation	• Comfortable with ambiguity
• Strong ethical foundation, trustworthy	• Coachable and value coaching
• Attitude to continuous learning	• Driven to accomplishment, success oriented
• Driven to be successful	• Focused on own self-improvement and development
• Engaging	• Relentless communicator
• Able to get commitments	• Detail oriented
• Delivers on commitments made	• Self-driven
• Able to deal with rejection	• Out of the box thinker
• Ability to navigate organizations	• Gives and receives feedback

Some of these are redundant and you may want to eliminate. Again, there may be some that are important to you that I've not included.

I've provided only a few words describing each characteristic, but it's actually more useful if you write a full sentence describing the characteristics. For example, what do we mean by "time focused?" A sentence clarifies this.

As you put these together, for each category, think about what you see in your best performers. For example, what behaviors and attitudes do they exhibit? What's their industry and market knowledge, and so forth.

For your first pass, brainstorm, go for volume. Set an arbitrary goal of identifying 30 characteristics in each category. After you have completed all the categories, you can go back and prioritize and narrow things down.

Having said that, I tend to prefer pretty comprehensive lists.

• **Step 3:** Once you've identified all the categories and competencies within each category, you are going to want to look at how they apply to each role or how they apply to the development of a person in a role.

Below you'll see a couple of examples. I've only used a few of major categories and a few competencies as examples. Naturally, you would want to put every category and the competencies within each category on this list.

Example 1: Different Sales Roles

Category	Competency	Sales Development Rep	Inside Sales	Salesperson	Account Manager	Sales Specialist
Behaviors and attitudes						
	Able to get commitments	2	4	4	5	3
	Strong technical aptitude	2	3	3	4	5
Sales process, planning, execution						
	Maintains a calendar, blocking and scheduling time to maximize productivity and effectiveness	3	5	5	5	5
	Understands the customer buying process and can align and execute the sales process in tandem with the customer buying process	2	3	4	5	4
	Maintains an accurate pipeline and funnel with high integrity	1	3	4	5	3

Example 2: Development Within Role

Category	Competency	Recruiting	After Onboarding	After 1 Year	Senior Level	Manager
Behaviors and attitudes						
	Able to get commitments	4	4	5	5	5
	Strong technical aptitude	2	3	3	4	4
Sales process, planning, execution						
	Maintains a calendar, blocking and scheduling time to maximize productivity and effectiveness	3	4	5	5	5
	Understands the customer buying process and can align and execute the sales process in tandem with the customer buying process	n/a	3	4	5	5
	Maintains an accurate pipeline and funnel with high integrity	n/a	3	4	5	5

You'll notice I've created a ratings scale, applying a rating to each competency. In this case, I've used a 1-5 scale with 5 being "High."

When you develop your scale, you will want to make sure you've identified what each means. For example: 1: Basic capabilities or 5: Able to teach/coach/mentor others in this competency.

As you start to fill out these matrices, you start developing a more complete picture of what the "ideal" person looks like in each role, or as they progress through their careers.

HOW DO YOU USE THIS?

I'm sure you can start to see lots of applications for this. First in recruiting, now that you've developed a rich profile of the ideal competencies and characteristics for the role, as well as the level or competency and capability the candidate should have, you have a clear method of evaluating candidates based on how they rate or fit.

You can use this in developing their onboarding plan to make sure they get to the skill level needed to perform on the job.

You can leverage this in developing the skills and capabilities of each person, growing their ability to contribute and preparing them to step into higher levels of responsibility.

Likewise, you may have various sales roles on your team. You may have SDR's, Inside Sales, Sales People, Account Managers. This framework helps you identify the skill level needed for success in each role.

SOME CAUTIONS!

- **First, take the time to develop a very comprehensive model for your people.** If you don't know what "ideal" looks like, how can you coach and develop your people appropriately. When I say "comprehensive," I mean make sure it's complete. It does you no good to focus just on the top two or three in each category. I've seen some models having well over a hundred competencies.

   Being a salesperson requires a huge number of skills, capabilities, and experiences. It requires certain behaviors and attitudes. Take the time to develop a strong model.

   I'd start with one model that covers the various roles in your organization, like the one in Example 1. After you get comfortable with that, apply the same model to your recruiting criteria. Over time, I'd expand it to cover all the areas in Example 2.

- **Second, don't manage to the "boxes."** Too many efforts in developing sales competency models are derailed by people trying to manage to each box or element of the competency model. It's not only impossible, it just doesn't make sense. No individual will ever meet your "perfect" picture across all elements. The model provides a framework for moving people to that goal— and it will change, based on where they are in their job and careers.

   Think of this as providing general guidelines. You want to meet as many as you can. Some are critical, "must haves." Be sure to identify those.

- **Third, use it!** Too often, we look at sales skills, behaviors, and competencies and rely on past experience or gut instinct. While these are important, they can't provide a basis for disciplined, consistent, and systematic development of individuals or a team. Our worlds are too complex to be managing by instinct or intuition. We need processes and tools to help and enable us to continually improve. That's our goal with this tool.

- **Fourth, keep updating it!** The extraordinary skills of today become table stakes tomorrow. Take a good look at the framework at least once a year. Think of what's working, what's not. Think about what's changed or different—both within your company, but more importantly in competing and creating value for the customer.

An outdated/obsolete set of criteria can be very damaging!

FINAL THOUGHTS

You will find great ways to leverage this framework as you read this book and as you coach and develop your people.

This is one of the single most powerful tools a sales manager can have. Take the time to develop something that's helpful to you and use it!

32

INTERVIEWING AND HIRING

You may think interviewing job candidates is primarily about the questions you ask a person and how to evaluate their responses. When I talk to new managers, they generally think the key to an interview is: "What are the ten killer questions I need to ask?" Alternatively, they are looking for "chemistry" with the candidate.

Too many people think of just "the interview." In reality the interview is a process. We want to design this process with two objectives in mind: Is the candidate a good fit for our organization, and is the candidate likely to perform at the level expected?

We need to make sure the person is a great fit for both those objectives. I don't know how many times I've seen managers hire sales people that can perform at the level expected, but are terrible fits for the organization. Culturally, personality-wise, or behaviorally, they just don't mesh.

As a result, they won't be successful. While they may be good in front of a customer, ultimately, they won't get the internal support needed to be successful.

In developing the interview process, you want to consider a number of things:

- **What do you need to do to be prepared for the interview?**

- **What do you need to tell the candidate to be prepared for the interview?**

- **What do you want to learn or discover about the candidate in the interview process?**

- **Who will be involved in interviewing each candidate?**

- **What do you want each interviewer to focus on?**

- **How will you assess the person "situationally?"**

- **How will you leverage external assessments?**

- **How will you collect and what will you do with the input from each interviewer?**

- **How will you leverage references?**

- **What feedback are you going to provide each candidate?**

And you thought interviewing would just be a 60-90-minute conversation between you and the candidate? Right now, you're probably thinking, "Dave, you're making this far too complex. I've been selling for years, I know a good salesperson when I see one."

But remember how we started this section. You are making a multi-million dollar investment decision! Do you want to make this decision based on a casual 60-90 minute conversation?

In reality, after you develop this process for the first time, you can apply it to every candidate, every time you have a job opening. So it really isn't that complicated or time consuming.

WHAT DO YOU NEED TO DO TO PREPARE FOR THE INTERVIEW?

The ideal candidate profile is the cornerstone for interview preparation. You want to design the process around determining how close a fit the candidate is to this profile, and where the big gaps are.

In a moment, we'll talk about external assessments. These are basically "tests" administered by organizations expert in these assessments. You will want each candidate to take the assessment before they interview. So you need to get those scheduled with the candidate.

You will want to set up the schedule for the interview day, and arrange all the logistics including the interview schedule, the candidate travel arrangements, and so forth. Right now, you are probably thinking, "I'm just interviewing for a sales role. Can't I save some money and get this done over the phone?"

Again, remember you're making a multi-million-dollar investment. You will want to meet face-to-face with the prospective salesperson. You want to see how they present themselves, how they interact and engage with a number of people. Likewise, you want them to have a good understanding of the company they may be joining.

You have to think about what you want the candidate to learn about you and the company during the interview. Remember, the interview is also their opportunity to evaluate you and the company. They will be making an assessment, "Is this a place I want to work? Am I likely to be successful with this company?"

You want to make sure everyone involved in the interviewing process is prepared, briefed, and knows their role.

WHAT SHOULD YOU ASK THE CANDIDATE TO PREPARE FOR THE INTERVIEW?

There's all the logistical stuff—travel, schedule, and so forth, you need to discuss with the candidate, to make sure she is prepared.

You want to send them information to help them prepare for the interviews. Ideally, this will include background information about the company—perhaps annual reports and other information about the company, its culture, the markets, customers, and so forth. Nothing confidential, obviously, but you do want the person to understand the company before they come in—you'll actually be testing them on this.

You want to make sure they have the job description and anything available to describe the responsibilities accompanying their potential position. You want them to have whatever information they need to understand the role and your expectations of performance in that role.

You will be assessing them situationally, and doing so through role plays or presentations you will ask them to give. Inform them of this in advance, and you may want to send materials to help them prepare.

Finally, make sure you send them the schedule for the day. Make sure you tell them who they will be meeting with and the process they will be going through. Again, you want them as prepared as possible.

WHAT DO YOU WANT TO LEARN IN THE INTERVIEW?

We've covered this a bit already. Basically, you want to determine if they are a good fit for your organization, and if they are going to perform as expected in the job. But let's dive into this a little more. There are additional questions whose answers will help you make your decision.

HOW PREPARED IS THE CANDIDATE FOR WHAT THEY ARE GOING THROUGH?

Think about it a moment. You want your sales people to research and prepare for each customer meeting, you want to have them conduct high impact sales calls, and you want them to plan and prepare deal strategies.

So you will want to assess the research the candidate has done to prepare for the interview. Did they actually read the materials you've sent? Have they researched the company on the Web? Have they looked at your customers, markets, competitors? Have they looked at your business strategies, products/solutions, and company performance?

What research did they do on the individuals they will be meeting with? Did they look them up on LinkedIn? Did they "Google" them?

You would be amazed at the number of people who do very little research and preparation. They may have skimmed through the web site, but have done nothing more. These people think the purpose of the interview process is to present themselves and their capabilities to do the job.

Sound familiar? Isn't this the same problem we have with bad sales people? All they know, all they all they prepare for, is to "pitch their product." So they don't take the time to research, understand the customer, and prepare for how they present themselves.

If they don't do this for the crucial interview when they are "selling themselves," then they are never going to do this selling your products and services!

How do you judge and evaluate their preparation? Part of it is the questions they ask. Ideally, they've prepared, and they've actually written down the questions. Sometimes, I've startled candidates by simply asking them to give me their list of questions. In just looking at their questions, you can get an idea of how well they prepared and how well they think.

In the conversations themselves, get an idea of how well they researched you. Do they know your background? Do they know the backgrounds of the other people they are meeting with? You don't necessarily need to ask them direct questions, but you do need to look at how they leverage that knowledge in the discussions.

HOW DO THEY ENGAGE YOU?

Is the candidate's engagement with you a pitch, is it a conversation, or is it a dialogue? Are they asking questions? Are they listening? Are they interacting? Do they respond appropriately? Do they push back and challenge, or do they rollover and seek only to please and tell you what they think you want to hear? Do they ask the right questions, the right follow-ups? Are they just too busy "pitching" themselves? Are they too busy bragging about how wonderful they are? Are they situationally aware, acting appropriately, or are they oblivious?

You also want to look at whether it's just question-answer-question-answer. Do they incorporate stories and examples appropriately?

Again, you want to remember, if they don't do this well in the interview process, they will absolutely fail in front of the customer. The interview is a powerful snapshot of how they will be selling every day.

HOW EFFECTIVELY DO THEY COMMUNICATE?

This is very similar to how they engage you, but you want to assess their sensitivity to different communications styles and whether they adjust appropriately. This really has more to do with assessing their emotional intelligence.

Everyone has a different communication/social style. Our effectiveness increases tremendously when we are able to adjust how we communicate to the communication styles of the people we are interacting with.

Consequently, it's important to assess this in the interview process.

HOW DO THEY PRESENT THEMSELVES?

Presence is important for sales people. You want to look both at how they physically present themselves, and how they conduct themselves in the meetings.

In most organizations, the only dress code is that there is no dress code. But you want to look at whether they are dressed and groomed appropriately for the interview. Generally, they should be a little better dressed than the people they are meeting with.

How do they look during the interview process itself? Are they nervous, do they have any distracting "ticks." It's natural for there to be some nervousness, but is it excessive and distracting? Is there anything sloppy about their demeanor or the way the present themselves? What's their body language telling you? Are they mirroring you at all?

Are they confident, aggressive, assertive? Do they try to take control of the interview and situation? Some of these approaches may be good, some may be bad. You want to assess the appropriateness of all these behaviors.

Look at how they interact with other people they meet through the day. Clearly, they are going to try to impress/sell you and all the people interviewing them. But how do they interact with the receptionist or your assistant (if you have them)? Take them out to a meal, whether it's in your cafeteria or to a restaurant. How do they engage with people they encounter? What are their table manners?

Some of the most important sources of input when I worked for big companies was what the receptionist or my assistant said about the candidates. I remember one time, when a receptionist reported that a candidate had been very loud, talking to a friend on his mobile phone, and talking fairly disparagingly about the company. He didn't present any of that in the interviews, and tried selling himself, but in front of the receptionist (and everyone else sitting in the lobby), he presented himself very differently.

In the end, do they have the presence that will command the respect of the people they will be working with and the customers? How well do they demonstrate this in the interview?

HOW DO THEY REACT UNDER PRESSURE OR WHEN CONFRONTED WITH A DIFFICULT SITUATION OR DIFFICULT FEEDBACK?

Are they defensive or in denial? Do they take things in, reflect, learn from the situation and improve?

One of the reasons role plays or presentations are so important is they give us the ability to assess the candidate in a pressure or difficult situation. Can they think on their feet? Can they adapt quickly and correctly based on the situation? Can they even read the situation?

In these simulations, you are looking less for whether they have the right answers, and more for how they act, respond, learn from adversity, and respond to coaching, and how they think. Make sure you build something into your interview process that enables you to see how they deal with difficult situations and difficult feedback.

Consider having them re-do the role play or presentation, so you can see how they may have incorporated the feedback you provided. If they can't learn from their experience and coaching, then they will probably not be great performers.

HOW DO THEY TALK ABOUT THEMSELVES AND WHAT THEY'VE ACHIEVED?

Are they braggarts? Are they stretching the truth or even lying? Are they taking too much credit, or do they acknowledge the help they may have gotten?

If teamwork and collaboration is part of your culture, you don't want someone who brags about what they have done and doesn't acknowledge the role of their team in supporting them.

Is what they've achieved appropriate for the job they are being considered for? You probably covered some of this in the pre-interview, but you also want to assess this in the interview.

Not long ago, I was interviewing a candidate for a senior sales management job at a client. I hadn't been involved in the pre-interviews, and on paper the guy looked pretty good. He worked for good companies, presented his performance well. There were typical indicators, "I led my team in growing sales 25% each year in the past 4 years." On the surface, that seemed awesome.

During the interview, however, I discovered a few things. One, he had only made quota two out of four of those years. Second, he was in a very hot market, with a very hot company. Much of the achievement was the result of his being in the right place at the right time.

The guy was being totally honest and forthcoming in the interview, but my client hadn't asked enough of the right questions in the pre-interview. The job he was being considered for was in a very difficult, lower growth market area. So, while he had great experience, it wasn't the appropriate experience for the position we were looking to fill.

WHAT ARE THEIR BEHAVIORS AND ATTITUDES?

They probably will be assertive and positive. After all, they are selling themselves to you. But watch for consistency over the interview process, and across all the people involved in interviewing.

They may display certain behaviors and attitudes to you, as the hiring manager, but may have completely different behaviors and attitudes towards others they perceive to be less important in the hiring process.

As I've mentioned earlier, my assistant and the company receptionist are important parts of my interviewing process. I've seen too many candidates treat these people poorly because they think they are less important. These people just don't fit in any organization I'm a part of.

WHAT DO THEY ACTUALLY KNOW?

Do they understand you, your company, your markets, your customers, your competitors, your industry? What's their business acumen? How do they think? What's their approach to problem solving?

I tend to think we ascribe too much importance to market, customer, industry understanding. While those are important, the ability of the person to figure things out, to learn, to think critically and solve problems is more important. If they can do these well, then they will be able to pick up all the other stuff.

It will be difficult for you to assess all these things by yourself; that's one of the reasons you want a team involved in the interview process.

THE INTERVIEW TEAM

Never trust your own instincts or abilities as the sole interviewer of a candidate. You should always involve others in the company to get their views and perspectives.

The candidate may present herself differently to each person. Other interviewers will see things differently from you. But the differing experiences each has with the candidate will provide you with a more complete and accurate view of the candidate's capabilities and fit.

Make sure each person on the team understands their role and what they should be looking for. You may want to assign different responsibilities; you may want different people to explore different things.

Make sure they understand specifically what they should be looking for. Make sure they understand the questions they should be asking, where they might probe. Make sure they have a convenient way of documenting what they discover. You may want to provide a specific interview guide.

In some parts of the interview, it may pay to have a couple of people involved in interviewing the candidate at the same time. This isn't to purposely create a pressure or "grilling" situation, but each of you will have differing perspectives and will see how the candidate responds in the same situation.

When all of the interviews are over, get the group together (either physically or virtually). Walk through their perspectives and feedback. It's not necessary to get agreement, it's only necessary to understand their perspectives, then use your own judgement on whether the candidate is a fit or not.

If there is great disagreement between interviewers, it will be important to understand, assessing whether the candidate will be the best fit for the organization.

SITUATIONAL ASSESSMENT

Situational assessments are critical for every role; I touched on these a few pages back. These may be case studies you ask the candidate to assess and present recommendations. They may be role plays, or formal presentations to a group of people. These situational assessments give insight into how they actually conduct themselves in front of customers. It gives you a chance to consider, "Is this the type of person who will represent us and engage customers the way we know will be successful?"

These situational assessments give you important insights into critical thinking, problem solving, adaptability, and the ability to react under pressure.

The purpose is less to see if they come up with the "right answer," and your purpose shouldn't be to "trick them." What you are trying to learn is how they approach complex problems and tough situations.

Giving them feedback in these sessions is a great way to assess their ability to take feedback and coaching. Are they open to learning, do they listen, ask good questions, challenge appropriately?

Test their ability to leverage the feedback by asking them to do another role play or presentation. See how they have incorporated your feed back into the situation.

OUTSIDE ASSESSMENTS, TESTS, AND BEHAVIORAL ANALYSES

I'm a great fan of using some of these instruments as part of the candidate evaluation process. There are a lot of different assessments out there. Some are pure garbage, so be careful with your selection.

You may want to have some of your top performers take these assessments, as well. This provides you a basis to compare their results with those of candidates you are interviewing.

You will want to use the same tools, consistently, with all candidates over time. Don't be using a different set of tools for each round of interviews.

I use these tools differently than many others. Some people or organizations use these to screen initial candidates or before the interviews. While these assessments may provide good information about how good they are as sales people, they are unlikely to say how good they might be for your company or the specific role you are looking to fill (unless you've had an assessment that is highly customized and constantly updated for each role.)

I never look at the results of assessments until after the interviews (or at least the initial round) have been completed. This way, I can use the results of the assessments to reflect on what we discovered in the interview process. Sometimes they help me understand something I saw in the interview process, but couldn't put my finger on. Occasionally, they reconfirm things we might have observed, or point out things we might have missed.

Remember, though, however good these tools may be, they can never predict likelihood of success in your company or your situation! They were developed for general use, across hundreds of companies and thousands of candidates.

Never make a decision based solely on the results of these assessments. Their value is an independent set of data and analyses that you can include as part of your consideration for candidates.

Ultimately, the assessment that counts is yours and that of the interviewing team.

REFERENCES/EMPLOYMENT VERIFICATION

I'm always amazed at how poorly most hiring managers use references. We always ask for them, yet most managers actually never check them out. It's a huge missed opportunity.

Many managers don't like to follow up on references because it takes even more time, all when they are anxious to fill the role. Others have the feeling, "Well, they are just going to tell me good stuff about the person anyway, so why should I check?"

I like checking the references of the top candidate(s) after they've been interviewed Because, inevitably, there may be questions. Talking to references can help you address those questions or open issues.

When I talk to references, rather than the classic "What are their strengths and weaknesses," I tend to ask about their observations of the candidate in certain situations. I tend to ask, "When you observed Amanda in this kind of situation… How did she handle it?" Or, "When something like this happened…How did she react to it?"

Finally, you will want to do some level of employment and educational verification. There've been too many stories of people at very high levels (some CEO's of very large companies,) who have falsified work, educational, or military backgrounds. So check them out!

Clearly, you won't be able to check them out with their current employer, but check them with previous employers. Companies are limited in the information they can provide, but they can at least verify that a person worked at an organization during a certain time. They may be able to provide titles or positions; they may be able to provide income levels. Not all will, but get whatever information you can.

One caution-both in checking verifying employment and in looking at resumes. Realize the actual titles used may have very different meanings to you. I remember once, an angry recruiter calling me and saying I had totally lied about my background. I was interviewing for a high level sales role, but the recruiter in checking me out said, "You've never had the sales experience you claimed. Your company says you are a marketing representative—you've never been in sales!" It turns out that all the sales people in the company at the time were called "marketing representatives."

In seeking to understand the candidates' "titles" make sure you understand what they actually did, not just their title.

As a quick side note on titles, be very careful about how much weight you put on titles. They often don't represent the level of responsibility and what they actually did. I don't know how many "Senior Directors of Business Development" with only 12 months of sales experience I've met. Or the number of "Vice Presidents of Sales" who have never had management/leadership responsibility.

Titles are very deceptive—after all, it's easy to go to your local printer to get business cards with the title, "Chairman, CEO, and Supreme Being." I know, I have those cards!

MAKING THE OFFER

At some point, you've found your ideal candidate, the person you want to hire and you make an offer. Your company probably has different ways of doing this than mine, so I'll offer some supplementary thoughts.

You may make an offer orally, but always follow it up with a written offer. Make sure you describe the specific role, compensation, and anything else so there will be no misunderstanding. I like to make sure they have the job description, how they will be measured, and any expectations about ramp time well defined.

Some people think this is a negotiation process. There are some fair and legitimate requests the candidate might make. For example, they might negotiate start date, location, or some other things.

Some may try to negotiate their compensation packages, guarantees, and other things around money. It may just be my personal style, but I never like these discussions. I don't tend to play games with an offer, starting low with compensation, to leave room for negotiation.

I also don't want anything with the candidate to be special and unique from their peers. Like it or not, people compare compensation and other things. We want consistency in how we compensate and incentivize everyone in the organization, or to have clear understanding about why we are doing something different.

CLEANING UP

You've made an offer to the best candidate, hopefully, the offer is accepted! But you haven't finished. You owe everyone else follow up and feedback.

I'm amazed at the stories I hear about people applying for a position, perhaps going through a phone interview, even going through a more comprehensive in person interview, who hear nothing at all or get no feedback.

It's a sign of professionalism and personal respect to provide feedback to everyone. The further through the process you've gotten, the more feedback you should provide.

It's not only a mark of professionalism. Remember the advice: Always Be Recruiting! Those people you didn't select this time may be good candidates for future jobs. You want them to feel as though they've had a good experience in their interaction in the interview process.

Also, remember, you now have a great candidate about to start the job; the next critical thing is successfully onboarding that individual, getting them productive as quickly as possible!

REMEMBER, YOU ARE MAKING A MULTI-MILLION DOLLAR DECISION!

This has been a very long discussion. I hope you made it this far and didn't skip to the next chapter. Interviewing and hiring is one of the most important responsibilities of a manager.

Whether you are interviewing for an entry level salesperson, an inside salesperson, a senior account or territory manager, a specialist, or even a manager—every one of these is a multimillion dollar decisions.

Making a bad hiring decision can be devastating! Even a mediocre one will cause problems in the future. So make sure you invest the time in searching for and getting the right person on board!

33

ONBOARDING

In your past jobs as a salesperson, how were you onboarded? If you were lucky, your company had a strong onboarding program, including, training, coaching, and traveling with other sales people.

Unfortunately, if your experience was like too many others', your onboarding probably consisted of being issued a laptop, sign-ons/passwords, maybe some product pitches, being told where the bathrooms were, who your customers were, then given a handshake and a statement from your managers, "Welcome aboard, I'll need a forecast next week!"

I'm amazed at the number of organizations, large and small, that have no strong onboarding process.

We've invested in recruiting, interviewing, and hiring our "ideal" candidate. We want to get that person productive and successful as soon as possible.

The data shows the average time for a salesperson to get to full productivity is ten months. For more complex products/solutions it may take more than a year.

The lack of strong onboarding could have devastating consequences to the organization.

A number of years ago, a multibillion dollar organization asked me to help with their sales productivity problem.

As I dove into the challenge, the voluntary attrition of new hires (sales people in the company 12 months or less) was 72%. The people they were hiring were the right people, but the company had no onboarding other than product training.

These people were struggling, trying to figure out how to be successful. Most got frustrated and left. I did a back of the envelope calculation, and estimated that the lack of a strong onboarding process was costing at least $700 million each year in lost revenue!

As a manager, it's your responsibility to make sure your people are onboarded and become productive as quickly as possible.

In some sense, the first few chapters in the book, the 30-60-90 day chapters were a form of onboarding for you. Think of something similar for your people.

In looking at onboarding, there are a number of things the new salesperson has to learn as soon as possible:

- **The target customers and territory.**

- **Your products and solutions.**

- **Your sales process, how you engage customers, how you create great customer experiences.**

- **Your value proposition, how you create, communicate and deliver unique value to your customers.**

- **What are the sales enablement systems, tools, programs available to help them sell? How to use them?**

- **The company and how to get things done within the company. The company strategies, priorities, values, and how it wants to be perceived by its customers. What's the company's culture, how do you work together?**

- **Your specific expectations of them and their performance. How they will be evaluated? Consequences of poor evaluations?**

- **What are the best practices in each area—prospecting, deal development, call planning/execution, territory/account management? How do we get the people started doing the right things in the right way from day 1?**

- **What happens when they have problems and need help? Where to they go for answers, how do they get help?**

If your company has no formal onboarding program, you have to figure out how to get this done.

TARGET CUSTOMERS AND THE TERRITORY

It's critical that everyone on the team knows the "sweet spot,"—your target customers. These are the customers who have the problems your company solves better than everyone else. Time spent on customers outside the sweet spot is wasted time and lost productivity.

Learning who the customers are, and who in the customer's organization is typically involved in purchase decisions, their personas, what drives them, their buying processes, and how we help them achieve their goals — all of these are part of learning about the target customers.

Your new salesperson has to understand this sweet spot—and why. (This is tied to your company and its solution strategies.)

Beyond this, they must understand their specific territory—whether it's a customer, a collection of named customers, a geographic territory, or a vertical.

They have to know the specific customers and territory they are responsible for. Additionally, as much background and context to the customers is valuable. If they are inheriting the customer from another salesperson, that salesperson should give them a complete background, status, and review all commitments and open items. Ideally, the salesperson will take the new person to the customer and provide introductions.

If there is no salesperson turning customers over to the new salesperson, you may want to take the new salesperson to some of the key customers in the territory and provide introductions yourself—or at least do it via a conference call. Doing this gives you a chance to reconnect with the customers, and to help the new salesperson get the relationship off to a good start.

YOUR PRODUCTS AND SOLUTIONS

This encompasses not only training about the products—features, functions, feeds, speeds—but it should also focus on the problems your products and solutions help your customers overcome.

Your customers are concerned about their business opportunities and challenges. Helping the new salesperson understand these and how your solutions help the customer address these is critical. Helping them understand the business issues your customers face and how your solutions help them improve their business will drive greater success for the salesperson.

The new salesperson is going to have to find these customers, as well. How do they do this? How do they research and analyze the customers in their territories to target those customers that are in the sweet spot and may have a real need?

How do our products and solutions specifically help the customers address these opportunities and challenges? Who are we likely to face in competing for the customer's business?

All of these go beyond the classic features, functions, feeds, and speeds of product training, but they are critical to accelerating the salesperson's ability to be successful.

YOUR SALES PROCESS

In addition to the product training, you need to train the new person on how to sell them. You need to teach them the selling process and how your customers buy. You need to make certain they understand how the company holds customers and how that is reflected in the customer experiences you create through the sales process.

Your sales process represents your best practices in finding, qualifying, and engaging customers. It's critical your new sales people understand the sales process, how it aligns with your customers' buying processes, and how they leverage to accelerate their success.

YOUR VALUE PROPOSITION

You don't win by having great products and services. You win by consistently creating superior, differentiated value. It's important for your new sales people to understand a number of things, some of which we've covered already:

What's your sweet spot? Your value and uniqueness is maximized when you focus on your sweet spot. If your salesperson doesn't understand this, he will waste a lot of time chasing things that are simply bad deals.

You differentiate yourself and create huge value by the way you engage the customer in their problem solving and buying processes. Train your new sales people in your engagement model. How do you create value in each interaction? What kind of leadership can you offer as the customer is struggling to buy? How do you incite customers to change? How do you quantify the value of the solutions you are proposing? How to you equip your customer to sell the solutions within their own company.

SALES ENABLEMENT

In addition to learning about the products and how to sell them, they need to be taken through the details of marketing materials/programs, sales enablement, support tools, how do you configure, propose, price the solutions. You should make sure the salesperson fully understands all the details from prospecting, through qualifying, discovering, proposing, closing, and implementing. Make sure they understand all the tools available to them, make sure they learn how to use the tools and programs. Assure they learn the great examples of how others use these programs.

They need to understand all the tools available to support them—CRM and other sales enablement tools, marketing programs and prospecting tools, analytic and customer intelligence tools. Demo, benchmarking, configuration, pricing, proposal tools. What materials, collateral and other things are available, how does the company handle references, and so forth.

THE COMPANY AND HOW THINGS GET DONE WITHIN THE COMPANY

The new person has to learn about the company that has hired him or her—its history, values, how it wants to be perceived by the customers, how it is perceived in the markets. The person needs to understand the strategies, priorities, positioning with customers, competitors and others.

Most importantly, the new salesperson needs to know how to get things done within the company. Where to go to for presales support, proposing and bidding, pricing and proposals. How do orders get entered, what about contracts, credit checks?

It's crucial for the person to meet key people in the sales, sales enablement, sales support, marketing, customer, product marketing, and product management organization. Even finance and legal can be important. All of this is focused on helping the salesperson learn how to get things done within the organization.

They need to understand how customer problems with your products and are solved, since it's likely they will be one of the first contacted if customers in their territory have problems. Make sure they understand the problem management and resolution process so they can set expectations appropriately. Make sure they understand the escalation process if problems aren't being addressed on a timely basis.

YOUR SPECIFIC EXPECTATIONS OF THEM AND THEIR PERFORMANCE

They need to know your expectations in the next 30-60-90 days. They need to know when they should be fully onboard and up to speed, and your onboarding plan for them should support this.

They need to understand expectations on reporting, CRM utilization, forecasting, activity management and so forth. They need to understand what they can do without escalating things to management, what commitments they can make without management approval.

They need to know where to get help when they need it.

AN ONBOARDING PLAN

If your company doesn't have a formal onboarding plan, you need to work with the salesperson to establish one. This should be a documented calendar of what should be accomplished each week for, perhaps, several months. This is the salesperson's and your road map for developing them and getting them up to speed over several months.

If you have the luxury, they should be able to spend a few weeks, or more, just learning without having to start calling on customers at all. If you can, have them shadow a top performer for a week or two, so they can see how that person works, how he engages the customers, how he gets things done within the organization.

You may want to assign the salesperson a pseudo-mentor. This would be a high-performing peer the new salesperson can go to for advice and help during their first 3-6 months. Being a mentor is great for developing your top performers for future leadership roles.

If the salesperson does have to start meeting with customers, be reasonable with your expectations of time they spend with customers and the time they spend learning. Realize that time spent with customers is probably not as productive as it could be—simply because the salesperson hasn't had the chance to learn.

Be reasonable in terms of performance expectations. You can't expect them to be hitting full quota in 30, 60, or even 90 days. You want to see a track record of progress. If you have a very long, complex sales cycle, focus on the leading metrics and where they should be as they go through their onboarding.

ONBOARDING-SPECIFIC COACHING

The time you spend teaching and coaching the new salesperson is critical. Investing time up front, making sure they have a solid foundation will save you hours and a lot of hassle, dealing with poor performance in the future.

Presumably, you've developed an onboarding calendar. This calendar should include scheduled weekly meetings to help the new member of the team move through the onboarding process and to make sure they are picking up the skills and knowledge critical to their success.

34

ATTRITION IS A LEADERSHIP PROBLEM!

At some point you will have to face the issue of attrition. People leaving voluntarily because they've found a better opportunity, or having to terminate people—involuntary attrition.

These days, many of the discussions revolve around the specific challenge of attrition with Millennials. Generally, the view is something like, "They will always be moving to other jobs…"

Many observers accept this insight as a fact, but don't look at the underlying issues or how to change it—if you want to.

I want to try to take the issue of attrition head-on. Before I go on, though, I have to offer a disclaimer. There will always be attrition—both voluntary and involuntary. People will find great opportunities and move on, and managers will never be perfect in finding people that meet our performance expectations.

I think we treat the issue of attrition far too lightly — as mentioned in the chapter on the true cost of a salesperson, the impact is millions of dollars and up.

In one very large organization, we looked at the very high attrition of first year hires and determined the adverse revenue impact to be greater than $700 million.

Attrition is a leadership problem. If we are to point fingers, we must start with executive management. Despite all the corporate culture, recruiting posters, and other PR efforts, too often, "People are our most valuable assets," is nothing more than lip service to many managers and executives.

Let's break down attrition.

INVOLUNTARY ATTRITION

Actions taken by management to terminate employment are all grouped under involuntary attrition. It happens because of several reasons:

1. **Performance problems with individuals.** Individual performance issues are usually driven by a few things: the wrong person in a job, the person doesn't understand expectations of the job, the person doesn't have the skills or capabilities to perform in the job. Too often, we tend to look at these as "That's the individual's problem," because it's that person that's performing badly. But really it's started with mistakes management has made. Bad hires, poor onboarding, poor training, poor performance planning/feedback, poor coaching. Yes, often, it is also attributable to the individual. For various reasons, despite all the training, coaching, and help, they just can't perform.

2. **Systemic performance issues with the team/organization.** Often, this is manifested by large numbers of people not making their numbers or other goals. The root of this problem lies with management, as well. It could be the business/markets have changed, yet we haven't changed how we go to market. We continue to do the same things, perhaps faster, with greater intensity, or more frenzy; somehow expecting the results to change.

Often, I see this in troubled organizations. Organizations that are somehow failing. For example, I've been involved in a lot of turnarounds. Often, there are very good, very skilled people, but they aren't producing results. Perhaps the markets have changed, and they haven't, perhaps they have, for various reasons, been disrupted by competition.

Systemic issues driving involuntary attrition are serious, they can mean the future viability of the organization. Usually, these result in Layoffs and RIFs.

3. **We may be changing our deployment strategy**—a shift from direct, to inside, to channels, or something else. What worked in the past, may no longer be the best route to markets today. Very often, we see organizations shifting their sales deployment models, as a result it changes the people and talent needs.

4. **Layoffs/RIFs.** This is closely related to the previous two points. Layoffs are the result of a massive strategy/execution failure on the part of management. Unfortunately, it's the sales people that bear the brunt of this action. Layoffs and RIFs s are massively disruptive to the organization and to your customers. In layoffs we lose very talented people through both involuntary and voluntary attrition (they lose confidence and want to go someplace better). It used to be, and I'm dating myself, that management did everything possible to avoid layoffs and RIFs. Sometimes they were unavoidable—a major layoff was required for the survival of the company (usually these are actions taken by the new managers replacing those that failed). Too often, however, I see

organizations leaping to this alternative too quickly. It's an "easy way" of dealing with performance problems—we don't have to go through a measured mile, we just get rid of them through a layoff and some minimal package. This is management/leadership at its worst!

VOLUNTARY ATTRITION

Voluntary attrition is when our people, usually our best, leave for another, possibly better opportunity. It happens for a number of reasons:

1. **They see no future for themselves in their current roles/organization.** Perhaps they are stuck in a job, they don't see a growth path to grow their capabilities, skills, and ability to contribute at a higher level. Management is not coaching them or developing them to step into bigger levels of responsibility. They want a bigger challenge, but see no opportunity for those challenges in the current company.

2. **They see no loyalty from the company to its employees.** (See items 2 and 3 in involuntary attrition). They believe they are being treated as commodities, they see the company has no respect for individuals, or don't see the company valuing the knowledge/experience of its people as a differentiator. They don't see management investing in the people, developing them, helping them grow, develop, and contribute at higher levels. All development and training is focused on optimizing current performance. Usually, there is a gulf between management and the people in the organization. Coaching is virtually non-existent, people aren't valued for ideas. While companies like this may have suggestion boxes, but they are always empty because people recognize management doesn't pay attention.

3. **Management has unrealistic expectations.** They are setting goals that are unrealistic—based both on past performance, investments, and an unrealistic assessment of future opportunity. (Usually these companies suffer from the same issues described in items 2 and 3 of Involuntary Attrition.)

4. **The company isn't doing "exciting things."** This doesn't mean a company has to be a "Hot," or "High Growth" company. Being "exciting" means the company is continuously learning, improving, innovating, changing. Being part of this is challenging and exciting to everyone. Companies focused on doing this always create new opportunities for individual as well as organizational growth.

5. **They aren't learning anything:** People want to grow in their current jobs and careers. If they don't see themselves learning, developing rich new skills, getting new experiences, they fear becoming uncompetitive in the job markets—or become bored.

6. They can get more money someplace else. This is the excuse that's given far too often. There are some individuals who are solely focused on compensation—these are probably bad hires in the first place. Sometimes, the company compensation is out of sync with others in the industry. Recently, I saw one organization losing very good people after a few years because their compensation was about 50% less than similar organizations. The executive team had some "old/bad" ideas involving sales compensation. As a consequence, they were hiring great entry level sales people, and training them for other companies to hire—never achieving what they could in growing the sales organization. But unless, something is really wrong with the compensation plan, money is seldom the driving reason people leave.

THE (NOT SO) "SPECIAL CASE OF MILLENNIALS"

There's been a lot written about Millennials. The generation born between the 1980s and early 21st Century does want to work differently than previous generations. They need to be led, motivated, and managed differently (but isn't this true about each individual?)

It seems there is a foregone conclusion and acceptance that Millennials will job hop and never be loyal to a particular company. I don't buy that. I think it's an excuse too many managers fall back on to justify high levels of voluntary turnover with Millennials.

Millennials come to work with a slightly different, perhaps jaded, perspective of the "workplace." They were raised in the late 80s, 90s and early 2000s. They saw their parents being subjected to layoffs and RIFs time and time again. They saw the rise of outsourcing, temporary/contract employees, flexible workforce, and other "employment practices." Where many of their parents expected to work with two or three organizations for their careers, Millennials saw a different reality. Having seen what their parents went through, they come into the workplace with some healthy and natural skepticism of management and companies, realizing they have to look out for themselves.

But for management to accept as a foregone conclusion that Millennials cannot be retained, that they will move from job to job every year or so, and that this is simply the "new work place," is to accept defeat from the outset.

Millennials are no different than any other individual. They want to learn and grow. They want to be challenged and see future opportunity. They want the opportunity to contribute and be recognized for that contribution. They want to be associated with organizations and people doing exciting things. Like anyone else, if they don't find that in their current job, they will look elsewhere—as they should. But if they are in an organization that enables them to learn, grow, be challenged, contribute, and can see a future for themselves, there is no reason they won't stay in the organization that provides that workplace environment.

ACTION STEPS

So now that I've painted a pretty dismal attrition picture, what are managers to do?

1. **Understand attrition in your organization.** Measure managers on both voluntary and involuntary attrition. Understand why people leave, conduct exit interviews for every person leaving the organization (voluntarily or involuntarily). Collect and analyze the data, understand the patterns so you can determine the problems.

2. **Avoid the factors that drive attrition.** Some of the major things that drive involuntary attrition are having the wrong business or sales deployment model, or massive failure on the part of the entire organization. Management must always be attentive to shifts in the markets, competition, in the most effective ways to reach and engage customers. Talented people we have today may have to be retrained and re-tasked to meet emerging market needs.

3. **Focus on retention.** Recognize that people want to grow and develop. Make sure each person in the organization has not just a performance plan (focusing on current performance,) but they also have a development plan in place. Understand their aspirations, coach them on their development, provide developmental opportunities. Remember: Not everyone wants to or should move into management, but there are extensive career/development paths for individual contributors.

4. **Train managers on recruiting/hiring, performance management, development planning, coaching, and dealing with problem employees.** One of the biggest challenges I see is that managers simply have no training in these areas, so they don't know what they should be doing or how to do it effectively. Senior management needs to take on the coaching and development responsibility for managers reporting to them. Just as attrition is a problem for individual contributors, management attrition (voluntary or involuntary,) is a major business problem. Organizations that don't invest in the development of the leadership and management skills of its management team will face all sorts of challenges, with unusually high attrition numbers being just one of them.

More broadly, people—their knowledge, experience, capacity to innovate and contribute—is the single most important part of the organization and its ability to grow, innovate, and thrive. People are the ultimate and most sustainable differentiator. Somehow, it seems too many organizations have lost sight of this. Without attracting and retaining the very best in each function, no organization will achieve its goals, grow, or survive.

CONCLUDING THOUGHTS

Attrition will never and should never be eliminated. We will never be perfect in recruiting, hiring, and onboarding. Some people will not fit, despite everything we do. Business needs and conditions will change, requiring changes in our people requirements. People will move on for very good reasons, creating opportunities for us to backfill and continue to improve the capabilities of the organization. We have to understand the causes for attrition and seek to eliminate them.

Our jobs as leaders and managers is to maximize the performance of our people in executing company growth strategies. We cannot treat this casually. As you should know *very* well by now, the all-in cost of each bad hire or lost person is millions of dollars. Cumulatively, the impact of attrition on results can be tremendous. Attrition is too important for it not to be a top priority with all leaders, executives, and managers.

PART FIVE

PERFORMANCE MANAGEMENT

35

MANAGING AND EVALUATING PERFORMANCE

Ugh! I can hear you thinking:

"Dave, can't we just skip this section? Performance plans and reviews suck!"

And, unfortunately, too many of them do.

Each of us can recount painful hours spent in performance reviews. Usually, it's a terrible process HR forces us to go through once a year.

Performance reviews never seem to be connected with reality. More often, the review is connected with how we allocate money for pay increases, more cause for anxiety.

Managers are never happy writing up and giving performance reviews.

Unless you receive a 5-star review—and weren't expecting it—no one is ever happy with being reviewed. But it's something we have to do, so we go through the same painful motions every year, with the same hours wasted, and the same painful outcomes.

And it shouldn't be that way! It should be an opportunity to learn and grow. It should be an opportunity for people to understand what they are doing well, and where they have opportunities to develop and do much better.

There is no doubt the majority of performance review processes are flawed, even broken. Most companies I've worked with provide no training or coaching to managers about the process and how to conduct effective performance reviews.

I won't be able to correct these shortcomings in a few chapters on performance. Clearly, you have to live within the boundaries or constraints of the system and processes your company has put in place.

What I hope to accomplish in these chapters is to provide some guidance about how you can harness these systems, or even go outside the systems to set expectations, to review performance against expectations, and to help your people perform at the highest levels possible.

Simply stated, it's our job to set performance expectations—whether part of a formal performance planning process or an informal one. (I believe it should be part of a formal process.)

Our people both deserve to know and need to know what's expected of them. Not establishing these expectations, not periodically reviewing where your sales people are, not assessing how they've done cheats them and is simply bad management.

It's also important to recognize that the performance of our team reflects as much on our own performance as it does on the performance of each individual.

If our people aren't performing at the levels expected of them, their failure is, in part, our own. We haven't put the right people in the right jobs. We haven't provided the right training, the right coaching, the right tools and support.

In the following chapters, we will address setting performance expectations, conducting performance reviews, and dealing with various types of performance—inspired performance from our A players down to non-performers, with whom we may have to take action to move out of the company.

We'll look at how to manage current performance and how to look at developing people over the longer term—raising their contribution and performance to meet their full potential.

As I mentioned at the beginning of this chapter, your company probably has a performance planning process in place. There are inevitably forms, reviews, and a calendar against which these reviews have to be held. Usually, these are universally despised by managers and the people being reviewed.

The purpose of these chapters is to help you and your people, perhaps in spite of the systems you have in place. My goal is to help you and your people recognize value in setting expectations and evaluating performance against them.

Likewise, your company probably has a process that you have to go through in dealing with poor performers. Whether it's the Performance Improvement Plan (PIP), the Measured Mile, or something else, it's tough on both the manager and the salesperson. These chapters will help you and the poor person who is on the plan deal with this challenge in a more humane manner.

Finally, remember that performance management goes hand in hand with coaching.

We coach every day, whether in deal or other reviews, or the "windshield time" you may spend with a salesperson, or while standing in line at Starbucks.

Mastering and practicing coaching is critical to your ability to get people to maximize their performance.

36

SETTING PERFORMANCE EXPECTATIONS

Our job as managers is to set performance expectations with every person that reports to us. If we don't do this clearly, our people don't know what they should be doing. And if we don't do this, we have no basis for assessing their performance.

Too often, organizations and managers do a terrible job of setting performance expectations. It's no wonder people are confused: They aren't doing what we expect them to do, or they aren't displaying the behaviors we want. But, if we haven't made expectations clear, and if they haven't understood and internalized those expectations, then we shouldn't be surprised if they are confused.

Setting performance expectations isn't just giving them a quota and saying "Good luck and Godspeed."

We have to look at performance across all dimensions of behaviors, attitudes, what their job is, how we expect them to do it, and the results we expect. We have to make sure people understand these expectations, that they have internalized them to the point they own them for themselves. We have to give our people periodic feedback about where they stand against those expectations. If they don't know where they stand, they don't know what they need to be doing to meet our expectations. Finally, we have to be clear about the consequences of not meeting those expectations.

WHAT SHOULD THE PERFORMANCE PLAN INCLUDE?

The process starts with establishing the performance plan. Whether or not your company requires you to establish a formal performance plan with your people you must do this. You and each of your people have to establish and agree upon performance expectations.

I think there are a number of critical elements to a strong performance plan:

1. **Clearly defining the job and performance responsibilities:** As you would expect, these include standard items like achieving quota. But sales people have far more responsibilities than just achieving quota—unfortunately, too many managers stop there.

   But there are lots of other things critical to success in the job. They may include prospecting, maintaining a healthy pipeline, maintaining accurate account plans. There may be customer service and customer satisfaction goals. There may be internal teamwork and collaboration goals. There may be financial objectives, beyond just the quota targets.

   Additionally, your team members must have strong knowledge of your products and services, and be able to demonstrate that knowledge. They must have knowledge of target markets, industries, and customers; having some level of business acumen is a critical responsibility for the salesperson. If these are expectations of the salesperson, we need to define what those are.

   Finally, there may be reporting or other requirements like keeping CRM updated, forecast accuracy or other internal and administrative responsibilities. There may be expense and budget management responsibilities.

   Being clear about performance expectations in doing the job, making them specific and quantifiable, where possible, is critical to establishing an effective performance plan. If a person doesn't know the goal and how it will be measured, then how do we expect them to meet our expectations?

2. **Clearly defining expected behaviors:** Do you expect people to be "team players?" How do you want people to represent your company to customers, prospects, and others? What levels of professionalism do you expect? It's important to discuss and define these matters in detail with each person on your team. These may not be as quantifiable as job expectations, but they are equally important.

3. **Developmental expectations:** We and our people need to be continually improving our skills and capabilities. It may be to perform at higher levels in the current job, or it may be to prepare them for future responsibilities and career growth. In establishing the performance plan, it's very powerful to have a discussion with the individual about how they want to grow and set goals to help them achieve it.

4. **Conditions of employment:** There are some things we never talk about, never define, but are "conditions of employment." They may be things involving ethics, legal requirements, maintaining confidential materials, or other "big issues." There may be things like showing up for work on time, spending/

budgets, and so forth. Generally, these are matters that, if violated, may result in immediate termination.

Why put them in a performance plan? Simple: too often, we don't define these explicitly.

Sometimes they are uncomfortable issues, like harassment or ethics. Sometimes they seem mundane or things we assume they "should understand," like showing up every day for work. But if we aren't explicit about these things, and their consequences, our team members won't know. Since they don't know, they may maliciously or accidentally violate them. Not defining these conditions, explicitly, is our failure as managers. In some cases, the personal and organizational consequences for violating conditions of employment are very severe, including legal prosecution.

EVALUATION SCALE

Another element of the performance plan itself is the evaluation scale. There are all kinds of evaluation scales. One example is a numeric scale from 1-5, with 1 significantly below expectations, up to 5 as significantly exceeding expectations.

Every company has its own scale for evaluating performance.

As you establish the specific performance criteria for the performance plan, it's important to set expectations on the evaluation scale. For example, if one of the performance line items is: Develop and maintain strong product knowledge. You may want to give examples: "People performing at a level 5 demonstrate their knowledge by doing things like this…" "At a 3 level, this what we would expect to see…"

You may not need to define this for everything, but give examples for the most important performance criteria. People need to know what they should be aiming for.

37

PERFORMANCE REVIEWS

Just mentioning the words *Performance Review* creates anxiety on everyone's part. It shouldn't be that way. The performance review should be part of an ongoing discussion about improving people's abilities and helping them more effectively achieve their goals.

I think some of the anxiety is created around the process as it exists within corporations. The performance review is a formal requirement; the evaluation becomes a part of the individual's record in the organization. Often, the outcomes of the review impact compensation and their futures in the company.

We have to live within the processes and policies of our organizations. The purpose of this chapter is really to put all the "corporate stuff" to one side, allowing us to focus on how we leverage the process to help our people grow.

In the previous chapter, I addressed setting expectations and developing the performance plan itself. We've learned the plan should be established collaboratively, producing mutually agreed-upon goals for the plan period. At the end of the process, both the salesperson and you have a clear understanding of those goals, of your respective roles in achieving them, and have established a general plan of execution.

In periodic (e.g. quarterly) performance reviews, you are reviewing the progress being made in executing the plan. You and the salesperson are discussing where they are doing well, where they can improve, and what actions they should be taking.

Ideally, you have the progress reviews quarterly, so by the time you reach the end of the year, there will be no surprises on either of your parts.

There may be areas where the person is falling short in performance. We want to identify these and address them as soon as possible. The real challenges in managing performance come when we don't identify these deficiencies early or when we avoid addressing them until they are major issues.

There are areas where we may excel. We want to continue to improve these, raising the bar on personal expectations and what we can contribute within the organization.

The performance plan and performance reviews provide us a way to sit down with our people and look at how they can constantly improve.

WHAT'S THE DIFFERENCE BETWEEN THE PERFORMANCE REVIEW, OTHER REVIEWS, AND COACHING?

As I've said, the performance plan/review and coaching are tightly interrelated. But there are differences. When we coach, we generally focus on a specific area, helping people improve performance in that area. This may be improving their ability to prospect, or develop and execute strong deal strategies, or manage their time more effectively.

When we look at the performance review, we are looking at *all* aspects of their performance in the job. We aren't focusing on a specific part of the job, but we are addressing total performance.

Here's where it may get a little confusing. The way we conduct a performance review is exactly like how we coach. We use the same techniques we do when coaching in reviews, one-on-ones, or anything else. You may want to review the chapters on **Conducting Reviews**, as well as the chapters on **How To Coach**. A person gets the most out of a performance review in exactly the same way they get the most out of a coaching session aimed at improving prospecting skills. This should be a collaborative discussion. The most effective way to conduct the review is to use a non-directive approach.

Many people think the performance review is about "telling," or is very directive. That's a mistake too many managers make. People don't learn and develop much through this; they learn and improve by being actively engaged in a discussion.

Also, just like coaching a sales call, performance reviews offer us a chance to provide and receive feedback. So the principles of **Giving and Receiving Feedback** apply very well in conducting the performance review.

While the performance review has different objectives than other reviews, the coaching techniques and the review process are precisely the same as what you've learned earlier.

NO SURPRISES

When you talk to people who are unhappy with their performance review, a couple of things come up.

One is that they didn't know or understand performance expectations in the first place. If you've done a good job in setting those expectations and developing the performance plan up front, they should clearly understand the expectations.

The second reason is they were surprised by the evaluation. They may have thought they were doing very well, then in the review they are surprised when they learn they weren't doing as well as they thought.

There should be no surprises in the performance review.

The salesperson should have a good understanding of where they stand. They should have a good idea of what they are doing well, where they need to improve. Ensuring the salesperson has this level of understanding is part of your job as sales manager.

Our ongoing coaching in business reviews, and other activities help in making sure people understand how they are performing. If they struggle with prospecting, and we are constantly working with them on improving prospecting skills, then they shouldn't be surprised to hear that feedback in doing the performance review.

But remember: we want all of our people to exceed expectations in their performance reviews. It's impossible for them to do this, if we only let them know how they are doing once a year.

That's why it's really powerful practice to conduct interim performance progress reviews, for example the quarterly updates. Some companies require this. But regardless of whether your company requires this or not, the interim review is an important tool for helping improve performance and eliminating surprises.

In an effective interim review, you and the salesperson sit down and review their entire performance on the job—not just one aspect of the performance. The performance plan is the reference document against which to conduct the discussion.

If you are constantly coaching people, providing powerful feedback, and conducting quarterly interim performance reviews, there should be no surprises in the annual evaluation.

If there are no surprises, then all of the anxiety that traditionally accompanies managers and sales people entering the review disappears completely. Each of you can focus on learning. Understand where the person is against expectations, and how they continue to grow and improve.

IT'S NOT ABOUT FINDING DEFICIENCIES

Too often, both sales people and managers think the performance review is about what the person is doing wrong.

Discussions focus on where people have failed to meet expectations. As a result, the discussions tend to be negative, and don't create learning moments.

In the performance review, we want to review *total* performance. We want to reinforce the things the person is doing well. Where they've met or exceeded expectations, where they can improve.

The real objective of the performance review is not the evaluation, but helping people continue to learn and develop as professionals.

IT'S A REVIEW OF YOUR PERFORMANCE AS WELL AS THE SALESPERSON'S

If a person is failing to meet expectations, if their performance is not satisfactory, their shortfall is a reflection of your own performance as a manager.

You are probably sick of this by now, but your job as manager is to get each of your people to perform to the highest degree possible, achieving expectations and fulfilling their potential.

If they are failing in their performance, you've failed in some way as a manager.

If they've done extraordinarily well, take some quiet pride in your influence and effectiveness as a manager, but make the extraordinary performance all about them and not you.

CONTINUOUS IMPROVEMENT

Corporations, and too many people, tend to treat performance reviews as a discrete event. "You did well, you did poorly." Performance reviews are uncomfortable discussions no one wants to be part of. We hold performance reviews because we have to, because HR forces us to do them.

Alternatively, I see some organizations that have no performance review process at all. Either they don't believe in them or they don't know how important and powerful they can be.

Everyone needs to know how they are performing. Everyone should be looking to see how they improve, how they grow, how they develop, how they achieve more.

The performance review is an essential tool for each of us to evaluate the progress we are making against our goals. The performance review shows us how we are doing, and provides an opportunity for learning how we can improve our effectiveness and better achieve our goals.

As managers, if both we and our people look at the performance review as part of the growth, continuous learning, and continuous improvement process, performance reviews become things we look forward to. They become learning moments, important steps in our development and progression through our careers.

CONDUCTING THE PERFORMANCE REVIEW

As you read this, you might get a sense of "*deja-vu*." Conducting the performance review is exactly the same as doing a pipeline, deal, call or whatever review.

You've learned there are four critical elements: Preparation, Conducting the Review itself, Agreeing On Next Steps, and Follow Up.

The performance plan itself provides the foundation for the review.

PREPARATION

I think it's useful for both the manager and salesperson to write down their own assessments of performance. Each person should go through the performance plan evaluating performance against the agreed upon objectives.

To do a thoughtful job, you must allocate time for this preparation. Too many managers take this process too casually. They quickly write a meaningless assessment. But this is important to the person you are evaluating. They deserve your respect and the time to do a thoughtful review.

CONDUCTING THE REVIEW

Generally, I like to have the salesperson present their own self-assessment first. Your role is to listen, probe, understand and explore. Your questions shouldn't be oriented to proving them right or wrong but understanding their point of view.

As with other reviews, you may want to challenge them a little with questions that prompt them to reflect on and think about their performance and assessment. As you listen to them, you may also be learning things they have done, but which you were unaware of.

Non-directive coaching techniques are most effective in this discussion.

During the discussion, you will want to share your evaluation and point of view. Encourage the salesperson to question, probe, and understand how you came up with your assessments.

If you've done a good job throughout the year, both in coaching and in interim performance discussions, there probably isn't a big gap in each of your perspectives. If there is, take the time to really understand the gap. Did they misunderstand expectations? Did you not understand or see some of the things they were doing, perhaps evaluating performance incorrectly?

Your responsibility, with the salesperson, is to understand where the gap in perception or differences in opinions are, and to close the gaps in those perspectives.

Sometimes, though rarely, you may not close the gap and agree to disagree. In this case the next steps and actions become very important.

The review will probably take some time, so make sure you allocate enough time. Make sure you aren't interrupted. Sometimes, conducting the review off-site, but not in a public area, is helpful in eliminating distractions.

One thing I see few managers do during this process is ask the salesperson for feedback on how the manager is doing and where the manager can improve. You might consider making this a part of the discussion. It should focus on how you can be more effective in helping the person meet their goals.

ESTABLISHING THE NEXT STEPS

Once you have completed your discussion of the plan, reconciled any gaps in perception or misunderstanding, you need to agree on next steps. What are the things the person needs to focus in improving to continue to meet or exceed expectations? What are the things they should do to grow even further?

Some of these actions and next steps actually become the basis for establishing the new performance objectives for the next performance planning period. Some of the actions and next steps require more immediate focus, for example getting some training, or completing some specific activities.

Be sure you agree on these next steps and actions:

- **Make sure the person clearly understands what expected performance "looks like."**

- **Give them a picture of what the right outcomes are, what the right behaviors are.**

- **Let them know what "success" looks like so they know how to evaluate their own performance.**

Some action items become part of the next performance plan, some become separate activities with specific responsibilities and target dates. Make sure all of these are documented.

FOLLOW-UP

Performance planning and evaluation is an ongoing cycle. Much of what you agree on as next steps become part of the next performance plan. You work with the people on an ongoing basis, providing coaching and feedback and reviewing progress in the interim performance reviews.

There have been some specific actions and target dates that require follow-up. If these aren't done, as scheduled, performance won't improve. So it's critical to close the loop in following-up, and in the discussions that occur with the follow-up.

Again, this process is exactly the same as what you do in coaching deals, accounts and similar sessions. You should be getting a lot of practice in this, so it should be becoming second nature to you.

38

PROBLEM PERFORMANCE

Everyone, at every level, has performance problems. You no doubt experienced this from time to time in your past jobs—or even in your current job. I know there have been times where my performance in certain areas wasn't where is should have been.

Making mistakes, sometimes failing, is a critical part of the learning and growth process. Understanding these as early as possible, taking corrective action is critical in driving top performance.

Our day-to-day coaching, one-on-ones, performance planning discussions, training, and other activities are intended to identify these improvement opportunities as early as possible. Once identified, we need to help the person understand the issue, correct it, and reinforce it. Ideally, these corrections stick, and our people meet our performance expectations.

It is unrealistic to think your people won't have performance problems every once in a while, it's unrealistic not to think your performance won't meet expectations from time to time.

Great professionals recognize this; they see it as part of their overall professional and personal growth. They are attentive to their own personal performance. When they see they are failing, they don't get defeated or blame others. Instead, they seek coaching and help to improve what they are doing.

Performance becomes *Problem* Performance when people don't recognize they have a performance issue or the poor performance is sustained.

As a manager, you will have problem performers and you will have to work with them to get their performance on track.

PROBLEM PERFORMERS

Every organization has them: problem performers. They come in all shapes and sizes.

There are problem performers who don't have the right knowledge, capabilities or skills. Probably they should never have been hired in the first place, or they are in the wrong job. But since they work for you, you have to step up to this issue and address it.

Other problem performers are those who should have the knowledge and capability to perform, but aren't meeting expectations. They may have problems in consistent execution. They may know *what* they should be doing, but for some reason they just aren't doing it.

Some may actually be top performers, at least from a numbers point of view. But they may have bad attitudes or destructive behaviors. These are actually toxic. They impact everyone in the organization, and may be impacting customer relationships.

There are many things that impact performance, but whatever form they take, they're often difficult to deal with.

Too often, our natural reaction is to ignore the problems performers, or avoid those uncomfortable conversations. Talking about performance is difficult in the best circumstances, but addressing unsatisfactory performance is always difficult, both for you as manager and for the salesperson who isn't performing as expected.

There's conflict and confrontation. Dealing with poor performers can take a huge amount of time. Time we probably don't have or time we would prefer investing somewhere else.

It's so much easier to turn a blind eye to the problem performers. Sometimes, the attitude is, "They aren't hurting that much, they just aren't contributing."

Ignoring them, or avoiding them, is the worst thing we can possibly do!

Early, in my career, I almost lost my job because I didn't have the courage to address a poor performer. I was a mid-level manager, and one of the managers, Ron, working for me was incompetent. He knew what he needed to be doing to lead the team, but he was just unwilling or unable to do those things.

We had some conversations about the issues in his team, but I danced around (read *avoided)* confronting him about his performance. As a result, performance continued to erode.

Rather than address his performance, I tried to put "fences" around him—effectively isolating or protecting the organization from him. I started reaching out to his people, coaching and leading them myself. While he participated in staff meetings, he was ignored.

I thought I was getting away with it. He wasn't doing much and I had isolated him, so he wasn't creating big problems.

After some time, my manager called me into his office. We talked about Ron. I told him I was managing it. At that point, Jerry gave me an instant performance review. His words have stuck with me since then:

"Dave, the problem isn't Ron, the problem is you. You have neither the courage to step up to Ron's performance, or the personal respect for Ron to address his performance. You've fenced him off, you've isolated him.

"Don't you realize, no one in this organization respects you. Everyone, including Ron's People, recognize Ron is a problem. But *you*, Dave, are the bigger problem. You aren't stepping up to the performance issue and addressing it. The fact that you aren't is eroding your reputation and effectiveness in the organization.

"If you don't address it immediately, Ron will be the *second* person I change out!"

By not addressing Ron's bad performance, I had become a bad performer myself. People are smart: major performance problems are obvious to everyone in the organization. Managers are expected to address these problems, If you aren't, if you are avoiding the issue, you become the problem performer yourself. You lose the respect and confidence of the organization by not addressing them immediately.

Not addressing bad performers erodes the performance of the organization overall. If people see that others aren't held accountable for their performance, they'll start thinking, "Well, maybe I shouldn't be busting my rear end. Maybe I should just coast."

Top performers will leave. They want to be around top performers. They want to be challenged to up their game. No top performer wants to be a part of a "loser organization."

Soon, overall performance of the organization erodes, and morale follows. With the exception of truly toxic performers, it's not the bad performer who is the problem, it's the manager's bad performance that creates the problem.

The manager's performance problem is also an issue of respect for the poor performer himself. We and, hopefully, they want to get their performance back on track. We've invested a lot in them. We don't want to lose them. We want them to perform as they and we expect them to perform.

As managers, we owe it to them to give them feedback about their perform-ance. We owe it to them to help them improve their performance. It's simply good business, responsible management and leadership.

IT'S ONLY ABOUT PERFORMANCE

Before going further, there's an important issue that must be addressed:

Sometimes we confuse the performance with the person.

When we do this, a poor performer becomes a "bad guy." In management meetings, talking about these people, we refer to them negatively. I don't know how many conversations I've sat in where managers talk about the "turkeys."

Addressing poor performance isn't about the person. It isn't about whether they are a good or bad human being. It's simply about their ability to perform as expected in the job.

I once hired a very close friend to work for me. I didn't hire him because he was my friend, but because we both genuinely thought he was the best person to do the job. After about a year, things changed.

Previously, he had a track record of great successes, but in this role he was just not performing. He was wrong for the job. I ended up having to fire him. It was a really tough decision. My friend actually made it very easy for me. He recognized he wasn't performing and was the wrong person in the job. So the "firing" part of the discussion was very easy, and we shifted into how I could help him find the right job. He ended up getting a much bigger job, at much higher compensation, and he was a stunning success.

As a leader, it's important for you to recognize this and not make it about a person and who they are, but focus just on their performance and what needs to be done to get performance to an acceptable level.

THE GOAL IS A POSITIVE OUTCOME

Another problem is that too often when we are working with problem performers, we start the process with a negative mindset. We think they won't be able to improve their performance; they think they won't be able to improve their performance.

Guess what, we've created a self-fulfilling prophecy. If we both think they will fail to correct and improve their performance, that's what will happen. Regardless how hard each of us tries, or how much time we invest.

Remember in the Secrets of Coaching chapter, I said, "You have to believe in them more than they believe in themselves." In dealing with problem performers, this is sometimes very difficult, but this is where it's most important.

When we address problem performers, we have to do so with a positive attitude. With them we have to see there is a way to improve performance, and both you and they have to be committed to that successful outcome.

Without this, you are wasting each other's time and just going through the motions.

IDENTIFYING THE PERFORMANCE ISSUES

Bad performance has to be addressed immediately.

The first thing to assess is: "What's driving or causing the bad performance?" As outlined above, there could be a number of reasons: lack of knowledge, poor skills, poor execution, not leveraging systems/processes or tools effectively. More complex issues are attitudinal and behavioral issues.

KNOWLEDGE, SKILLS, EXECUTION BASED PERFORMANCE PROBLEMS

Ideally, your coaching has identified knowledge, skills, execution and related problems. You should already be coaching them and helping them improve. With these types of issues, teaching, helping them learn, demonstrating the right way to do things is critical.

Sometimes, you may have to get the problem performer some special training.

The worst thing to do is getting into "tell mode," particularly telling them they are doing everything wrong. They clearly don't know how to do things, or struggle with doing the right things consistently.

Sometimes, there may be lots of areas of skills, knowledge, execution problems. Too often, we try to fix all the problems at once. Doing this confuses the salesperson.

To illustrate this, sometimes I think back to some of my golf lessons. I'd have well-intended people telling me ten things to do at once, "Keep your head over the ball, bend your knees, line up your feet, keep your weight evenly distributed, take the club straight back, keep your arms straight…"

I'd end up twisted like a pretzel, slicing the ball 50 yards off the fairway and getting no distance.

Professional instructors take things step by step, focusing only on one or two things, making sure you have mastered them before moving on.

As you are working with your people on knowledge and skills issues, focus on no more than two things at a time. Coach them, perhaps get them some training—but be sure to reinforce that training as they try to apply it. Consider pairing them with someone who has mastered the skills. Watching someone doing things the right way, leveraging the skills in an impactful manner, can have a huge impact in helping people learn.

Most of the time, if the issues are a lack of knowledge or skills, these can be easily corrected with training and coaching.

If there are lots of issues on skills, knowledge, execution, and if you aren't seeing improvement over time, it could be the person is a bad fit for their job. Someone, hopefully not you, has made a hiring error.

It's not the person's fault, they don't have the skills or capabilities to do the job, and they shouldn't be in the job in the first place. Can you redefine the role, can you move them into a role where they can perform well?

As Bradford Smart discusses in the book, *Topgrading*, a "B" or "C" player might be an "A" player in another role.

Our job is to help them find that role. That role may not be with the company, and so they will have to be exited.

As you look at people with skills, knowledge, and execution problems, it's important to recognize that addressing these will take time. The person has to be willing to learn and change, if they aren't, it becomes more of an attitudinal issue, which I'll cover later.

There is always an issue about how much time it will take to resolve the performance problems. We can't afford to take forever, nor is it fair to the individual. At some point, it may be necessary to set a specific time period during which certain improvements *must* be achieved.

Often this process is called a Performance Improvement Plan (PIP).

ATTITUDINAL/BEHAVIORAL PROBLEMS

These are very difficult problems to address. These are typically the issues we have with toxic employees. Their behaviors and attitudes are poison in an organization.

There can be all sorts of attitudinal or behavioral problems. Some of these include a disruptive or abusive behavior, inability to work with team members/colleagues, being uncoachable, being unwilling to do certain parts of the job, being unwilling to comply with certain policies or practices, refusing to change things they are doing that aren't appropriate or are ineffective, constantly complaining or blaming others for failures, representing the company inappropriately or incorrectly to customers, refusing to accept responsibility for their actions, or sometimes just pure laziness.

One of the biggest challenges is that sometimes the people displaying these problems may be your "top performers." I don't know how many times I've heard, "Mark is so disruptive, even toxic in his interactions with everyone he encounters. But I can't afford to lose him. Somehow he always makes his numbers!"

This is another case of, "If I had a nickel for every time I've encountered this scenario…."

Toxic people are toxic people. Bad performers are bad performers. What we are looking for is not only their ability to execute against their performance expectations, but how they interact and engage others, in and out of the organization.

While their individual performance may be OK, their impact on the rest of the organization adversely impacts the performance and morale of others. Eventually, if managers fail to take action, the organization figures out a way to isolate these toxic individuals, making them totally ineffective.

This is why it's important to look at performance plans more broadly. You don't just want quota attainment, but things like "plays well with others," is important to their and your overall effectiveness.

Attitudinal and behavioral issues have to be addressed with great urgency.

We have to sit down with the salesperson to make sure she understands the specific issue. It's important to have specific and current examples about where their attitudes or behaviors have created issues. They should be direct observations you have made, not things that you suspect or that have been reported to you by others. You have to be able to say, "I observed this behavior…on this date… It is inappropriate for these reasons…" They have to understand, specifically, why the attitudes or behaviors are unacceptable. They have to understand what the correct attitudes and behaviors are. Again, very specific examples of the correct attitudes or behaviors are critical.

Finally, the person needs to understand the consequences of not changing their attitudes and behaviors. These need to be documented, a plan for correcting the behaviors established, and you have to continue to follow up to make sure whatever changes you agreed upon are actually taking place.

CONDITIONS OF EMPLOYMENT PERFORMANCE ISSUES

I talked about *conditions of employment* earlier. These include a certain category of behavioral and attitudinal performance issues. Many times, violations of these conditions of employment require immediate termination.

Conditions of employment are mandatory behaviors required to maintain employment. They include some very serious issues, where failure to comply creates legal exposures, threatens the well-being of others, or creates exposures or risks to the company, its customers, suppliers, or community. Some of these include ethics, fraud, harassment, collusion, theft, misuse of confidential/proprietary information, doing something illegal, and other issues. (In some states and countries, murdering a bad sales manager is not a criminal offense ;-)

Recently, I was involved in a very difficult situation with a client. One of their very best sales managers was caught booking false, fraudulent orders. My client's accounts payables department discovered this when customers began disputing invoices.

The reasons for the sales manager committing this fraud are irrelevant to this story, or to the actions we took. Despite how good his past performance appeared, his actions were illegal and he was immediately terminated.

The issue was more complicated. In the investigation, we determined there had been a pattern of fraudulent activity connected with this individual. Turned out he wasn't the high performing manager we thought he was. It also turned out his manager wasn't paying attention to what was happening. There were clear signs something wasn't right for a number of months. But his manager was closing his eyes to these signals, and didn't have the right controls in place to prevent this fraudulent activity. As a result, his manager was also terminated.

A friend shared an unpleasant experience he had. It involved his top regional manager and the top salesperson in that region. The salesperson bought $10K in "gift cards" to be used in a contest with channel partners. Instead of implementing the contest, the salesperson and regional manager split the cards and used them for themselves. Both were immediately terminated and required to repay the $10K.

While some of these conditions of employment issues may not be illegal, for example, certain ethics issues, they are still wrong. These, also, will require immediate termination.

Some conditions of employment issues may require a formal warning. For example, bad or inappropriate expenses (not fraud), attendance issues, and similar issues. The warning must be provided in meeting with the salesperson discussing the issue very specifically, with examples of the bad behavior, examples of the correct behavior, as well as the consequences of not changing.

They should be given a very short period of time to correct these issues. If they aren't corrected after being warned, it is unacceptable, and the employee must be terminated immediately.

Conditions of employment issues are very serious. They cannot be ignored. They must be addressed with great urgency. In addressing these, it's important you do the research and have documented the issues as completely as possible. In these cases, you will always need to involve HR and probably Legal because of the severity of these issues and the potential impact and exposure to the organization.

When you are discussing these conditions of employment issues with an employee, you may want to consider having your manager, or someone from HR or Legal participating in the discussion. HR—or perhaps your own manager—can advise you on whose presence is required, and why.

FINAL WORDS

It's worth repeating:

> ***Dealing with problem performers is always challenging.***

The situation creates anxiety and stress for everyone involved, the employee and you, the manager.

Avoidance is not the answer—as I've shown, avoidance only indicates there are two problem performers, the employee and you.

Dealing with problem performers takes time. There are no shortcuts. Use your manager as a sounding board as you address these issues. Undoubtedly, your manager has more experience than you, sometimes, her advice can be very helpful as you think about what you need to do.

The best ways to minimize the challenge of problem employees include:

- **Hiring the right people in the first place.**

- **Having strong onboarding procedures.**

- **Constant coaching and development, to minimize the potential of performance problems.**

- **Establishing clear performance expectations so people understand how their performance is evaluated.**

Having said this, despite all of you best plans and intentions, you will have problem employees and you will have to address these performance issues.

39

THE MEASURED MILE

At some point, we may have to put a poor performer on a formalized performance improvement plan, sometimes called a PIP or a Measured Mile (Kilometer for those of you in metrics countries).

Undoubtedly, your company will have a formal process for doing this.

The purpose of this chapter is to help you think differently about the PIP, and, perhaps, get your company to rethink its policies around Performance Improvement Plans.

GETTING TO THE PIP

Bear in mind, when placing a problem employee on an improvement plan, you and the employee share some history. You don't all of a sudden decide a person is a marginal performer and needs to be put on a measured mile.

You have provided the employee a lot of coaching, many discussions, perhaps some training, and other efforts aiming at improving the salesperson's performance. But for some reason, performance is not yet at a satisfactory level. You have to take definitive action, within a short and clearly defined period of time, performance has to be improved to a certain level or the person will be terminated.

The process of establishing a PIP is emotion-packed, on all sides—the salesperson's, the sales manager, and HR, since Human Resources is inevitably involved in the process.

Putting a PIP in place, and the work that goes on while a person is on a PIP, requires careful attention

IS IT THE RIGHT THING TO DO?

The problem I've seen with so many PIPs is that there is a foregone conclusion about the outcome. Too many people, the salesperson, manager, and HR, and the salesperson believe the only outcome will be termination.

The plan may be constructed in such a way that the person cannot be successful, or even if he is, some excuse will be found to terminate the person anyway.

If you think there is no possibility for a successful outcome to the PIP, why do you want to start the process in the first place? Yes, I know HR is telling you that you must, but is it really the right thing to do?

Are you just prolonging the salesperson's agony and consuming the sales manager's time for something that you know will result in a termination?

If no one believes there can be a successful outcome to the performance improvement plan, isn't everyone better off calling it quits upfront?

Think of the time, emotional trauma, and agony that will be saved on everyone's part. The salesperson can get on with his life, finding a new job. The sales manager can focus her time where she can have the biggest impact—either recruiting backfill for the soon-to-be vacated position, coaching and developing others, or helping the team grow the business.

If everyone is agreed there can be no possible recovery, just don't go through the motions the plan forces you to go through. Don't waste time. Terminate the person with grace.

Don't be greedy if this is the most likely outcome. Typically, measured miles are somewhere around 90 days. Pay the person for the 90 days they would have been on a PIP, but let them get on with their lives. If you put them on the PIP just to go through the motions, you will be paying them anyway. But the cost will be much higher in sales management, HR, and other people's time.

BE COMMITTED TO SUCCESSFUL OUTCOME

In putting someone on a PIP, that person, you, and the rest of the organization must be committed to a successful outcome. That is, everyone is committed to do what it takes to get performance in line and sustain it.

Anything else is just going through the motions and a waste of time and money.

The salesperson, naturally, will say he is committed to a successful outcome. But what else would he say? After all, he's struggling to keep his job. So it's important the salesperson clearly understands the commitment, work, and change required to be successful and maintain that success.

If they are merely going through the motions, if they've already given up, discuss the potential of an immediate departure, with the 90 day (or whatever it is,) payout. Help them understand that it's better for them to get on with their lives and careers.

You and the rest of the organization have to be totally committed to a successful outcome as well. Be honest with yourself. Getting to this point has undoubtedly been rough. Helping the person achieve and sustain adequate performance levels is not going to be easier. You will have to be meeting with the person at least weekly. You'll probably have to spend a lot more time helping show them the right way to do things.

If you aren't committed to a successful outcome, if you can't visualize the person getting through this successfully, then your attitude and mindset will betray you to the person. You won't be doing the things you need to do to have the person be successful.

The rest of the organization has to be focused on a positive outcome as well. If your management or peers don't see any possibility for improvement, they will not provide you or the salesperson the support needed for the improvement plan to be successful.

BE FAIR IN YOUR EXPECTATIONS

You won't get the salesperson to suddenly become a superstar at the end of this process. All you are likely to do is to get them back to minimal acceptable performance. They will likely be a "C" player.

Likewise, they are probably very far behind in quota attainment. It's unrealistic to expect them to get back to plan in the 90 days of the formal plan. Determine what's reasonable and acceptable, being very realistic.

Remember, if you aren't realistic in your expectations, you are just setting the person up for failure.

DOCUMENT THE PLAN

Developing the PIP must be a collaborative effort with the salesperson. This is critical; if it's something you dictate, they will have no ownership.

Make sure each of you fully understand the goals. Make sure the goals are easily measureable and trackable, so both you and the salesperson clearly understand what is expected. You don't want to end up in conversations like, "I thought I was doing what was expected of me. I don't know why you think I'm not performing as expected!"

Don't focus only on the end goals, but define the interim metrics, or milestones. For example: "Every week you should be doing X number of prospecting calls which produce these results, at least Y number of customer meetings producing these types of outcomes," and so forth.

Don't overburden the person with too many of goals and activities. All you are trying to do is to get them back to a minimal level of acceptable performance. If you inundate them with too many objectives, they will get confused and fail. So focus on the three or four most important things required to recover performance.

Make sure you and the salesperson are in lockstep as you develop the plan. If they have concerns, be sure to take time to understand and address the concern. Don't be locked into your position: Their point of view may be very reasonable.

At the end of the process, make sure you have a detailed follow-up and review plan. You can't send the salesperson off by saying, "Good luck and Godspeed, see you in 90 days!" You will have to meet with the salesperson weekly to track progress against the goals.

There's another good reason to have the interim goals in place. If the salesperson is consistently missing the interim goals, they won't meet the end goals. You might face the option of terminating the PIP plan (and the person) more quickly. (Yeah, your HR and potentially your legal people may go crazy in such a situation, but in reality neither you nor the salesperson should have to be committed to 90 days if you know it's not possible to achieve the plan.)

When putting the plan in place, it's critical to be crystal clear about consequences. This is no time to be fuzzy, or for the salesperson to engage in unrealistic thinking. Not meeting the objectives of the plan means termination— no if, ands, or buts.

You should also be clear about the consequences of not consistently meeting the interim goals.

TRACK, MONITOR, COACH

Now that you both are committed to a successful outcome, and have a clear understanding of the path to achieving it, you are in execution mode. This requires weekly follow-up progress reports, with written feedback. It requires constant coaching and support in achieving the goals.

Committing to the coaching is critical. Think about it: The person wouldn't be in this position if they were responding to your normal coaching, they would be performing well. For them to be successful, you are going to have to go above and beyond.

If they start falling behind, don't just tell them. Sit down and help them figure out what they need to do to get back on track. Do everything you can to help them find the path to success.

REACHING THE END OF THE PLAN

At the end of the period there are only two outcomes: They succeeded or they failed. The plan shouldn't be renegotiated based on the final outcome, otherwise you are likely to find yourself in the same place with the same individual sometime in the future.

If the person succeeds, as everyone hoped, first congratulate him. But then map out some clear goals and actions so the person can sustain the expected performance levels. The person is probably a solid "C" player—which means they need very focused attention and direction to sustain performance.

If you don't develop a detailed plan and goals, there is a high probability the person will slip again. No one wants this to happen. But if either of you go back to "business as usual" it's almost guaranteed to recur.

A NOTE OF CAUTION:

My approach to the PIP is very non-traditional. But when I put someone on a PIP, I use this process rigorously. Most of the time, when we get to this point, if given the opportunity to opt out, particularly if they feel there is no chance for a successful outcome, people will do so.

When people opt to go through the PIP, they are usually successful. Because they have had direct and honest discussions with me, because they know what they must do, because they have been given the option to opt out; those that go forward have a different mindset—which is key to their success.

But make sure you have the full support of your management team and HR. If you are doing something that doesn't align with corporate practice, you could create huge problems for the salesperson and yourself.

Some companies force you to go through the process, even though the outcome is pre-determined. If you can't get them to change, then you have to do it. But be as fair and honest with the person as you can be.

There has to be some human respect and pragmatism in this process.

40

ON TERMINATIONS

At various points in their careers, every manager will have to terminate people. It's never an easy thing to do, regardless of how justified the termination is.

Obviously, a termination meeting creates great anxiety for everyone involved. Each person, the manager and the employee, knows what's going to happen.

There are two types of terminations—Performance Related Terminations, and Reductions in Force (RIFs or Layoffs).

Performance related terminations are the result of the employee not being able to meet performance expectations on a sustained basis.

Reductions in Force, RIFs, Layoffs have nothing to do with the employee, but have to do with poor management decisions and execution.

PREPARING FOR PERFORMANCE-RELATED TERMINATIONS

At some point we have to meet with someone to terminate them. It's important to prepare for this meeting in advance. Things you want to look at:

1. **Who will take over the person's responsibilities?** You will have to reassign accounts and customers to other sales people. You will have to have sales people pick up deals that are in the pipeline. You want to know who will be doing this and have a plan for how these will be transferred to the appropriate sales people.

2. **What assets, for example, computers, company cars, demo equipment, and so forth does the person have in their possession?**

3. **What systems and tools do they have access to?**

4. **What IDs, building passes, keys, and other access do they have?**

5. **Is there any restricted IP or other sensitive data they may have or have access to?**

6. **Are there any non-competes in place? What restrictions might be in place?**

7. **You will want a clear understanding of the person's termination package.** You will have to explain these things when you are terminating the individual:
   - Is there some sort of severance?
   - Are there commissions or other bonuses they may have earned? If they were on some sort of draw, are there unearned payments that have to be recovered?
   - Are there accrued vacation days?
   - Are there stock options that may be terminated?
   - What happens to their medical, 401Ks, insurance and other benefits?
   - Is there any sort of outplacement services that will be provided?

8. **You will want to have a copy of their termination package for them to take with them.** In spite of telling them everything clearly and carefully, they won't hear 75% of it.

9. **Are they to be terminated immediately and escorted out of the facility, or will there be a two week, or some other period of presence in the company?**
   - If people are being terminated for Conditions of Employment, Attitudinal, or Behavioral reasons, generally you want to escort them out of the office immediately.
   - For people who can't improve their performance, you may want to give them two weeks' notice. That time should generally be spent on their turning over current activities to the people who will be taking over their responsibilities. Don't hold them firm to the two weeks. If they finish it in a day, let them leave; don't force them to stick around.

10. **What is their reaction likely to be?** If there is a concern about a possibly violent reaction, do you want security nearby?

11. **Where do you want to hold the discussion?** In your office, in a conference room, off-site? Think about who will see them afterwards, if they are in the office and their peers see them before or after the meeting, it may create some feeling of embarrassment or shame with their peers.

12. **When do you want to do it?** What day, what time? Some people say never terminate some on Friday, others say always do it on Friday. I don't know, but you may want to think about the timing. They are going to have a few bad days whenever it happens.

CONDUCTING THE PROBLEM PERFORMER TERMINATION MEETING

Most managers make a mistake by making termination-for-cause meetings too long and offering too much in the way of explanation. The time has passed for explanations. If you have been working with them on a performance improvement plan, they will know they haven't been meeting expectations.

As you start the meeting, be very clear that the only thing you are addressing is their unsatisfactory performance in the job. You are not making any judgments about them as human beings.

Be respectful of them as people. Remember, in the majority of cases, the termination is the result of a good person in the wrong job.

The meeting should actually be very short. You should say they are being terminated for performance reasons. You need to tell the effective date. If they have any turnover responsibilities, or will be in the office for another couple of weeks, be very clear about what they are expected to do. Generally, you want to minimize the amount of time they are around after they are terminated—both out of respect to them and their feelings, and because you both need to move on. The sooner both of you get on with it, the better.

Before you go into their separation package, give them a chance to react. Ask them if they have any questions. They may ask for long explanations. They may ask for another chance. They may want to argue and debate. They may want to try to change your mind. They may be angry and want to vent. Give them a chance to have their say, but don't react to it,

There is no need for long explanations. You and they have gone through much effort and spent plenty of energy trying to get their performance back on track; it hasn't succeeded. There are no other chances.

After they have had a few minutes to ask questions, provide them the termination package. Walk them through it. They won't hear about 75% of it. That's why it's important to have a copy they can take with them. Make sure they know who they can contact if they have questions later.

Conclude the meeting by thanking them for what they have done, and genuinely wish them luck in their future endeavors.

Be sensitive about where and when the meeting is. They will be shocked. Some will cry; others will be visibly shaken. You don't want them to be embarrassed by having to run a gauntlet of their peers.

I may sound crass, but these meetings are generally very short. Longer than 15 minutes is very unusual.

Immediately after the meeting, take some time for yourself to decompress.

Maybe go for a short walk, grab a cup of coffee at Starbucks, do something. Don't immediately roll into your next task. No matter how often you do this, it is a stressful situation. You should never become comfortable or callous about terminating someone.

TERMINATIONS FOR CONDITIONS OF EMPLOYMENT

Since I brought the topic up a couple of chapters ago, I need to address it. I hope you will never have to face this situation.

There are some conditions of employment terminations that are pretty easy and can be handled like the performance based terminations. These generally have to do with things like not showing up for work, not adhering to certain standards of reporting, and so forth.

There are other conditions of employment issues that are very serious and require careful deliberation and planning. These include illegal activities like embezzlement, fraud, harassment.

Generally, in preparing for these terminations, you will want a legal review and opinion about the situation. Are there any responsibilities, liabilities, or other exposures the company or individual face? Are there releases or legal agreements that may have to be completed as part of the termination? Are there any obligations the company has to the individual, or the individual has to the company following the termination? Does the company face obligations to report the cause of termination to legal authorities or others?.

In the case of these terminations you want to make sure you have a complete review by legal and your management. If it's very complex or high exposure, you may want legal or another manager to participate in the meeting. Yes, you may need to cover your ass by having witnesses in the room.

I've had to do a few of these. They make me angry with the person. I feel the person has cheated the company, customers, his peers, his management, and me. But this is an area where you have to be very cautious. As much as you may want to express your anger, it will only make a very bad situation worse. It's a no win for you. Expressing your anger will likely provoke a negative reaction or excuses from the person. None of this helps the situation or gets you past it quickly. The best thing is to get rid of the person as quickly as possible.

I mentioned the situation where a client discovered a sales manager had fraudulently entered orders just so he could make his numbers. It was in the millions of dollars and created huge problems with the customer getting products and invoices they hadn't expected.

His manager and I conducted the termination meeting. Both the manager and I struggled, we were so angry with the individual. As you might guess, the individual denied doing these things and created all sorts of excuses, which made both of us more angry, though we didn't react.

We powered through, got the termination done, had the person escorted from the facility, and went out for a cup of tea to decompress.

Getting angry and lashing back could have created great difficulty if the person decided to take subsequent legal action.

THE SALESPERSON'S POINT OF VIEW

A good manager understands what the salesperson is likely to be thinking, and what they will be going through when they are terminated.

If you have done the right job, with the exception of Conditions of Employment terminations and layoffs, the salesperson should not be surprised. However, they may be in denial. They may seek deeper explanations, make excuses, or ask for more chances.

Even if they aren't surprised, they will be shocked. There is no way they can't be. It's normal for them to be angry, and they may express that anger. Just let them vent. It's fair for them to be upset and angry.

At termination, and during the weeks following, they will go through several phases. The first will be anger. It's fair and natural. Hopefully, they get through that in a few days. The longer they are angry, the longer it will take them to move past this.

The next stage will be grief. They will have a deep sense of loss, not only a paycheck, but their job, what occupied their time, and perhaps much of their identity. Since we spend so much of our time working, a lot of our personal identity is wrapped up in, "I work for…" Losing the job means a certain loss of identity.

The grief may persist for a long time. The person may move into the third phase, denial, but lapse back into grief for short periods of time. They will blame everything and everyone but themselves.

When I was fired from a job (and I deserved it,) it took me a number of months to work through the grief, even some of the anger. I was several months into my next job before I was completely past the termination.

The fourth and most productive phase is acceptance and moving forward. The more quickly a person can get into this stage the better they are. Sometimes outplacement organizations are very helpful in getting people to and through acceptance. If that's part of your separation package, encourage the individual to use it. If it isn't, encourage them to seek this kind of help on their own.

It's important at some point for the individual to reflect on what happened and try to learn something from the experience. If they don't take the time to learn as much as they can, they may find themselves doing the same things again, in a new job, perhaps facing a similar future.

AFTER THE MEETING

You need to think of the rest of the organization and the customers the terminated salesperson was responsible for. You need to communicate something to them.

You need to let them know the person is no longer with the company. You don't need to offer any explanation and should not discuss the termination was for performance reasons. It is none of their business. The line, "pursuing other interests," is sufficient.

Make sure your customers know who will be working with them now. If your salesperson did turnover calls that's great. Otherwise, make sure the new salesperson is with you or on the call, so you can introduce them and make that connection.

It may be more a matter of personal style, but I always like contacting the customers myself, as manager, at least for the major or active customers in the salesperson's territory. It allows you to do a few things:

- **Announce the change. The new salesperson shouldn't have to answer questions about the change.**

- **Talk a little bit about what's happening with them. If your salesperson wasn't performing well, he may have been blind to issues, concerns, or opportunities. Talking to the customer about the change enables you to identify these very quickly.**

- **Re-establish your own personal relationship and connection with them.**

- **Demonstrate your respect for the customers by taking the time to personally speak with them.**

Finally, perhaps a few days later, conduct a "loss review" just for yourself. Think back on the history. Did you make a bad hiring decision? Did you not see performance problems early enough? Were you blind to what was really happening? What did you do well in identifying the performance issues and addressing them? What would you change? What might you do to avoid this in the future?

In every termination, there are issues about your own performance. Things you might have done better, or differently. Think about them and how you can do better in the future. All of these moments are learning moments.

You need to provide information, you need to treat the terminated employee with respect, and most importantly you need to put everything behind you and move forward.

FOR THE PARANOID, SOME REALITIES AND CONCERNS

There are, unfortunately, some things through this process you should be worried about. You may not be able to do much about them, but you should at least be aware of the risks and exposures so you can choose how you want to deal with them.

1. **Your salesperson may copy a lot of customer information and company information and take it with them.** You can prevent them from doing this by taking away access to any of this information immediately after terminating them (or have IT do it at the moment you are having the meeting.) If a person

is on a PIP and they see the outcome is not likely to be successful, they may start copying data long before the termination meeting.

2. **Beware of the actions of angry people.** Unfortunately, some people will react in anger and be destructive. With one client, a salesperson tried deleting all the CRM records and history of the customers in his territory. Again, you may want to assess the likelihood of doing this, taking appropriate actions.

3. **If the salesperson has any prepaid commissions, draws, or advances, it may be difficult to recover them.** While legally you can recover them, it may not be worth the time and hassle. It is far better to put the whole thing behind you and move forward.

4. **Be aware the terminated person may bad mouth you and your company.** There's not much you can do about it, so don't worry about it.

5. **In some cases, the performance issue is one of a very good person who is just in the wrong job.** In these cases, I may modify the termination "script," investing time in coaching the individual, if they are willing to listen. The individual is a good person, you want to see them in a role where they can be an "A" player. It's worth the time to help them think about it.

ON LAYOFFS

I've saved RIFs and Layoffs to the very last part of this chapter on terminations. Layoffs do not represent the failure of an individual to perform. They represent a massive management failure. We need to think of these differently.

At one point in my career, I was brought into a troubled organization to do a turnaround. I was the EVP of Sales. For years, the company missed goals and expectations. New management was brought in to correct the situation.

After spending some time evaluating the organization, I determined we would have to reduce the organization by close to 50%—well l over a thousand people would have to be let go. This was one of the most tragic decisions I've ever had to make. My decision would impact the lives of over a thousand families.

Largely, the layoffs were through no fault of the people themselves, but a result of tragically bad management and years of horrible decisions made by that management team, each of whom was gone, and each of whom had a "golden parachute."

While we were as generous as we could possibly be with separation packages, the day the layoffs were announced remains among the most tragic of my career. The thought of impacting over a thousand families still haunts me. I don't question the decision. This was a survival issue. But I was angry with the management that created this situation. I had a huge amount of compassion and empathy for the people and families whose lives would be disrupted by my decision.

Layoffs are a reflection of your and your management's bad performance (or perhaps previous management). You must do everything possible to avoid layoffs. This means continued sharp execution, attention to market dynamics, precision management/leadership, accountability, and strong sustained performance in the organization.

But as much as we try to avoid layoffs, sometimes they are unavoidable. We decide to exit a business or market, there have been sudden disruptions in the markets, there is a massive switch in strategy.

When we have to resort to layoffs, they must be done with the greatest compassion. It is never the fault of the employees being impacted; it is the result of management decisions, which ultimately impact them. We should do everything we can to be generous in their severance packages, and to support them in getting new jobs.

Most of all, remember a layoff decision isn't just about the people you are laying off: it is about their families and community.

Layoffs, also impact the people left behind—those still on the job. Sometimes they don't know whether they are the winners or losers. They've lost friends and colleagues, undoubtedly, they have to pick up many of the things they were doing.

In recent years, however, I've seen real abuse in using layoffs. I've seen a trend of managers using the layoff mechanism to address individual performance issues and problems. Rather than understanding the performance issue, working with people to try to improve performance and address performance issues directly, managers get lazy and terminate people through a layoff.

This is the highest level of cowardice and bad management. Managers using layoffs to address performance issues are cheating the individual, cheating the company, and not doing their job.

Lazy managers resort to layoffs because they lack the respect of the individual in helping them understand and improve performance problems. They simply don't want to take the time to do their jobs. They use the layoff as a fast and easy way to get rid of someone.

Managers using layoffs to address individual performance problems are wrong. They are not doing their job, and this needs to be addressed by senior management as a performance issue of the manager himself.

THE LAYOFFS MEETINGS AND ANNOUNCEMENTS

Layoffs are different. You are not just terminating one person; you are probably terminating a number of people at the same time. They are devastating for the people being laid off and for the people being left behind.

While as a first line manager, you may be instructed what to do, and much of the timing may be out of your hands, as much as possible, you want to do the following:

1. **Get it done all at once.** I've seen some organizations do layoffs over a number of days, even weeks. This is devastating! No work gets done, everyone is waiting to see if they are going to be next.

2. **Recognize the rumor mill will be in overdrive leading up to the layoff and for some time after the layoff.** If you don't address people's concerns

individually or as a group, they will be harboring doubts and worrying about their role for weeks and months to come.

3. **I prefer to tell the whole organization what is happening up front.** To let them know about the layoff, the reasons for the reductions. It's important to own up to management's role in this. The layoff never has anything to do with individual performance, but it is an unfortunate business and organizational decision. Make no excuses. Give everyone the chance to ask questions.

4. **Immediately conduct one-on-one meetings with the individuals.** Realize, the moment they have been asked to sit with you in a private meeting they already know what's happening. Tell them about the package they will receive, any support they can get in getting a new job. Give them a chance to ask questions, even to vent. They will be shocked; some will be in tears not knowing what to do, others will be angry. Every reaction is a fair and probably deserved reaction. They need and deserve the opportunity to express their views.

5. **Be sensitive to the logistics and how it will be perceived by both the people impacted and others.** Everyone knows what is happening when individuals are being called into your office. Try to avoid the "walk of shame."

6. **Be aware there is a need for grieving in the group and for people to say their good byes.** Normally, when terminating a person, you want to get them out of the office as quickly as possible. In the case of a layoff, people will want to be able to say good bye to friends and colleagues. Make sure you show the respect they deserve by giving them the time to talk to other and grieve together.

7. **Be aware of the "long tail" of the layoff. People left behind will be shaken.** They will be wondering if something else will happen and if they might be next. Make sure you are sensitive to this and are constantly communicating telling people what's going on and what they can expect.

8. **Also be aware the workload hasn't changed, so this means the same work now needs to be done by fewer people.** Make sure you have a plan for tis. Make sure you sit down with each person to review the plan so they understand the new expectation. Re-prioritization is seldom thought of, but critical. The people remaining were probably fully busy before the layoff, They now have a dramatically increased workload. Realize everything can't and won't get done. Help them figure out what they need to be doing and what is OK to stop or let slip.

I can't emphasize this concluding point enough. Layoffs are only done for business reasons and have nothing to do with the performance of people. Layoffs are a management failure, not the failure of individuals in their performance.

Using the layoff as an excuse for addressing performance issues is sheer cowardice. I've had managers in my organizations trying to do this. They never remained managers because they didn't have the courage to do their jobs.

NEVER GET COMFORTABLE

Terminating a person is stressful for you, the manager, and for the salesperson. In some sense, it should be that way. We should never treat terminating someone casually. We should never be comfortable with it.

When we become comfortable with terminating people, we have lost our humanity and ability to connect with our people. At that point, you should be questioning your own future as a leader.

YOU WILL BE FIRED

Sales managers and sales executives, unfortunately, tend to have short tenures. Industry data puts it at around 14 months. The job is a tough job, sometimes, we just don't have the ability to meet expectations, sometimes, we are caught up in a "changing of the guard," regardless of our performance.

But odds are, at some point in your career you will be fired.

Realize, like those employees you've terminated, you will go through the stages: Anger, grief, denial, moving on. It's important to recognize the process you are going through. If you have a friend or mentor or spouse, leverage them for help in getting through it.

Get through it as quickly as you can. Put it behind you and move on.

But before you put it behind you, do a "loss review." As dispassionately as you can, walk through what happened and why. Resist the temptation to blame someone else. While it may be tough to accept, most of the time, you probably deserved it. In some way, you were not meeting expectations.

As part of the loss review, think, "Were you in the wrong job?" "Did you thoroughly understand what was expected of you?" "Did you recognize and understand the gaps in your performance?" "What did you and your management do to close the gaps?" "What should you have done differently?"

It's important for you to learn as much as you can from what happened so that you can move forward and improve. Too often, I've seen people, managers and sales people alike, who haven't taken the time to learn from the situation and improve. As a result, inevitably they are condemned to making the same mistakes again.

While it may sound crazy, one of the benefits of being fired or laid off, is that it helps you develop compassion and empathy for others. Too many managers, are very cavalier about the process. They don't understand the range of human emotions that arise in these situations, they are callous and hardened. If you have been through the experience, it will make you better—a better manager and leader, and a more compassionate human being.

PART SIX

TACTICAL BUSINESS MANAGEMENT: MANAGING THE BUSINESS WEEK TO WEEK, QUARTER TO QUARTER

41

BUSINESS MANAGEMENT IS IMPORTANT: THE DAY-TO-DAY BUSINESS OF MANAGING THE SALES TEAM

Leading a sales organization involves doing a lot stuff that's not directly related to the day-to-day coaching and development of your team. Some of these things include performance analysis, reporting, budget management, compensation/ commission planning, workflow and forecasting. Stated differently, there are a number of necessary business management, administrative, and day to day management tasks that aren't directly related to coaching and developing your people. They have to be done, but you don't want them to consume too much of your time.

If you are in a larger organization, you may have a separate sales operations organization. In a smaller organization, you may have an individual performing the sales operations function, or you may have to do a lot of this yourself.

Regardless of whether or not there is a sales operations function, and an individual responsible for this, or you have to do it yourself, these matters will impact you and you will need to be involved in some way.

The purpose of this section of the book is to introduce you to some of these areas, and identify important things to be aware of with each one.

Before you jump into this, let me offer a HUGE word of warning. While these business management tasks are very important in looking at the performance of the overall sales organization, they can grow to consume all of your time.

There is a real danger you spend all of your time doing analysis, paperwork, and all of the other activities we will be discussing in the following chapters.

Some managers, the weakest ones, find solace in doing these sorts of things, and hiding from their real responsibilities of helping the sales people. These people are actually acting as administrators and desk jockey's, shirking the responsibility of leading and developing their teams.

There will be a great temptation to spend a substantial portion of your time doing "sales analysis and operations stuff." It's important, but it cannot be your top or even one of your top three priorities.

The moment you find yourself giving up time for one-on-ones with your people, coaching, developing them, being out in the field working with them and your customers, you are doing the least important part of your job.

Day to day "Business Management" or "Sales Operations" cannot and should not occupy more than a small part of your time.

With that warning in place, let's look at what you need to know. I can't cover everything that might need to be done in your organization, but I'll cover the major and most common pieces that will require and impact your time.

42

IF YOU CAN'T MEASURE IT...

Anyone who's been in sales for more than a few seconds knows how important metrics are. We're driven by the numbers.

The problem is, too often, we are measuring the wrong thing!

Quota attainment, for instance, is a terrible metric. But that's the one that first comes to mind when we think about metrics. It's probably the key measurement you grew up on as a salesperson. It's probably what your manager asks you about every week.

Don't get me wrong, quota attainment, revenue, orders, sales, gross margin are all important metrics, but they are *output metrics* or historical metrics.

Using these to manage the performance of the sales organization is like driving a car by looking in the rearview mirror. You are always looking at what has happened, not what is happening, or is likely to happen.

By the time you know you are in trouble, you probably don't have the time to take action to recover.

It's important to trace things backwards from quota attainment, understanding the key activities that drive the output—quota attainment. It's critical to understand the right level of activities required to assure you are going to make your numbers.

As a first line sales manager, it's important that you understand these leading metrics and are identifying the right goals to drive the results you want.

Let me give a simple example. In our own organization, we have a really good understanding of what drives revenue results. Our win rates are pretty consistent, usually around 82-87%. Our average transaction size is pretty well known, as is our sales cycle. While we constantly refine our sales activities to improve, we have a good idea of what drives our ability to win qualified deals.

But, for our business to grow, for us to achieve our numbers, we have to look back even further. We have to look at our prospecting activities. We have to know that we are having a sufficient number of prospecting conversations, to create the volume of opportunities necessary to achieve our business goals.

We know how many unique prospecting conversations we need to have to qualify a sufficient number of opportunities to make our numbers. Each of us has a "magic" prospecting number I measure people on. My own number has typically been six to eight unique prospecting conversations a week. (This isn't dials, they are substantive conversations with executives matching our target profiles.)

That means if I consistently miss hitting my weekly target, I will be lucky if I'm making my number about 11-14 months later. However, if I have those six to eight conversations a week, I have great confidence I will be able to make my number 11-14 months later.

It turns out, the more complex and longer your sales cycle, the more important it is to have a strong base of leading metrics.

There are a number of other metrics that may be important to your organization. They may be things like product mix, new customer acquisition, customer retention, and so forth.

As a first line manager, you may have a lot of goals assigned to you and your team. Certainly, your quota may be assigned. But often, it's those leading metrics that aren't developed that become your responsibility to determine and agree upon with your team.

It's those metrics you will rely on every day, to make sure you and your team are doing the things necessary, in the volume required, to make your numbers.

A FRAMEWORK FOR METRICS

In establishing a good base of metrics, it's useful to have a framework to understand how things fit together. The following figure provides a simple but powerful model.

Strategic Goals	Business Management Goals
Operational Goals	Developmental Goals

Let's walk through these so you can have a better understanding.

BUSINESS MANAGEMENT

These are pretty much the classical metrics we know and love as sales people. They are the metrics associated with the organization—or your part of the organization and roll up into the overall corporate business plan. The classic metrics are Quota/Quota Attainment, Orders, Revenue, Sales, Gross Margin. Sometimes we might see other metrics like market share, growth, customer satisfaction.

The common thing about all of these is they are output or trailing metrics. So it's impossible to use them to manage day to day performance. Think of it this way. Say you have a three- to six-month sales cycle. Let's say you have a big miss on Q1's numbers. You not only have to find out what's wrong, so that you can make your Q2, but you have to recover the volumes you missed for Q1.

If you have a three to six month sales cycle, you can start to see the problem right away. At the end of Q1, when you make the miss, it will take you a little time to figure out what's wrong and what you need to do to fix it. Maybe some deals fell through, maybe you had some unexpected losses, maybe you had a weak pipeline.

Now that you've figured out what went wrong, you have to fix the problem. Remember, you are already some weeks into Q2. But here's where it gets sticky: You are probably well into the sales process for the Q2 deals, so changes you make now will not have a real impact on those Q2 deals, in fact you may have another shortfall if there was a big problem, but are more likely to have an impact in Q3. (That's if you can change really fast).

Also, you have to make up the gap from Q1 and any gap you might have in Q2.

So in the best of cases, you start seeing recovery in late Q3 and Q4. But it's just the end of the first quarter and all of a sudden you see your whole year threatened.

And that's probably the best case, it usually takes time to determine the problem, time to figure out corrective action, then you have to go out and execute. Here's where your sales cycle comes into play, and really puts your numbers at risk.

That's why the Business Management Metrics are bad from a day to day or even quarter to quarter performance management point of view. We'll see how to complement Business Management Metrics with leading metrics to provide you a real time capability to make sure you can hit the numbers.

STRATEGIC METRICS

Organizations don't want to just book revenue. They want to make sure the composition of that revenue is aligned with the goals of the company. There are important things like:

- **Are you selling the entire product line?**

- **Are you investing enough time in selling new products, or are you just selling what you are comfortable with?**

- **Are you growing your key accounts?**

- **Are you growing in your target markets?**

- **Are you acquiring the right number of new customers?**

- **Are you retaining your current customers?**

- **How are you doing in competitive win backs?**

There are all sorts of thing that may be important to making sure you are driving the right mix of revenue, and supporting the execution of the corporation's overall business strategy.

These metrics tend to be trailing or historic metrics, like the Business Management metrics. There are some things you can do to establish some leading metrics. For example, if you have a goal to acquire new customers, a leading metric to support this goal might be number of prospecting calls on potential new customers. This is actually a great example, of an operational metric.

Strategic metrics are important in aligning what your team is doing with the overall strategies and priorities of the organization. It's important to pay attention to these.

OPERATIONAL METRICS

This is where you and your people live your lives. These metrics are a reflection of what we do every day to make sure we are doing the things that enable us achieve our numbers at the end of the month, quarter, or year.

Pipeline metrics represent a great example of a good operational metric. If you know your win rates, sales cycles, average deal value, you can figure out how many deals you need to win to make your annual quota. Stepping backward from this, you can determine how many qualified deals you must have in your pipeline to produce the number of wins.

Let's look at a quick example. Say one of your sales people has a $10M quota, and your average deal value is $500K, and to make the math simple, let's assume you have a 12 month sales cycle. For him to make his number, he must win 20 deals.

Now if his win rate is 25%, how many qualified deals must he be working to make the number? The answer is easy, it's 80 deals.

Now you can look at the actual number of deals in his pipeline. If he has fewer than 80 qualified deals working now, his ability to make the number is seriously threatened. But knowing this early means you and he have a chance to take corrective action.

To fix this problem, you and he have a number of alternatives: improve his win rate, increase average deal size, reduce the sales cycle, or prospect to find more deals.

Let's run the numbers even further back. Let's say he qualifies one in five deals that he prospects. That means, over the course of the year, he has to prospect 400 deals or about eight per week. (Now you can see the methodology of how I came up with my six to eight unique prospecting conversations per week.)

These operational metrics are really critical to making sure the things your people are working on each day produce the end results you need.

The pipeline and its metrics are fundamental operational management metrics. Other activity metrics are also very powerful. Things like the number of prospecting conversations a day or week, the number of customer meetings a week, the number of quotes or proposals a week/month can all be useful in making sure your people are spending their time on enough of the right things to produce the numbers.

I'm sure you've had operational and activity metrics before, and I'm sure you may have been very frustrated about them. That's usually because managers do a terrible job of setting operational metrics.

Usually what happens is they establish relatively arbitrary metrics, more focused in "busywork" than understanding what really drives business results.

To establish meaningful metrics, you have to have a strong understanding of your business and what produces results. You have to be able to work the number backwards—to close 20 deals, you need to qualify and work 80 deals, and you need to prospect 400 deals.

The other problem is managers apply the same goal to everyone. Really, the goals need to be individualized.

Go back to the example of producing $10M in a year. Let's imagine for a moment, those are the goals and operational metrics for one of your sales people. But imagine another salesperson who might have the same quota, but has a 50% win rate, double his peer. That means to make his numbers, he has to have an active pipeline of 40 deals, not 80.

But too many managers, in their inevitable wisdom—or laziness—establish the same goal for everyone. So if you establish a goal of 80 active deals in the pipeline for the second salesperson, the same as the first salesperson, you are really forcing him into a higher level of work, not commensurate with the results he produces. He's likely to be very upset.

Or maybe you do the reverse, you say each salesperson has to have 40 active deals in the pipeline. You've just set yourself up for a big miss in your number, because if the first salesperson has the 40 deals, closes his 25% for ten deals at $500k each, he'll hit $5 million or about 50% of his plan.

Or even worse, managers haven't taken the time to understand the link between the leading and trailing metrics, so they just make and arbitrary guess. What it a manager said, "You've got to make eight prospecting calls per day." There is no reason other than it feels like a good number. But from the example above, we know the salesperson only needs to make about 8 per week. By forcing the salesperson to make eight per day, the manager is taking him away from the other important things he needs to do to make his numbers. So his performance and morale will sink!

Now you see how activity metrics can go awry. You may have the wrong metrics, you may have the wrong goals. In addition to pissing off your people, you expose yourself to a big risk in making the numbers.

But there's one more level of even more leading metrics, things that are important to achieve your operational metrics.

DEVELOPMENTAL METRICS

These metrics are the most leading you can get. They really focus on issues of:

- **Do you have the right composition of your team to make the numbers (skills, experience, capabilities)?**

- **Do your people have the right skills, knowledge, tools to achieve their goals?**

Let me pick up from the previous example of the first salesperson. Remember he had a $10M quota, 25% close rate, $500K average deal size. To make his quota, he had to have 80 qualified deals in his pipeline. To find those 20 qualified deals, he has to prospect 400 hundred deals, or eight per week.

But what happens if he doesn't have the skills or tools to prospect effectively? What if he doesn't know what prospecting techniques work, where to prospect, or how to have a prospecting conversation with the customer?

Or what if he's very weak in developing and executing deal strategies? What if you determine he needs to increase his win rate, or increase his average deal value, or compress his sales cycle? Does he have the skills, tools, capabilities, and time to do these things?

So by taking your operational metrics and thinking, "What do I need to have in place for each salesperson to make sure they can achieve these goals," you start to establish the leading actions to enable them to be successful.

It might be training, it might be providing prospecting tools, or other tools. It may be you don't have the right skills and experience, and you may have to rebuild your team to meet the new needs for success.

USING THE FRAMEWORK

Now you can start to see the power of the framework and how the different elements complement each other.

Building the Goals: Starting at the upper right hand side, Business Management Goals, working backwards, or counterclockwise in the matrix, you can start to construct the strategic, operational, and developmental goals and metrics necessary to achieve your numbers. You will clearly be able to identify the leading goals, metrics, and activities critical to hitting your numbers.

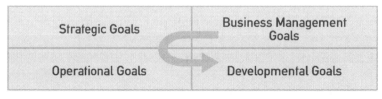

Executing to achieve the goals: Working forward, from Developmental Goals, moving clockwise around the matrix, you now have the sequence of things that have to be done to achieve success.

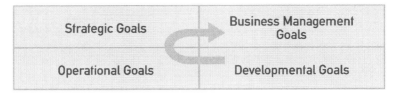

Strategic Goals	Business Management Goals
Operational Goals	Developmental Goals

WHAT SHOULD YOU MEASURE?

As you might guess, you need to have goals and metrics in each quadrant in the framework outlined above.

But as you think about establishing metrics, you may also want to think of a few other items:

- **What behaviors do you want to drive?**

- **How do you ensure quality in the achievement of the goals?**

- **How will the salesperson "game" the metrics?**

- **Do they allow you to achieve both your business management goals and your long term growth goals for the organization?**

When you think about behaviors, think about what it is that you really want the salesperson to be doing, what has the greatest impact?

For example, I get into a lot of discussions about whether sales people should be measured on sales/revenue targets, or gross margin. It seems these days it's very fashionable to put a gross margin metric in place, thinking that will limit discounting. It may or may not (more often, except in very sophisticated organizations it doesn't limit discounting).

But what if you gave the salesperson virtually no freedom in setting prices and discounting. To get anything non-standard, management approval is required. So in this case, a gross margin metrics is virtually meaningless to the salesperson, he has little control over pricing. So a revenue metric might be a better metric. You just want the salesperson to chase deals. And since they will be at relatively standard pricing you have great control over gross margin.

What about the quality in achievement of goals? You'll actually find this related to the "gaming a salesperson might do."

I had a client with a large inside sales organization. They set a goal of a certain number of calls each person had to make every day.

When I talked to the sales manager, he said, "You have to talk to Ray, he always far exceeds his goals for calls per day. He can set the example for everyone else."

Since they had a phone system where I could monitor calls, I started listening to Ray, unbeknownst to him, to learn what he was doing and how he could always overachieve his number.

After a few hours, it was obvious. At least 50% of the calls Ray was making were to his buddies. He'd have great conversations about what they might do in the evening or the weekend. He had a wide network of friends. Since he was being measured on average call duration as well, a conversation might last over several dials.

It turned out, Ray was falling very short of the goal because he wasn't making the right calls, but rather gaming the system. When you looked more deeply at his performance, you could see he was struggling to make his numbers.

So this was a case where there was no definition (or at least inspection) of what a quality call was and whether the people were making quality calls.

The quality of the activity can have a devastating impact on overall goal attainment. Let's look at how bad quality can impact pipeline metrics. Let's go back to our first salesperson. He has to have 80 qualified deals in his pipeline. If he works those 80 deals effectively, he should be able to make his number.

But let's imagine he only has 60 qualified deals in the pipeline. As manager, you put him under tremendous pressure. "You have to prospect and find another 20 deals in your pipeline."

Under pressure, this might drive the wrong behaviors. The salesperson might relax his qualification criteria just to fill his pipeline. So he ends up having the 80 deals in his pipeline, but the quality of those deals is significantly lower.

This is where people and pipelines go into a death spiral. As we relax qualification criteria, our win rates decline because we're chasing lower quality deals. Perhaps our average transaction values decline, or our sales cycle increases because it's tougher to close these deals.

So where 80 highly qualified deals might have been the right number, it's now far too low.

Let me run the math on that so you can understand more vividly. You recall the average transaction value was $500K, the win rate was 25%, and the salesperson had to close 20 deals to make his $10M quota.

But if he relaxes his qualification criteria, his win rate will decline. Let's say it declines to 20%, but that means his pipeline metrics have changed. To make his number he has to have 100 deals in the pipeline, not 80.

This usually isn't people "gaming" the system, but people who are trying to hit the metric, and under pressure reduce quality and start chasing the daily number rather than really looking at what they are doing. You have to pay attention to this; it's human nature to take shortcuts. So consider designing it into your thinking. As you put a goal in place, think about the short cuts the salesperson might take. If they take those short cuts, do you still have the quality you want, do you still achieve the goals you want? If you do, you've designed a great metrics. If not, go back to the drawing board.

43

PERFORMANCE METRICS AND ANALYTICS

The previous chapter provided a foundation for a system of metrics—connecting the dots between the leading metrics and trailing or output metrics. We'll continue this discussion as we look at how you might analyze your own performance or the performance of the overall organization.

Many of these metrics are things you would never use in measuring individuals, but they provide interesting insights about how the organization is performing and how well aligned you may be with the overall priorities of the company.

Understanding the numbers is critical in understanding sales performance. It's not just a matter of making quota, but there are a whole variety of areas in which it's important to assess the performance of the organization.

We'll scan through a laundry list of what they are and how they are leveraged. As you look to your own needs, choose those that are most meaningful to you and your organization.

ORDERS/SALES/REVENUE/PLAN

Depending on your business you may actually look at several different types of overall goals.

1. **Orders are POs you have gotten, but that have not yet been invoiced.** They are recorded on a company's books as backlog—indicating potential future revenues. Sometimes, with service sales or embedded components, orders may remain on the books for a long time, with portions being converted to

revenue as products are shipped and invoiced, or as services are delivered and invoiced.

2. **Sales/Revenue represents orders that have been invoiced.** Financially, sales/revenue is important to your company because revenue is what is reported in your company's P&L and to shareholders.

3. **Why are the two important?** If all your business is shipped and invoiced immediately on receipt of orders, tracking both numbers is probably unimportant. If there are long time gaps between orders and revenue, it's important to track both. Typically, top management wants to maintain order flow, but they want to make sure revenue numbers are hitting corporate and market expectations. So timing of order to revenue recognition is important for managers to understand.

For example, if we make our order number but invoice nothing in a quarter, the quarter will be deemed a disaster because there is no revenue. (Which could stimulate spending cutbacks, freezes or other things.) If you are measured on both, you want to make sure you are hitting both numbers and your understand the relationship/lag time between revenue and orders.

4. **Plan is a term sometimes synonymous with quota.** It's the goal the organization has committed to achieve. You may have order and revenue plan numbers to achieve.

OPERATIONAL PERFORMANCE MEASURES

We talked about this in the previous chapter; you will have any number of operational measures. These are metrics about current activities and performance. Their purpose is to see if the organization is on track to achieve its goals.

Operational/activity measures include pipeline metrics, activity metrics (e.g. calls per day, connects, call duration, meetings per week, proposals, quotes, etc.).

Now here's some of the challenge with operational measures. They can't be set arbitrarily, that's the mistake too many managers make. They pull a goal out of the air, "You need to make 50 calls per day, you need to have five prospecting meetings per week, and you need to have three times coverage in your pipeline."

These are all arbitrary and not tied to the outcomes they need to generate. The only way to set these goals is to start from the end outcomes and work your way backwards. Let's walk through a simplified example of the problem with arbitrary metrics.

Think back to the last chapter, where we went through various examples of pipeline metrics. In the examples, we discussed, one salesperson had a 50% close rate, another had 25%, and a third had 20%. Setting an arbitrary number for pipeline coverage can be devastating. Let's say you arbitrarily chose "four" and required everyone to have four times coverage.

Clearly, this coverage goal is only appropriate for the person with the 25% win rate. Your high performer will be required to have two times as many opportunities as she needs—adversely impacting her morale and possibly her performance (because she has to try to manage twice as many deals.) Likewise, the lower performer could have the four times coverage, but based on his win rates, that doesn't enable him to achieve his goal. He'll miss by a huge amount—even though he's met your operational target.

Hopefully, now you can see the flaw in pulling arbitrary numbers out of the air or even

using the same number for everyone on the team.

You can see how to develop the operational and activity metrics that are tied directly to the outcomes you are trying to drive. These are leading metrics. These are really important, because you know when you start failing to meet those goals, your ability to hit your numbers is threatened. But since they are leading metrics, you have an ability to fix them, changing the outcomes and making it more likely that you will make your numbers.

There are dozens of operational and activity metrics you can establish. Most of the time, I find managers establish far too many. Sales people get confused about what's important and what's not.

It's critical to establish the "critical few." But to do this, you need to really understand the operational and activity drivers for your team and the business. As a very general guideline, other than pipeline metrics, two to three key activity metrics are usually sufficient.

Here's a laundry list to help you think about what might be most relevant. Remember, whichever you choose, you have to establish a goal, then track actual attainment against that goal. Also, these are ideally individualized for each person on the team. They become unreliable if you use general numbers.

PIPELINE

- Total qualified deals in the pipeline, deals at each stage.

- Cycle time/velocity, both through the pipeline and from stage to stage.

- Average deal size/value.

- Number of deals progressing from stage to stage each month.

- Win rate, abandonments, losses, no decision made.

- Stalled deals, slipped deals, deals that keep changing value in the sales cycle.

- Net new deals added to the pipeline.

- **Deals that have moved to a new stage (a velocity measure).**

- **Pipeline coverage.**

ACTIVITY MEASURES

- **Prospecting meetings per week.**

- **Number of first calls (telephone calls) per day or week (make sure these are actual conversations, not dials—dials are probably one of the most meaningless numbers around. Any salesperson not meeting your daily dial requirement is just not being creative.).**

- **Number of proposals per week or month**

- **Number of email campaigns (responses, follow-up, etc.)**

- **Number of demonstrations (I'm not a fan, but this might be relevant).**

- **Select social media activities/engagement (follows, likes, etc. tend to be irrelevant, but there may be some good social engagement metrics.)**

This will give you a starting point. Again, focus on identifying the very few that are most important. Be careful about numbers that can be "gamed." That's why dials are so bad as a metric: It's easily gamed and irrelevant to the results. (Imagine how easy it is to make 100 dials a day, but if you have no conversations, it's meaningless).

OTHER PERFORMANCE MEASURES

Depending on the priorities of your company, there may be some other things you will want to analyze, perhaps even setting performance goals. These may be some of the strategic metrics we discussed in the last chapter, they may include developmental metrics. Some of these may be metrics you establish for your salespeople, others may be important metrics to look at your overall organizational performance—but you won't want to assign them to each individual, perhaps you want to track them for the team. A few of the more common ones include:

- **New customer acquisition:** Acquiring new customers is important in growing a business. They are both new sources of revenue, but can become sources of future recurring revenue. You and your people may have a goal around new customer acquisition. Another measure within this is CAC—Customer Acquisition Cost.

- **Customer retention:** Keeping customers, growing them is important to the overall revenue growth of a company. General wisdom indicates it's cheaper to retain and grow a current customer than it is to acquire a new customer. Another measure within retention is LCV—Lifetime Customer Value.

- **Product line performance:** Sales is responsible for executing the corporate strategy with the customers. As a result, we have to pay attention to all the products and services, for which we are responsible.

It's important to drive balanced performance across the product line (unless you are accountable for only one product line). Too often sales people sell what they are most comfortable with. But that leaves products ignored and ultimately makes the company uncompetitive and unprofitable.

As sales managers, balanced performance across the portfolio is critical. Think of this:

You have two sales people, each making their $1M quota's. One has only sold one product line, it's his favorite, one he's been successful with for years. The other made her number by selling the entire portfolio. She sold the old products as well as the new products and had balanced performance across the entire portfolio.

Which salesperson is the better performer? Both made their quotas of $1 million, but who's contributing most to the company? I hope your answer is the second salesperson. Her performance is balanced with the overall company strategy for growth. The first salesperson is not executing the company strategy, but selling only what he wants to sell. Only focusing on what he wants to sell, not what he needs to sell to support the company priorities, is a huge performance issue. While he is creating revenue, he is doing nothing to execute the company strategy with the customer.

- **Year Over Year Growth:** Companies want to grow; their investors and shareholders expect them to grow. While you may not have a metric on YOY growth, sales operations is probably tracking this number. They want to make sure the company is meeting its growth commitments.

  Be careful, meeting plan and YOY Growth may not be aligned. I worked with a company that was in deep trouble. In reviewing performance with the VP of Sales, he stated, "We are X% above last year's attainment. We aren't meeting our goals, but we're still doing very well!"

  It's that kind of distorted thinking that causes companies to be troubled. They hadn't met last year's goal, they were far from meeting this year's goal, but all the sales manager was concerned about was YOY growth. Fortunately, his successor knew his goal was to meet or exceed plan.

- **Win/Loss Analysis:** As natural as it would seem, very few organizations do good win/loss reviews. Usually, it's something a salesperson enters into CRM, with very little additional inspection. (When I casually inquire, the reason for wins is always superior selling, and the reason for losses is never sales error, most of the time it's price). There is huge value in analyzing wins and losses. There's huge value in looking at the patterns of wins and losses over time.

Do we lose against certain competitors, in certain types of customers, with certain products? How do we learn and improve without understanding what works and doesn't work?

I don't recommend doing reviews for every win/loss unless most of your deals are very large. Instead, look at deals of a certain value, or with certain types of customers or competitors or other criteria important to your business.

A good win/loss review isn't about assigning blame. It's about learning and figuring out how to improve for the future.

- **Competitive Analysis:** This is less about your competition's products and positioning, but more about your success in competing against certain competitors. You, also may want to look at how they engage the customer through the buying process to make sure you are addressing competitive threats. As manager, you will see more competitors than your sales people since you are seeing all your sales people's deals. So you will see the patterns in terms of how they engage, their strategies, and approaches. In deal reviews, you can really help your people think about the competition and develop better strategies.

- **Customer Satisfaction:** This is one of the most important pieces of analysis you can do. It's critical to have a formal way of measuring and tracking customer satisfaction (sometimes we call this customer experience or customer success,) but you should also spend time with customers, trying to understand their attitudes and opinions about your company, products, services, support. You can use these conversations to understand what they think about the sales team, and what might be improved. Generally, I like to do these calls without the salesperson, just so I can talk about customer satisfaction and not be worried about selling them something.

- **Value Realization:** This is connected to customer satisfaction/success. Presumably we base this on the value proposition we created and the customer expectations of the outcomes they would achieve. If we want to grow our relationship with the customer, if we want to maintain their loyalty, if we want to leverage them for references, it's important we validate that they have achieved what they hoped to. If not, figure a way to address it. While this may not be the direct responsibility of your team, it certainly impacts their future with the customer. As a result, it's critical for you to understand.

- **Pricing/Margin Analysis:** This is one of my favorite areas. I want to look at pricing and margin trends with the team. This enables me to start understanding what's happening with "discounting" and other pricing activities that may be eroding our overall profitability.

In our normal day to day activity in helping people win deals, we may choose to take certain pricing actions, or provide certain discounts. Often, we have all sorts of rationalization—good or bad, about what we've done for a specific deal. Over time, however, if we aren't tracking pricing and margins across all our deals, we may find we've gotten into very bad discounting practices. We may be doing special discounts on virtually every deal, seriously impacting our overall financial performance.

It's important for you to periodically look at what you are doing in the aggregate. You want to maintain your pricing and margins at the highest levels possible.

There are more, but these are some of the key performance management areas you will want to look at. Some may be important enough to establish goals and metrics for your people, while others may be more relevant to you. But be careful about trying to measure too much.

BUDGET/EXPENSE

There are things critical to your performance and the overall cost of selling that you will have to track.

1. **Labor/People expense.** Generally, this is salaries, commissions, bonuses.

2. **Burden.** This may be tracked with labor expense, but these are generally the health care, social security, taxes and other expenses for each person. While they don't see them in their pay checks, these are real expenses the company incurs.

3. **Other sales people overheads or expenses.** These may include things like cars, computers/tools, office space and others expenses incurred by the sales people.

4. **Travel and entertainment.** These are expenses incurred in supporting sales people activities with customers. They may be mileage or other travel expenses incurred in meeting with customers, meals, entertainment and related sales expenses.

5. **Other expense areas:** Programs, tools, trade shows, channel support, recruiting, training, onboarding, rent, facilities, office, and other expenses in supporting the organization and its operation.

As a manager, you will want to understand those expenses you are measured on and accountable for.

PEOPLE MEASURES

There are a number of people measures your company may have or that you may want to put in place. Most of these metrics are actually indicators of your own personal performance. While they measure people, when you look at the trends for the group over time, it's a direct reflection of your performance. If your company doesn't have these in place, you may want to look at them to evaluate how you are doing.

A few critical ones:

- **Voluntary/Involuntary Attrition:** Attrition is critical to pay attention to. Generally, attrition is a management problem, reflecting directly on your performance or the company overall.

  Voluntary attrition is very concerning. It's the type of attrition where people are choosing to leave the company. Perhaps they have a better offer, perhaps they are unhappy. A certain amount of voluntary attrition is unavoidable, perhaps even healthy. But if it is too high or increasing, you will want to understand what's going on. Additionally, you will always want to do exit interviews to learn from the departing employee perspectives they have on the company, suggestions they would make, areas of satisfaction/dissatisfaction, why they are leaving. (Be sure to wish them well in the new role, even if they are going to the competition.)

  Involuntary attrition is based on actions you take. It could be a poorly performing employee that is being terminated. It could be reductions in headcount/layoffs. Involuntary attrition, even a poorly performing employee, is largely the responsibility of management. There is always some level of attrition, but a growing or high number is an indicator of a deeper problem.

- **Stack Ranking/Other Ranking:** Some companies have some type of forced ranking process. The most famous is a stack ranking process, ranking people from top to bottom. There are lots of articles and opinions for and against these approaches. I actually like ranking systems, but implemented in a positive manner. The problem with most ranking systems is they are less oriented to driving top performance and more focused on being punitive. That's where ranking tends to fail. Stack ranking to create "friendly" competition within the team is sometimes very powerful. People like to see how they are doing compared to their peers.

- **Performance Plan Metrics:** Hopefully, your company has a formal performance planning process. There are a number of metrics companies might track to look at overall performance. Some might look at the distribution of performance (number of highly evaluated, number low, etc.). There are also metrics having to do with how well managers meet their commitments to have performance plans in place and to keep them current.

  One of the negative uses of performance plan metrics and stack ranking is the arbitrary elimination of X% of low performers. This creates a punitive and negative environment in the organization and is a misuse of these tools.

  We could be arbitrarily getting rid of very good performers just by adhering blindly to these goals.

- **Employee Development:** I'm a strong believer in employee development. People want to grow in their careers, both in their current job and to move into higher levels of responsibility. It's important to have individual development plans in place and to track those. It's in their, your and your company's best interests to grow their ability to contribute and to retain and promote them.

- **Recruiting/Onboarding Metrics:** These are measures looking the quality of the recruiting and onboarding process. For example, candidates seen, offers made, offers accepted, time to productivity, voluntary/involuntary attrition within the first 12 months, and so forth.

- **General Employee Metrics:** There are a lot of metrics around general performance: Employees at or above plan, YOY comparisons, and so forth.

- **Employee Satisfaction:** These are usually formal surveys assessing employees dis/satisfaction across a number of dimensions—sometimes including your performance. This is a very powerful way to get great feedback from your people—but only if you pay attention to the results and do something about them. Otherwise, it's just lip service.

- **Employee Perspectives On Your Performance:** How do you know how you are doing unless you get some feedback. Hopefully, your employees have the courage to be direct with you, but sometimes they won't. They will feel there may be some repercussions. There are a variety of tools that help this, 360 Reviews get the input of your people, your peers and your management. They provide very powerful information about your strengths and weaknesses and how you can improve.

As a Senior Executive, I always conducted "skip level interviews" with 100% of the direct reports of the leaders reporting to me. Their managers knew this—because I required them to do skip levels as well. After I got a good picture, I incorporated the feedback in a review with each manager.

Again, there are a lot more. The key thing I really like about these people-related metrics is they are tightly coupled to your own personal performance. Whether your management evaluates you on them, or you just track them to continue to improve your performance, these can be very powerful.

PRODUCTIVITY ANALYSIS

You will want to look at the productivity of your people. Quota performance is a little misleading. It doesn't give you a total picture of productivity. You want to understand your costs of producing revenue.

At the highest level that's cost of selling. On a corporate income statement, sometimes you will see cost of selling as a percent of net revenue.

At your team level, this is an important metric. One of my favorites is called CPOD (Cost per Order Dollar—or this could also be Cost for Revenue or Sales).

It's a pretty easy calculation. Basically you want to look at the total burdened cost of your sales people (salaries, variable, benefits, expenses they incur like computers, phone, travel, offices,) divided by the revenue they generate. Over time this should be flat to declining.

Some people, particularly if you are a senior sales manager, track Indirect CPOD. This looks at the indirect costs of supporting sales people. For example, this is where your costs are accrued, any sales support, sales programs, and other parts of the organization.

Again, over time, these should be flat to declining. Don't worry if one month they spike, just look at sustained trends. There are some timing effects that impact these on a month to month basis. For example, I may invest a lot of money in one month for training and tools to support a product launch. The revenues associated with that may be realized over a number of months later in the year.

WRAP UP

As a manager, one of the biggest challenges you'll face is figuring this out. As you go up the management ranks, figuring out how to constantly improve sales productivity will be where you will be spending significant amounts of time.

The discussion on performance analytics can fill many more chapters. As a manager, your job is maximizing performance, so you need to have metrics, goals, and data to leverage to see how you and your team is doing.

The biggest trick is finding the few key metrics that enable you to make sure everything is on track.

44

FORECASTING

Forecasting is another one of those difficult discussions. It's impossible to have a general discussion about forecasting.

Each company has a different methodology for forecasting. Some of the language around the certainty of the forecast can be quite colorful. One of my clients calls their most certain (absolutely will close when I say it will close,) forecast the "Blood Commit." I've often teased the exec, a good friend, "What is a pinky swear forecast?"

Instead, I'll discuss a number of issues about forecasting, and why forecasting matters. I'm surprised at the number of sales people and sales managers that really don't understand the purpose of forecasts. Most tend to think forecasting is just a way for senior management to harass us about making the numbers.

Often, it is, but there is much more to forecasts and the importance of getting it right, or as accurate as possible.

FORECAST ACCURACY

Too often, I see organizations and individuals addressing only a small part of what a forecast should address. Most often, the forecast is viewed as "Will we get the deal and how certain are we?"

But a good forecast has several other important elements. There is a time element. That is "will we get the deal when we say we will get the deal." A good forecast means we have not only gotten the deal, but we've gotten it within a certain time window of when we committed we would get it. For example, if we forecast getting a deal this month, and it comes in six months from now, we could create huge problems within our organization.

The second element is the value/content of the deal. Again, this tells us, "We expect the deal will be for these products and services and will be worth this much."

Why are these important?

Basically, the rest of the organization builds its plans on what is being sold and when it is expected to be delivered. Manufacturing doesn't know what products to manufacture or when until they have an accurate forecast. Purchasing doesn't know what parts to buy so that manufacturing can build the products.

If you are in a services organization, the people responsible for managing the service delivery need to make sure they have the resources available to provide the services when committed. They need to look at their people's schedules, other commitments, what skills and capabilities are needed to support the customer.

Financial management needs to understand cash flow, making sure we have the funds to buy, build, service the products, pay people and vendors, as well as predict when the company will be paid by the customer.

Top management needs to manage the expectations of shareholders, analysts, and investors on overall company performance.

The bottom line: Is the rest of the company dependent on getting accurate information from sales about what, when, what kind, and how much will be needed in order to deliver on sales commitments.

If we can't provide that information, or it is inaccurate, we cause havoc with the rest of the organization. They may have purchased the wrong inventory. Manufacturing may not have the products in the build plan. We may not have the right resources available, and so on. Have you ever faced a situation where you were about to get a deal, then all of a sudden it has a very long lead time? Trace back through history, one of the primary reasons might be the result of terrible forecasting-procurement and manufacturing may be very conservative, not wanting to be burned again. Bad forecasts end up impacting you and your success.

All of these impact costs, performance, and the ability to serve customers, fulfilling the commitments we make to them.

Implicit in this discussion is that we are forecasting specific deals, not dollar volumes. A forecast that we will close $1M in business this month is relatively useless to the rest of the company. They don't know what to order, build, or support. For example if you sell two products, apples and oranges, and you forecast selling $1M, what does procurement buy? $1M of apples, $1M of oranges, $500k of each?

Accurate forecasts are important because everyone else in the company depends on them to help us do our jobs.

BUT HOW DO WE FORECAST?

One of the biggest errors I see sales people and managers making is building a forecast based on progress we make through the pipeline. We assign a certain probability of getting a deal if it's qualified, another when we complete discovery, another when we propose, and another when we are closing.

Our CRM systems even assign these probabilities as we change stages in the sales cycle.

This is a huge error. All we are measuring is our progress through the sales cycles. This has no relationship with a customer propensity or willingness to buy.

Instead, we must base our forecast on actions and commitments the customer makes.

I'm not suggesting the customer is going to say, "There's a 75% probability we will select you in 30 days."

Instead we need to look at things like: Customer urgency and commitment to change. Customer willingness to take actions we have asked them to take, for example, committing to a proof of concept, naming an implementation team, establishing a target "go live" date. Other things may include: the customer attitudes toward us and our solution, as well as their attitudes toward the competition, or the customer agreement and support of the business case.

There can be many more elements, but fundamentally, we are looking at customer behaviors, commitments, actions, and attitudes that indicate their buying behaviors.

Second, we have to have a strong sales process—aligned with the customer buying process. And our people have to be using it rigorously. Our sales process is based on our best experience of winning business. If you don't have a sales process and/or aren't using it, understanding where the customer is in their process, understanding their commitments and actions, understanding what's next is just a guess. We have no idea what it takes to move the customer to a decision and win the business.

As a result, it becomes impossible to forecast.

Finally, the decision of what to forecast and when is based on explicit agreement between the salesperson and the manager. Too often, we see managers completing the forecast independently of the salesperson or "persuading" the salesperson to commit to the forecast.

This is wrong, and is a major reason why forecasts are inaccurate. The salesperson is the one responsible for and accountable for the deal. The salesperson is the one working with the customer every day and knows the most about the situation.

If the salesperson is not absolutely confident in forecasting the deal (winning it, when it will be completed, for what and how much), then it's wrong to coerce the salesperson into committing something to the forecast.

45

TIME PLANNING

Time is the only thing we can never recover. We can recover from lost deals, shortfalls, mistakes, but we can never recover lost time.

Yet time is undoubtedly one of the most wasted resources in sales. It's your job to protect your time and your people's time viciously. You want to make sure they maximize their time available for selling.

Bad time management comes from a couple of sources:

1. Poor planning and time management by the individual.

2. "System imposed" time drains.

Periodically, you may want to have your people track how they use their time. Have them look at a few days or a week. Give them a standard form to complete at the end of the day. They should fill in the form with the time they spend on different things.

The form might include:

____Time spent on the phone with customers on pipeline deals,
____Time spent in meetings with customers on pipeline deals
____Time spent researching/preparing/following up for customer meetings
____Time spent actually prospecting
____Time spent researching/preparing for prospecting
____Time spent doing administrative tasks/paperwork
____Time spent in team meetings
____Time spent in other internal meetings

_____Time spent in working on non-deal related, non-selling related activities.
_____Time spent in post-sales customer service, problem solving, or similar activities.
_____Time spent with manager
_____Time spent traveling to customer locations
_____Time spent in training
_____Time spent in daily/weekly planning
_____Non-scheduled time
_____Other time (meals, breaks, etc.)

You don't want minute-by-minute time recording, and you aren't using this to "catch" lazy people who aren't using their time well. You aren't using this to look at individual time management so much as you are looking at the group trends and how everyone is spending their time. Make sure the team is clear about this when you ask them to do the exercise.

What you are trying to do is get an idea of the *time available for selling*. For the purposes of this discussion, I include: time spent preparing for a sales call, time spent following up the sales call, and the time spent on the call itself.

You'll be shocked by what you learn. In most organizations, time actually spent on selling accounts for less than 50% of the salesperson's time! Years ago, we did this sort of study with the sales organization of a Fortune 500 organization. We collected data for two weeks, and at the end of the period we found they had *only 17% of their time available for selling*!

Some of this was poor time planning on the part of the sales people. But a large amount of their time was spent on "system imposed" activities and duties that diverted their time from sales-related activities.

There are a lot of related non-selling activities that are important for your sales people to spend time on: their meetings with you, training, even a certain amount of administrative time is all part of doing the job.

There will always be some "down" or unscheduled time, as well. We can never be 100% scheduled.

But what you are trying to do is understand where they spend their time and how they might better utilize it or manage it. You want to free up as much time as possible to focus on selling activities.

In that Fortune 500 company, we Identified some things the company was doing, inadvertently, producing huge time drains. By identifying and fixing them, we would get their selling related time to 30% (still pretty bad). But in just doing that, it gave them the potential of nearly doubling productivity and revenue! And it was only the start!

POOR PERSONAL TIME MANAGEMENT

You need to train your people to have a disciplined approach to managing their time during the day and week. It's useful in your one-on-ones to review their weekly or even biweekly calendar.

You want them blocking out time for critical activities and meetings. Too many sales people are very poor at managing and blocking time, instead spending time "reacting" to the latest crisis. They may spend a lot of time on email, or social media, or researching a specific issue. Because they haven't planned or structured their use of time, they end up doing the urgent and not the important, or simply wasting time on activities that don't drive results.

It's highly productive for team members to have a regular cadence for how and when they do things. Establishing time blocks and rigorously sticking to them drives good habits, good time management, and high performance. They should block certain time periods every day/week for prospecting. They should have scheduled appointments. Or at least time blocked for when they are seeing customers, or blocked work time for working on current pipeline deals. There are certain administrative matters they need to block time for—make sure they block these during "non-prime selling hours."

Get your sales people in the habit of blocking their time, then make sure they use the time they blocked for that purpose.

	Monday	Tuesday	Wednesday	Thursday	Friday
8:00	Daily/Weekly Planning	Daily Prep & Social Media	Daily Prep & Social Media	Daily Prep & Social Media	Daily Prep & Social Media
9:00	Prospecting	Prospecting	Prospecting	Prospecting	Mgr 1:1
10:00					
11:00	Prep Mtgs	Cust Mtgs		Cust Mtgs	Prospecting
12:00					
1:00	Cust Mtgs		Cust Mtgs		
2:00					Training
3:00		Deal and Call Reviews with Manager		Deal and Call Reviews with Manager	
4:00				Team Mtg	Planning Next Week
5:00	Admin & Paperwork	Research & Prep	Admin & Paperwork		Admin & Paperwork

I once coached a team that wasn't doing enough prospecting and was finding every excuse they could to avoid it. Initially, we set aside blocks of time— 9-11 every morning, for example — for prospecting.

During that time, people would find excuses to do other things. They were busy doing paperwork, proposals, all sorts of things. They weren't prospecting. I created a rule, "You can't do *anything* but prospect. You can't do paperwork, proposals, or other tasks. If you don't have prospects to call, you sit at your desk doing nothing."

There were some painful mornings when people were sitting doing nothing. But forcing them to think about prospecting and to start doing prospecting, with no distractions, eventually got them doing what they were supposed to be doing, rather than finding every opportunity to avoid it. Eventually, their prospecting became very productive, they even started enjoying it.

Get your people in the habit of blocking time for a week to two weeks in advance. Look at how they are allocating those time blocks. During the week, make sure they are doing what they said they would be doing during those time blocks.

On the following page is a sample of what a week might look like. It will be different for every salesperson, but you want them to be disciplined in blocking and using time for specific purposes. Some things that are critical:

- **Blocking time for prospecting.** Sales people hate prospecting and will find excuses to avoid it. If they don't block time and commit to it, it won't get done.

- **Customer meetings:** This is time they are spending with customers, working on their deals, moving opportunities through the sales/buying process.

- **They need to block time for prep, for things like social media, and research.** Sometimes these can be all-consuming; people spend hours on social media or research, so the time blocking helps them limit themselves. For example, I allocate 30 minutes from 6:00-6:30am every morning. At 6:30, I stop, regardless of how much I've accomplished.

- **Make sure they don't overschedule themselves.** The purpose of time blocking is to help them structure their time, not completely fill it. Things come up, so unscheduled time is important. I generally like to see 15-20% of their time unscheduled during the week.

- **Look at their calendars blocking for at least two, possibly three weeks.** Remember the prospecting calls made this week should turn into customer meetings the next or following week. If you don't see these things happening, something's wrong with their time allocation or their execution.

Don't forget to block your own calendar! These should include one-on-ones, deal/pipeline/call reviews, team meetings, customer calls with your people. Your planning, administrative, and reporting time starts at 8 PM or is done Saturday mornings. OK, I'm partly joking. This isn't a 40 hour a week job, use you're the time you need for planning/reporting/analysis when your people aren't around.

SYSTEM-IMPOSED TIME DRAINS

System-imposed time drains are the things others in the organization do that rob people of selling time. It's never done maliciously: the drains emerge from everyone just doing their jobs.

For example, a drain may take the form of a marketing meeting with your team to talk about the latest marketing programs, and getting the team's input. It could be product managers spending time interviewing sales people about their perceptions of customer needs and requirements. It may be some task force or project your people have been asked to participate in (for example looking at a new CRM system).

All of these are "good business" activities. They are the result of people doing their jobs and needing help, input, or support from sales, but they mount up. In the case of the Fortune 500 company I mentioned earlier, over 40% of the sales people's time was spent in these "good activities." Until we did the time survey, no one realized how big an impact it had on their selling time.

Another area that is a huge time drain is post-sales customer service and problem solving. This is a huge problem, but something sales people have to do if you have a customer service problem. Sales people are the "problem solvers of last resort" for their customers. Sales people will jump in and spent a lot of time in order to protect their relationships with customers and the potential for future sales.

YOUR OWN TIME MANAGEMENT

As I mentioned earlier, you need to look at how you are spending your own time. Too many managers allow "system-imposed" time drains to dominate their calendars. There are always too many meetings to go to. Management meetings, strategy meetings, meetings with product management, marketing, customer service.

These are very interesting meetings. You talk about and get to be a part of lots of cool stuff. But they take you away from helping your people. They take you away from your real job.

There is always a lot of reporting and analysis that "must be done." It's easy to get trapped behind your desk looking at endless CRM or other reports.

Or they get into crisis management mode, focusing on the urgent, but forgetting to block time for the important.

Too often, bad managers use these system-imposed time drains or crisis management to "hide out." Working with your people is tough, they face challenging issues. Some of your people are challenges themselves.

But it's your job!

Your job is to get your people performing at the highest levels possible—*all the time*. You don't do that by sitting in strategy and planning meetings, or hiding behind a computer screen doing analysis. You don't do that by constantly creating and responding to crises.

You have to be spending your time with your people. I hesitate setting a number, but if you aren't spending at least 50% of your time working with your people, you're spending your time incorrectly.

And by "working with your people" I mean being in the field or on customer calls with, coaching and developing your team and its members, solving problems or getting resources to make them more effective, recruiting/hiring/onboarding.

You have your greatest impact when your time is focused on working with and developing your people.

46

COMPENSATION/COMMISSION/INCENTIVES

I hesitated to write this chapter. There is just so much plain bad discussion and planning around compensation, commissions, and incentives. Writing about it is a little like opening Pandora's box. In addition, everyone has a strongly held opinion—and no two opinions are ever the same.

As a first line sales manager, you may not have any influence over these areas. You may be as much a victim of compensation mishandling as your people.

My goal in this chapter is to help you understand some general principles and challenges around compensation, commission, and incentive planning. Perhaps, they can provide a framework for questions you might have of senior management in understanding your organization's practice. It might also help in conversations you have with your people.

COMPENSATION AND COMMISSION FUNDAMENTALS

In deploying a salesperson or organization, a fundamental issue is affordability/ value. Simply stated, this means, "What am I willing to pay for a certain level of performance?" There are a lot of factors (some good, some bad,) that go into generating the answers to that question.

We have to be competitive in the marketplace in order to attract and retain the right people. Compensation has to be "in the ballpark," so we look at comparable compensation packages with others in the industry, or in the region. Typically, HR or Sales Ops, will look at competitors, similar companies, local companies to develop the "comps," and provide a framework for total compensation.

There are issues of affordability. That is, despite what the comps tell us, we still have to ask what is affordable? Clearly, if the comps are at a level that causes an organization to be unprofitable, then it's impossible to pay at that level. We may have to set total compensation at a lower level, recognizing it may impact our ability to recruit and retain people. Of course there's the tradeoff, "Could we get more done with fewer but higher capability people?"

As we make this assessment, it's critical to look at "Total At-Plan Compensation." That is the total base, variable, and burden (healthcare, insurance, taxes,) at the expected level revenue/sales performance.

Total At-Plan Compensation sets the bar at what we are willing to or can afford to pay people to achieve the expected level of sales. Remember, this will probably be a range, not an absolute number.

For example, if I'm willing to pay $100K for a person to produce $1M, the Total At-Plan Compensation is $100K, that sets the bar for performance expectations and affordability. Once you have this, then the rest of your compensation planning becomes figuring out how you will pay that $100K out. For example, what part is base salary, what part is variable, and what are the risks to achieving plan?

In my experience, determining Total At-Plan Compensation is always the toughest part of developing the compensation plan, but it gets the least attention. Set it incorrectly and you aren't able to recruit the right people, or your cost of selling is far too high.

Once Total At-Plan Compensation has been set, then you have to decide how you are going to pay it out. The first decision is what percent will be fixed—that is a base salary of some sort—and what portion will be variable. The variable piece can be commissions, bonuses, incentives, or combinations of those.

Here's where all the controversy surrounding compensation planning starts. Everyone has a different opinion about what this split should be. Some argue for very high leverage, less base, and other variables, while others argue for the opposite.

My opinion doesn't matter, but this decision really needs to be driven by what you expect your people to be doing, what levels of performance are expected, risks in achieving plan, and the behaviors you want to drive.

The heated debates continue with determining how to pay the variable portion of compensation. Generally, the variable piece can include commissions, bonuses, incentives/ SPiF's, contests, or other mechanisms.

Too often, people focus the variable part of compensation planning on commissions only, forgetting the other types of variable compensation might be more effective in driving behavior.

Generally, I like to have some part of the variable compensation reserved for bonuses that can be defined around specific accomplishments. For example, I might want to emphasize new customer acquisition, or penetration of a certain market, or growth within our existing customers, or focus on certain product lines. Reserving part of the variable compensation to reinforce those behaviors can be very powerful.

Having said that, I've always had a bias that the majority of variable compensation be allocated to some kind of commission payment.

There are all sorts of ways to pay commissions. Some are very simple. For example, a certain percent of every revenue dollar. Some are based on quota attainment, some kick in when you've achieve minimum goals.

What's best depends on what you are trying to achieve and the behaviors you are trying to drive.

At the end of this process you really need to test the design. Remember you are trying to manage these payouts to achieve a certain target and affordability level. This is what was set in your Target At-Plan Compensation.

Be careful here, do some simulations. Look at risks. Put yourself in the salesperson's shoes. They are going to study the plan to figure out how to maximize their income, as they should. The very worst thing that can happen is you pay a person $150K and they produce $100K.

These kinds of mistakes happen all the time. My very best compensation year as a young salesperson, I made over 200% of my targeted compensation and only achieved 87% of my plan. It happened with everyone in the organization, and the company vastly overspent on compensation (needless to say, a new compensation planning team was hired). The plan was poorly designed and they didn't "game" the plan to understand how sales people were likely to respond.

So game the plan, look for the loopholes, look at the risks.

At the same time, make sure it's achievable. Remember you really want each of your people to hit $100K in compensation. You should be ecstatic to be paying them that $100K, because it means they achieved the goals you wanted them to achieve. If you aren't paying that, if it's something less, you haven't "saved" on compensation—you missed your business goals!

This is the second mistake I see people make in commission and compensation planning. We want to have people hit their goals, but we want to be stingy at paying for it. That's why, setting Target At-Plan Compensation is so important. Remember, you WANT to pay that out. You WANT to see everyone hit that compensation level because it means they are doing their job at a level you can afford!

After you've done this basic level of planning on the compensation program, you want to look at the overattainment and underattainment accelerators. Remember, on overattainment of plan you are always looking at net incremental revenue, so the economics of bonuses become very attractive.

Finally, you want to keep your compensation plan as simple as possible for two reasons. First, you want your people to understand how they get paid. They need to think, "If I do these things (which is the stuff you want them to be doing,) I should expect to earn this much." It has to be crystal clear in their minds. If it isn't, then it will be difficult to drive the behaviors you expect.

Another reason for keeping it simple is that you have to administer the plan. If it's so complex you have to invest a lot of time to figure out what you pay each salesperson, then it's a bad plan. Or worse, you miscalculate, because of the complexity, and you pay people incorrectly, creating a lot of dissatisfaction and rework.

I wish I could stop this discussion here. Unfortunately, there are a lot of other factors we toss into compensation plans that increase the complexity. There are things like splits, for example, when multiple sales people are involved in closing a deal. There are draws (recoverable and non-recoverable,) generally used in bringing new people on board.

Then there is the endless discussion around caps or over-attainment accelerators.

How you handle all of these depends on your specific situation, what you are trying to achieve, and the expected return.

However, there is one very dysfunctional behavior we see, too often, in looking at caps accelerators and other things. It has nothing to do with sales people, but is all about management (sales or executive management).

This is the attitude that says, "Sales people can't possibly earn more than me!"

This is possibly one of the most destructive behaviors I encounter. It immediately limits the potential that can be achieved, and the growth of the organization. If you want to drive the highest levels of performance in the organization, this sort of ego or hierarchy-based limitation can have no place in the design of the compensation system.

As I wrap up this section, I know I'm repeating myself, but most people don't do this. Make sure, after you have designed the system, you simulate and game it. Try to break it. Put yourself in the shoes of the salesperson trying to maximize compensation. As they look at the plan, what are they going to do? How are they going to spend their time to maximize their income? What things will they not be doing as well?

If the behaviors that result from this test are the behaviors you want to drive, and your Total At-Plan Compensation goals are met, then you've designed a good compensation system.

INCENTIVES

There are a whole variety of things that may be part of the compensation plan or may complement the compensation plan that fall into the category of Incentives.

Sometimes these incentives consist of contests with cash or other types of awards for achieving a certain goal. Generally, these should be budgeted as part of the variable part of the compensation plan.

But there are other incentives which can have a huge impact on individuals in organizations that can be free or near free.

Management recognition of great performance has a huge impact on both the individual and the overall organization. The power of public recognition of a job well done, perhaps accompanied with a congratulatory letter, plaque, or trophy, has tremendous impact.

These shouldn't focus just on best sales performance. Recognition can be on any number of things: Biggest improvement in customer satisfaction, recognition for mentoring/helping team mates, new ideas that improve the organization. There is no limit to the kinds of recognition that can be provided.

Pay attention to the incentives for those who've earned recognition. Sometimes, there are developmental opportunities. For example, being able to spend time with a key executive, participation in certain meetings, or other developmental activities both provide recognition and the opportunity to further develop a person.

RECOGNIZING RECOGNITION

Everyone wants to be recognized. Whether it's a simple comment, "Jill did a great job in winning this tough deal!" or "Bob is doing some very innovative things in his prospecting," people crave recognition.

Somehow, in sales, recognition has been confused with "reward," or "incentive." While those are forms of recognition, it's a very narrow view of it.

As a manager, you want to find opportunities to recognize great performance. It can be a compliment you make to an individual. It may be something your call out in a team meeting. It may be telling your boss or other managers about a specific great performance. Look for opportunities to leverage all of these where appropriate.

A little recognition goes a long way!

At the same time, there is a danger in over-recognizing everything with everybody, "Bill, great job getting the forecast in on time; "Sue, thanks for keeping your desk neat; John, great visuals on that PowerPoint..." Soon the recognition loses value. Special performance no longer stands out.

Likewise, sometimes you are recognizing the same people—usually your "A" performers. They certainly deserve it, but what about the other people in your organization. Find something great that each person is doing. Spread the great feelings!

A WORD OF CAUTION

One of the biggest mistakes I see in overall sales performance management is using the compensation plan as the only lever for managing sales performance.

Too many managers are sloppy in how they do this—ending up spending more money than they should, not getting the results.

Compensation is only one lever or tool a manager has to manage performance. But there are a number of other tools the manager has in her tool box. Strong performance plans, strong coaching and development are some of the most impactful.

There's the saying, "If the only tool you have is a hammer, then pretty soon, everything looks like a nail."

If you are using compensation as your only tool for managing performance— pretty soon every problem becomes a compensation issue, and your ability to manage to a Target At-Plan Compensation, becomes impossible. Inevitably, you will be spending far more in compensation than you need—and you still may not be getting the results.

You have lots of tools at your disposal for managing and driving performance. Compensation is only one and probably the last one you should use in addressing performance issues.

The perfect compensation plan reinforces the strategies and priorities you have in place, complements your performance expectations of the team, and hits your At Target Total Compensation goal.

WRAP UP

I've just touched on a few of the most important areas of the business management and planning tasks that are part of your job.

There are any number of tactical things like workflow management, sales programs, resources planning, training, systems and tools, quota planning, territory planning, and others. Some of these, we'll cover in the next two sections of the book. Some we can't address here.

The most important thing to recognize is most of these activities don't drive revenue. They don't directly help your people with their day to day performance.

They may be urgent things, or they may be really interesting and cool discussions you have with peers and others in the organization—but don't let them consume you. They should always take a second priority to working with your people. As I've mentioned several time, I always like reserving my time to do these things early in the morning, late in the day, or on weekends.

I wanted to keep as much of the business day free—reserving that time to working with my people.

PART SEVEN

SALES ENABLEMENT: EQUIPPING YOUR PEOPLE TO SELL

47

SALES ENABLEMENT: EFFECTIVENESS AND EFFICIENCY

Sales enablement is a hot term these days. Everyone is talking about sales enablement, but too often they are talking about something entirely different from the term's actual meaning.

If you take the word "enablement" somewhat literally, it's really about providing tools, systems, processes, training, coaching and development that "enable" sales people to be more effective and efficient.

Since we toss around the words "effectiveness and efficiency" pretty casually, let's spend a moment talking about what these mean. Their meaning is important for you to understand as you evaluate what sales enablement programs you want to put in place and as you look at the performance of your people.

Effectiveness generally refers to doing the right things in the right way. For example, it may be planning high impact sales calls that maximize our ability to achieve the objectives of the call and move the customer through their buying process.

We know there are "best practices" for sales calls—pre-meeting research and preparation, establishing clear goals, making sure the right people are participating, having a clear agenda, knowing the questions/information we seek to learn, anticipating what the customer might want. Doing these things well, executing high impact calls really focus on effectiveness.

Making sure our people are as effective as possible is critical to driving high performance.

Efficiency is more focused on "time." Efficiency looks at how we accomplish what we need to do in the shortest time possible.

Using the high impact sales call example from above, we might improve our efficiency by conducting the call over the phone or via a video conference. This would save travel time, enabling us to get more done in the day. Or we might look at how we can compress what we might have done in two calls into a single call.

As first line sales managers, we want to focus on both effectiveness and efficiency.

What "experts" seldom tell you is that you can't do both at the same time. People like to make you think you can, but in reality, based on how people learn, we can't achieve both at the same time.

If you've ever been involved in sports, you'll recognize this concept immediately. Generally, in learning something new—whether it's a new play in basketball, tuning a tennis or golf stroke, or anything else, you first learn how to do it very slowly. Coaches purposely slow things down, they may run a new play in slow motion, or have you practice your golf swing in slow motion.

What they are trying to do is to train you in doing it correctly. For example, I race road bikes (at least I try to compete in those events). My coach spent endless time getting me to master my pedaling technique. He did this by having me ride slowly, focusing on pedaling "full circles" to maximize my power output.

Doing the right things in the right way is what *effectiveness* is all about.

Once you have mastered a capability or new skill, the coaches speed things up. You run the basketball play faster and faster until you are going full speed. In my case, when I mastered pedaling "full circles," my coach started speeding up my cadence. I went from 50-60 RPM, to 80-95 RPM. Now I'm trying to get to 95-105 RPM.

Efficiency is all about doing the right things faster.

It makes sense focusing on effectiveness first, then look at efficiency. After all, if your people are doing things wrong, doing the wrong thing very fast is a disaster.

As new sales enablement programs are implemented, make sure you look at how they first improve the effectiveness of your people, then look at improving efficiency. Keep them separate so you can achieve the results you expect.

In the following chapters, we'll look at a lot of the areas that are typically included in discussions of sales enablement. As you read these chapters, remember the underlying purpose of each one—the training, tools, systems, and approaches covered are supposed to make your people more effective and more efficient. If whatever you are doing in the name of sales enablement doesn't do this, then something's wrong!

48

TRAINING

Notice I didn't start this chapter with Sales Training. Too often, we have far too narrow a view about training and skills development. We focus on two areas: Sales Skills Training and Product Training.

Those are important, but in reality they are just table stakes. I characterize these as the Kindergarten and Grade School of training for sales professionals.

In today's world, there are so many other things that are important to the success of your team.

This chapter will provide some brief ideas to think about in training your people—or making sure they are getting the right training.

PRODUCT TRAINING

Your people have to understand the products and services your company sells. Product training is critical. However, most product training focuses on the products. There are endless materials about how wonderful products are, endless pages of feeds, speeds, features, functions. There may be some competitive comparisons—but it is always product focused.

Most product training stops there; it isn't very helpful in helping sales people connect with customers.

Product training should focus on customers, that is, it should answer questions:

- **What problems do our products and services solve?**

- **Who has those problems—both what types of companies, and what job titles within those companies?**

- **What causes those problems?**

- **How do we capture the customers' interest and get them to consider a new approach?**

- **What do customers generally look for when they are buying these products? What does their buying cycle look like?**

- **How do customers justify these solutions to their management?**

- **What concerns or objections are they likely to raise?**

I'll stop here, but you get the point. Our product training is best when it focuses on the customer and how we engage the customer in conversations about our solutions.

Probably marketing or product management is developing the product training for you and your team. Make certain they are addressing these and the other important customer focused questions in their training. You want your people hit the ground running with these products, make certain the training equips them to do that.

SALES SKILLS TRAINING

You've probably been through lots of sales skills training, so I won't spend a lot of time here. Sales skills training is important, but too often, I think we don't do as effective a job at sales training as we should. As you look at providing your team sales skills training, consider the following:

Look for training that helps your people think about what they are doing. There is too much training that focuses on "magic." Do these things, use these 12 closes, or these 15 prospecting opening sentences, or these 10 cool ways to handle objections. If you execute them perfectly, the customer will immediately succumb and give you a purchase order.

We all know training like that doesn't work. We need to get training that is not so much technique oriented, but that helps the person think about the situation—whether a deal, a negotiation, a sales call, an account. We need give them skills to analyze, develop plans, and execute those plans.

A lot of sales training comes under Sales Methodology. There are dozens of familiar names for Sales Methodologies: Solution Selling, Customer Focused Selling, Selling to VITO, Challenger Selling, Insight Selling, Large Account Selling, SPIN Selling, even our own—Dimensions Of EXCELLENCE.

These methodologies tend to be very comprehensive and based on solid research and experience. I've been through most of them and learn a lot in each one.

But in implementing any Sales Methodology, make sure you require the vendor to customize that training to your needs. First, it needs to incorporate your sales process at its core. Some vendors will claim to have a sales process embedded, but it's not yours. Think about it, these vendors sell to people who sell office supplies, jet engines, enterprise software, professional services, and more. Each of the sales processes for those customers is different. The markets, issues, and customers are very different.

Make certain they customize the program to your process and business. It's not useful if the case studies they use are for office supplies, and your team sells semiconductors. Likewise, if you sell office supplies, case studies for enterprise software aren't useful.

Any of these vendors, if they are using the latest technologies, will be able to easily adapt their programs to fit your business. They may provide a small customization fee, but it's well worth it.

Second, do not invest in any sales skills training without a reinforcement plan build into the offering. Billions of dollars of sales training investments are wasted every year because of the lack of reinforcement. Make sure they propose a reinforcement program and make sure you implement it. Otherwise you are throwing money away.

MARKET TRAINING/BUSINESS ACUMEN

These are two of the most important areas of skills development, yet most organizations provide virtually nothing to their sales people.

Market or industry training focuses on helping your people better understand your customers. They look at the markets, their structure, key metrics, business drivers, trends, major participants, their customer issues and other things.

When I first started selling, I sold to major money center banks in New York City. As part of my training, I was sent to a six week "Banking School" at Wharton. I was the only computer salesperson in the class—the rest were bankers. But at the end of that class I really understood banking. That was invaluable in helping me connect with customers on issues that were important to them.

Today, we can hardly afford to invest in six weeks of training, but we do need to make sure our people understand their key markets, customers and what drives them. There are all sorts of formal and informal programs that help people develop these skills.

Business acumen is a pet annoyance. Too many sales people lack basic understanding of how businesses work. They don't understand basic financial analysis, how to read an income statement, balance sheet or cash flow statement. They don't know how to translate what their solutions do to business relevant terms.

Again, there are a variety of formal and informal training programs that help develop skills here. If a salesperson expects to be competitive, this is critical.

If we want to drive our customers' thinking, if we want to connect with them in business relevant conversations, we have to know what they care about and talk to them in business terms. Market and business acumen training is critical to compete in today's world.

CHANGE MANAGEMENT/PROJECT MANAGEMENT

I think change management and project management skills are critical for all sales people today. There is plenty of data focusing on issues we and customers have with change. We know customers struggle with change; we know our customers struggle with buying.

A lot of the role of high performing sales people is to help facilitate the change process and manage their buying process. If we are to create value doing this, we need to develop those skills in our people.

Find some good programs, and leverage them with your team.

CRITICAL THINKING AND PROBLEM SOLVING

I'll get on my soapbox a little in this section. It seems we've stopped looking to recruiting for and developing our people's critical thinking skills. Instead, there is a huge trend to leverage software, tools, programs that minimize the need for sales people to use their minds.

We provide scripts—as long as the customer stays on script, the salesperson can execute the sales call. But how often does that work? As a prospect, I don't ever recall a salesperson sending an email, "Here's your script for our upcoming call."

As good as the tools are we can never predict what's going to happen between the customer and the salesperson. We don't know their attitudes, challenges, or concerns at the moment they pick up the phone, or when we walk into the office. Things constantly change, yet our sales people are so closely tied to the "script," or even the "bullet points." Some can struggle through, but they can't drill down, they can't push back, they can't challenge the customer. A lot of what we do is challenge the customer to think differently, but if we don't have those skills, how can we expect the salesperson to provide leadership?

One of the most important skills I look for in recruiting people and training them is their ability to figure things out. The better their abilities when confronted with a situation they haven't encountered, to analyze, question, probe, challenge, and figure things out, the more successful they will be—both in what you need them to do and what the customer values in their interactions with customers.

If we claim to be problem solvers for our customers, yet have no ability to find, identify, articulate, convince, and engage our customer in the critical thinking and problem solving process, then we are not exploiting the single greatest value we or the biggest differentiator we can create.

I've been on this soap box for some time. It's in the interests of a lot of the vendors to continue to provide tools/programs your people can't live without. I don't blame them; they've identified the same problem and are trying to provide a solution for it. And many of those tools are very powerful. But, at least currently, none of these tools are helping your sales people respond to situations or questions they haven't encountered before—but something they must deal with.

There is a lot you can teach and develop in improving your people's critical thinking and problem solving skills. Make sure you do this—whether it's reading books and talking about them, joining a discussion group, bringing in a training company.

The wonderful magical thing that happens is that once your people have these skills, their need for support/tools (crutches—pardon my cynicism) diminishes.

Why? Because they know how to figure it out *themselves*!

TRAINING, TRAINING, EVERYWHERE...

The old days of getting together in a workshop and learning something new are passing. Yes, there is still some good workshop-based training, but don't limit you and your team to this standard mode of training.

Take advantage of e-Learning tools as much as you can. They are both easy and fast to implement, but the person can acquire the skills "just in time." So often, the learning is more focused and valuable if the salesperson has the need to immediately apply the skills following an online program. Distance learning programs also provide a great deal of flexibility. People can find good programs they can take themselves.

Don't limit yourself and your team to courses. As a team you should adopt an "Always Be Learning" approach. Find books to read, find good blogs, find interesting topics to develop new skills. Spend a few minutes in a team meeting talking about these. Assign one of your people to lead the review and discussion of a book. Build a culture of curiosity and continued learning in the team. Without this, they will be left behind.

REINFORCEMENT

All the dollars and time we invest in training is wasted unless the training is reinforced. I have a good friend who finds opportunity for reinforcing new skills at least three times a week, and keeps it up for a minimum of four weeks. In his experience it takes that long for people to internalize and own the skills themselves.

Don't buy any training program unless the vendor also provides a "30-60-90" detailed reinforcement plan.

A lot of that reinforcement falls on your shoulders. Incorporate reinforcement into your coaching and into your review process. If you are coaching a deal, leverage the training they've had in developing deal strategies and reinforce what they've learned. Likewise, for every area you coach and develop people, find ways to draw their training into your coaching and development.

WHAT ABOUT YOUR OWN TRAINING?

Don't forget your own training and development! Hopefully, your manager is paying attention and getting you good leadership, coaching, and business management training. But don't let that limit you, be curious, figure out what skills you need to acquire. Invest in yourself, take courses, read books, find different ways to learn.

Your continued learning and development is critical to helping your people, growing in your current job, and moving into new jobs.

49

PROCESSES

In running the sales organization there are multiple processes and workflows we have to pay attention to.

Processes are simply the series of steps we go through to get something done. A process or series of processes may be related to a workflow.

For example, recruiting and hiring is generally a series of steps you have to go through Getting approval to hire, writing a job description, publishing it to get candidates, engaging a recruiter, screening candidates, interviewing, making a job offer, onboarding—all create a workflow.

Processes are important because they should define the steps to get our work done as effectively and efficiently as possible. If we've designed the process well, we will have achieved both goals. Well-designed processes represent our "best practice," the things that we consistently do to produce the best results.

Some of you may be scratching your heads; many of the processes that have been inflicted on you may be poorly designed, bureaucratic, cumbersome. They may slow you down; they may actually produce poorer results.

Part of the problem is clueless design of processes. We often believe the way we've always done things is "the process," but things change. What served us well in the past may no longer be effective, so we must alter or re-design the process.

Another problem with processes is the attempt by many to force rigid compliance. Perhaps rigid compliance is useful in a manufacturing process where you can minimize the variance of what happens within the process. But for sales, it's impossible to control this—we're dealing with people in various situations. Each will act differently; groups will act differently.

I prefer to think of processes more as guidelines. Most of the time it's important to follow the process as closely as possible. But when things don't fit, it's important to adapt to the situation. The great thing about processes is they provide a framework for making that assessment, for figuring out the best course of action.

Not following the process should be the "exception," not the rule. When you find your people consistently not following the process, dive in to understand. Are they just being sloppy, choosing to do what they want to do, rather than leveraging best practices? Or is the process outdated or wrong? Do we have to change the process?

Processes represent a paradox to sales managers and leaders. You want to leverage them and make sure your people are leveraging them, simply because they should be making you more effective and efficient. At the same time, you need to be skeptical. Do we have the right processes in place? Do they reflect our current realities? Are they achieving the goals of making us more effective and efficient?

THE SALES PROCESS

We talked about the sales process earlier in this book. This is one of the most important processes you must have in place. I can't keep from reiterating it.

The sales process is about deals or opportunities.

The sales process is the series of steps and activities your team undertakes to help move the customer through their buying process. The sales process is based on your organization's best practice at winning deals.

A great sales process should accomplish three things:

- **The sales process should maximize your probability of winning.**

- **The sales process should enable you to compress the buying/selling cycle.**

- **The sales process should enable you to maximize the deal value or margin.**

If your sales process doesn't help your people achieve these factors with every deal, then you have a bad sales process.

The sales process is critical to the effectiveness and efficiency of your sales people as they work on deals. If they aren't using the sales process rigorously, their performance becomes both unpredictable and bad.

Having a sales process your people rigorously use helps you as a manager. When you review a deal and see a salesperson leveraging the sales process effectively, you have high confidence they are doing everything possible to win the deal. You still have to coach them and help them come up with ideas to improve their ability to win, but without watching everything they do, you can be confident they are doing the things necessary to win.

It also means you don't have to review every deal your people are working on. If you see your sales people effectively leveraging the process in the deals you review, you can guess they are doing the same with every other deal.

By contrast, if they aren't using the sales process, if they approach each deal differently, then the only way you know they are doing what they need to do to win is to review every deal. It becomes impossible for you to do this.

Let's run some numbers to illustrate the point. Let's imagine you have ten sales people working for you. And let's imagine they each have ten very active deals, for a total of 100 deals for your team.

If your sales people aren't using a sales process, then the only way you can make sure they are doing the things critical to winning the deal in the shortest time possible, at the highest margins, is for you to review every deal. If it takes you 20 minutes per deal, then you have to spend 2000 minutes or 33+ hours a week in deal reviews!

Clearly, that's impossible. You have too many other things to do to be reviewing status on every deal every week.

If your people are using the sales process rigorously, then you only have to invest your time in the one or two most important deals each week, for each person. If they are using the process well, developing and executing winning strategies in those, then you can be confident they are probably being very impactful with their other deals.

OTHER PROCESSES IN THE SALES ORGANIZATION

There will be any number of processes in your organization. As mentioned earlier, there should be recruiting/hiring, onboarding, or performance management processes. There is forecasting, planning/budgeting, performance review, demand gen, order entry/management, customer service, new product introduction, problem management, and others.

These processes are really concerned with workflow and what needs to happen in the sales organization for it to work. These processes should support your team, making you more effective and efficient. But sometimes, they have the opposite effect.

Some organizations become process-bound. They have too many poorly designed processes. Rather than improving effectiveness and efficiency, they encumber the organization and slow it down.

There's a temptation to abandon processes at this point—with good reason. But abandoning the process is probably the wrong thing. If there is no process or structure shaping how work is done, things become chaotic, errors are made, and there is constant confusion.

Rather than abandoning critical processes in the organization, it's better to reexamine those processes, see where you can simplify them, and which you might eliminate.

Take the time to understand the processes and workflows that impact you and your people the most. Understand them, understand the impact on your people—are they making them more productive, more effective, or more efficient? If not, how can you change or eliminate them. Some simple ways to examine and simplify processes is to map or flow chart them and to look at people's roles and responsibilities in executing these processes.

FINAL THOUGHTS ON PROCESSES

This bears repeating: It's useful to remember that processes provide only guidelines. They shouldn't be rigid and inflexible, but provide guidance. Sometimes things come up that the process can't deal with. In such situations don't force fit it, but be adaptable. Be willing to make exceptions.

When exceptions become the rule, you know your processes aren't serving you, and you need to reassess, redesign them.

DRAW A PICTURE

As human beings, we tend to be visual. It's hard for us to understand things in the abstract. It's hard to define and refine a process by writing a lot of words, "Step A, Step B, Step C..." It's very powerful to draw a picture. It could be a flowchart, it could be a Mindmap, it could be a diagram.

A picture is worth 10,000 words, not only in designing and understanding processes, but in helping your people understand it!

50

SYSTEMS AND TOOLS

Read any article on sales today, go to any conference, sit with any group of sales leaders and the discussion will get around to systems and tools. There are thousands of automated and web based-tools focused on "improving" the productivity of sales people.

I can't imagine any high performance salesperson or sales manager not leveraging these technologies and tools to the utmost. Properly used, they drive huge improvements in efficiency. Some of the new analytic and research tools also have great potential for improving effectiveness.

Having said this, I'd also advise you to remember each of these tools is a double-edged sword. As much as they might help, they also enable us to "create crap at the speed of light."

Implemented incorrectly, sales tools can be huge productivity and money drains. They can consume you and your sales people's time, diverting you from the real business of producing results.

I like to think of tools as "amplifiers" of people's and the organization's capabilities. They don't discriminate. They help make great practice and methods far better and more efficient. Likewise, they make poorly thought out approaches, bad processes, weak thinking even worse.

Each of you has probably lived through or been the victim of a hellish CRM implementation. You may have tools your company has bought, but no one is using. So they sit there gathering digital dust.

As you evaluate tools, think about the following:

1. **They are for the sales people, not you!** Except for a small number of management focused tools, most of the tools you should be looking at are for the sales people. Yet too often, the people selling the tools focus on what they do for management.

   CRM is a great example. We're sold CRM tools based on the fantastic reporting and insights we get from using the data provided from these tools. The management uses of CRM are fantastic—but only if your people are using them.

   The key question in CRM or any other tool, is: "How does it improve the efficiency or effectiveness of the sales people?" If the tool doesn't do this, then it shouldn't be bought. If your people don't see this, then you are wasting your money. Involve your people in selecting the tools. Involve them in pilots to see if the tools produce real results. Make them part of the selection and decision making process. Again, if they don't see value, they won't use it—regardless of what rules you put in place.

   In implementing the tools, let the sales people define the implementation process. Make sure they are engaged and getting great value. If they are, they'll use it. If they use them, they will improve their productivity. If they use them, the icing on the cake is you get tremendous reporting.

   Pay a lot of attention to the implementation plans and training. Make sure you spend a lot of time making sure people understand how to get the most out of the tools, how to use them most efficiently.

   Know they will be concerned: Do they have to spend all their time entering data? Will the information they enter be used against them, "Big brother watching?"

   If they can't see the tool helping them make better use of their time and produce better results, then they won't use it—or they'll do the minimal work to get managers off their backs.

   Properly implemented, these tools should free up their time and help them engage customers with greater impact.

   The icing on the cake, if your sales people are leveraging the tools well, is that you have a tremendous set of tools understand what they are doing and help them improve.

2. **Be attentive to how the tools fit into your sales team's normal workflow and work life.** Some of the earlier CRM systems required connection over secured networks. Often, people had to be in the office to use these tools, and using them over the network was too complicated and cumbersome. But if your people spend most of their time in the field, then access to the tools from remote locations becomes a problem. Fortunately, WiFi and VPN's are making that easier.

   The point is, look at how and where people will be using these tools. Pay attention to the devices they use most. Laptops are giving way to smart phones and tablets. Those may be giving way to "watches" or devices we don't yet know of.

Make sure the tools support how and where your people work, not forcing them into a workflow that doesn't match what they do.

3. **Beware of the "sales stack."** There are literally thousands of sales automation systems and tools available. Some are broad platforms like CRM systems. Others are very narrowly focused on a specific function, for example, "improving call effectiveness on left-handed, blue eyed, blond decision makers."

OK, I'm exaggerating with that last example. But not by much. The specialized tools can be very useful. But beware of the challenges they present. They have to be integrated to your core platforms, they have different interfaces. They overlap with other tools, so pretty soon people get frustrated entering the same information multiple times. Or they get confused with which tool they should be using.

The number and variety of tools can be counterproductive and confusing.

Beware of how much you are spending. I believe in investing in these tools. In our own company, our people have a rich array of tools they leverage. We invest thousands of dollars per person, every year in providing them tools to help them improve productivity and impact. Having said all this, spending $20/month/person here, $15/month/person there, mounts up quickly. Make sure they are using the tools and you are getting the expected return.

4. **Use the tools yourself!** All right —I'm contradicting what I said earlier. These tools are for you as well. Plus, if *you* aren't using these tools, then why should you expect your sales people to use them?

I'm amazed at the number of managers and executives who don't use the CRM system. Either they haven't taken the time to learn, or they consider it beneath them. Instead, they insist on Excel reports, printed extracts, or other data views. All of this defeats much of the value of the tool, and creates extra work for the sales people.

I'll be blunt: If *you* aren't going to use the tool, then don't waste your people's time or your organization's resources. But then, remember, you'll be putting a huge limiter on the productivity of your people.

5. **Tools are useless if you have bad strategies, processes, sloppy thinking or the wrong implementation.** Buying and implementing a new tool will not cause you to make your number. Yet, I'm amazed with the number of managers that seem to think it will.

A great tool applied to a flawed strategy produces terrible results— sometimes across all your customers. (Take a marketing automation or sales automation tool applied foolishly to all customers.)

Tools aren't a crutch or substitute for bad thinking or a poorly performing organization. As much as vendors might want to claim that "buying our tool will improve win rates by 50%," a system or tool is just a tool. It is only as good as the people using the tool are. It is an enabler to improving productivity and efficiency.

Without the proper foundations, a tool will, at best, do nothing. At worst it could accelerate bad performance.

As much as I say this to the groups I work with, people always tend to think of sales tools and systems as miracle cures—and vendors tend to reinforce this thinking.

Don't get caught up in the craziness of buying tools to solve all your sales problems. Do the work first; make sure you have the right foundations of strategy, people, programs, processes. The tools will then amplify the ability of your sales people to produce results.

51

SALES TOOLS:
THE NUTS AND BOLTS

There are sales tools I think no sales professional can be without.

CRM SYSTEMS

Yeah, most CRM systems suck. There seems to be endless data that has to be input, so much that pretty soon we all feel like data entry clerks rather than sales professionals. The older, big name, CRM tools have terrible interfaces, the new ones look a little interesting.

Get past your resistance to CRM tools. I can't imagine not using them. In essence, CRM has become my and my organization's memory core to our workflow.

We first implemented CRM in the early 90s, when it was actually called Contact Management. We can track our relationships with tens of thousands of people we've worked with since then. We've moved with them from company to company and role to role, we know what white papers, webinars, and other content they've consumed, we have a history of the emails, and notes about every (at least) major meeting. Relationships are important and CRM is key to managing and building relationships.

We also track all our opportunities in CRM. It keeps me honest about the strategies I develop for my own deals; it keeps me thinking about, "What's next, with whom, for what outcome?" I can collaborate with our other partners on deals, get their advice and insights. While we could do the same through email or on the phone, CRM —since it is on all our platforms—is just easier.

I start and end every day in CRM. It is the core of my time management and planning. I know what calls I have to make, what deals I have to work on, what meetings I have to attend. My whole life is managed in the CRM calendar—I even schedule haircuts, dinner with my wife, and trips to the gym in CRM.

Keeping everything in CRM frees me up to think and be engaged. I don't have to remember things: I just refer to CRM. As a result, I can really focus.

CRM is for you! It's a phenomenal productivity tool. Adapt it, shape it to serve you.

Which CRM you choose—that's up to you or your company. But choose one.

RESEARCH TOOLS

I want to be prepared for every call or meeting that I have. I want to know about the individuals, their backgrounds, what they care about, who they are. I want to know about the organization they work for, its strategies, business drivers, competitiveness, products/services. I want to know about its financial performance and its positioning in its markets. I want to understand the markets they compete in and the customers they serve.

Being prepared maximizes my ability to connect and engage people in a meaningful way. CRM has some of that data (and links to others,) but there are a huge number of tools that complement CRM and flesh out your knowledge. LinkedIn is a critical tool for learning about individuals. The company website is a great tool for learning about the company. Edgar (at sec.gov) is powerful for digging deep into financials. Google Alerts are very powerful. I've set up alerts to track people, companies, and industries. Every day, I get emails updating me with the latest news on each.

There are a whole variety of tools that do analysis on companies, markets, competitors. They are reasonably affordable; you and your sales team should have one that you can leverage.

You can't be impactful unless you are in the "know."

NEWS READERS

I read over 150 blogs, newspapers, and publications a day. Well to be fair, I skim through them, diving deep into articles and subjects I'm interested in. I've set them up to feed a couple of News Readers. In the evening, I catch up on news and learning by spending a couple of hours going through what they have gathered. You can be relevant and impactful unless you keep up with the news.

By the way, I use Evernote to clip and retain articles that I like or need to take action on.

SOCIAL NETWORKING

These tools actually fit into a number of the categories I've discussed (e.g. research, news, collaboration/conferencing). But social networking tools are very powerful in engaging your people, peers, customers, and suppliers. "You get to hang out where your customers hang out," and increasing numbers of them are hanging out in the "social world," whether it's updates or discussion groups in LinkedIn, Facebook, Twitter, or any of the dozens of platforms available.

Beyond the research and news aspect, when I look at these tools for communicating and engaging, I treat them as an additional set of tools I can leverage to connect with people. Just as face-to-face meetings, telephone calls, emails, or even snail mail are tools we can leverage to communicate and engage people, the social tools provide additional means of reaching people.

Many of the "social selling" bigots say you should abandon everything else. Frankly, that's foolish, use whatever works!

EMAIL TRACKING SYSTEM

I like to know what's happened with emails I've sent. Have they been opened, when, how many times? Have the recipients forwarded them, have they clicked on embedded links? This is not just for prospecting, but it's also useful in communicating with my team and in working with customers on a project. There are a variety of tracking systems available: make sure you use one.

CONFERENCING/COLLABORATION TOOLS

Increasingly, more of our "meetings" are done virtually—even if we are in the same facility. Video conferencing tools, the ability to share documents, presentations are critical.

PORTABILITY

As much as possible, your tools need to work across all your devices: your Desktop computer, if you have one; laptop; tablet, smartphone, and whatever may come next. You never know where you will be and what you need to access on what device, so making sure the tools you use are supported on the devices you use is important.

BLACK COMPOSITION BOOK:

I think this ties with CRM in terms of value to me. I'm a write it down person; my black composition book is always with me. It's usually the only thing I carry into meetings (with the agenda and call plan stuck inside). I keep notes, next steps, reminders, actions in my composition book.

There is something about the act of writing things down, by hand, that cements them in your mind. There's a lot of research supporting it. Retention and comprehension is much higher if you physically write something, rather than type it (the challenge being reading my own writing afterwards—just kidding).

There's another thing about the notebook, a thing that may be generational.

Sometimes technology becomes a distraction. One of my people used to take diligent notes by typing into his smartphone. One day we were in a meeting, and both the customer and I kept getting distracted—just watching him type, wondering, "Is he taking notes, is reading text messages?" Finally, I asked him to put the phone down and pay attention. (I did notice his fingers twitching during the remainder of the conversation.) When your use of the tool or device becomes a distraction to anyone in the meeting, put the tool away.

Some of you are probably wondering: "If Dave keeps all his notes in his composition book, how does he get them into CRM?" It would be foolish to take the time and type them in. I just take pictures of the appropriate pages and upload/email them into CRM.

There are literally thousands of tools and apps you can leverage to improve your effectiveness and efficiency. Find those that are most helpful/indispensable to you and your people, and *use* them.

There are two emerging categories of tools that have huge potential that you should be looking at:

ANALYTICS

Analytics can be very powerful in helping get insights in to behaviors, trends, critical issues, customer activity and so forth. There are analytic solutions coming out every day—those that help you identify "purchase ready customers," those that help you identify performance issues in your organization, literally thousands of uses.

Spend time looking at them and understanding how your organization might leverage them. Some very powerful areas include: customer analytics, marketing analytics, sales enablement analytics.

COACHING TOOLS

These are relatively new, some are standalone, others are integrated into CRM, Sales Enablement, Learning Management or other platforms. They are tools specifically focused on helping you coach or helping reinforce the coaching you do. For example, you may be coaching someone on a specific skill and can point them to an online tool to reinforce that skill. There are tools that continually prompt and reinforce things you think are important. The salesperson can't ignore them and you see the results, complementing it with your own coaching.

Anything that can support and reinforce your coaching is probably worth considering. One word of caution, though: Make sure they support and reinforce your coaching, not displace the coaching you do. Nothing is more powerful than direct human-to-human engagement.

52

CONTENT AND COLLATERAL MATERIALS

One of the important areas of sales enablement is providing content, collateral, and materials to support your people.

One can be overwhelmed with the amount of content and collateral available. These include: brochures, data sheets, pitch decks, scripts, white papers, case studies, training materials, webinars, seminars, demos, playbooks, battle cards, competitive guides, configurators, proposal generators, business value justification web sites, microsites, landing pages, email campaigns, social media campaigns… The list could, and sometimes does, go on endlessly.

Occasionally, when I look at the content available to sales people, I'm reminded of the phrase "Water, water everywhere, but not a drop to drink."

I think sales people struggle with using the right content in the right way to have the most impact.

Here's where you can provide a lot of coaching and leadership to your people, as well as to the people developing content.

First, content will not win the day! If that were true, the entire sales process could be conducted electronically, through e-commerce.

Good professional selling is what wins. Content supports the salesperson in winning!

Make sure your people understand this. Too many sales people focus too much on content. They drown their customers in materials, perhaps thinking the person providing the most "poundage" in paper wins.

Or they use content as a poor surrogate for questioning, probing, understanding, and engaging. This is creating no value—which is probably why customers spend so much of their time "digitally teaching themselves" on the web. If the salesperson is just delivering brochures, data sheets, or reading from scripted decks, the customer can get their information more effectively searching the web.

Various research reports tell us the customer is 57-90% of the way through their buying process before they engage with sales. While there are problems with this, it does indicate that the customer has self-educated before seeing your salesperson. So if all your salesperson is doing is providing more content or parroting content, then they are creating no value.

> *Content needs to support and reinforce the salesperson's strategy, not be a crutch for poor salesmanship.*

The second area where managers can play an important role is to make sure sales people are actually putting the content to good use. This may seem a contradiction to the previous comment, but it isn't. Too often, I see sales people not leveraging content in impactful ways.

Several years ago, I was consulting with a sales organization. They paid another company a lot of money to develop a series of playbooks and battle cards. When I looked at the materials, they were actually quite good.

The problem is the sales people weren't using them! They knew they were available, but they didn't know how to use them, nor were they reminded about them. Unfortunately, the sales people hadn't been trained on how to use the content, the managers hadn't been trained in how to coach sales people in using the playbooks effectively.

A great resource that could have helped sales people be more effective was not being leveraged. Make sure you have an understanding of the content available to support your sales people's efforts. As you look at their deal strategies, review call plans or look at account plans, think of how they might use the content available to help them.

Make sure you understand the content and tools your people have, help them learn how to use them to help win more deals more quickly.

PART EIGHT

LONGER-TERM SALES MANAGEMENT ISSUES

53

STRATEGIES FOR THE OVERALL SALES ORGANIZATION

The next set of chapters focus on longer term issues for the sales organization. This is probably where your boss or your boss's boss spends a lot of time (unless you are running the entire sales function yourself).

In looking at the overall organizational strategy issues, you aren't focused on tactical day to day, week to week, or even quarterly performance. You are looking at longer term issues about your company's overall Go-To-Customer strategies.

Undoubtedly, you may be asked to serve on project groups or for your opinions on these strategic issues. Also, it's really helpful to understand what's keeping your manager awake at night.

We won't go very deeply into each one, but just cover enough to whet your appetite to learn more.

WHAT DOES ALL THIS INVOLVE?

The sales organization is responsible for the execution of the organization's strategy in the face of the customer. In some sense, you and your team are the "tip of the spear," with the entire organization aligned behind you, helping you execute.

While marketing organizations do all sorts of things to drive overall visibility for the corporation, the positioning in the market, and what products the company offers, sales translates the strategy into action and revenue.

The strategies and priorities of the sales organization have to be in lockstep with those of the organization (or the part of the organization your team is responsible for). Clearly, top priorities are revenue and margin growth. Your company has a plan (revenue/margin) it has committed to the owners or board.

Questions and issues top sales executives will be concerned about include:

- **What are the overall enterprise strategies, goals, priorities?** What is sales' role in implementing and executing those strategies? What is our purpose, vision, goal? What strategic initiatives do we have to put in place to support this?

- **How do we think of customers?** How do we want our customers to think of us? What's our customer experience model, positioning, and strategy? What are the principles around which we will create our distinguishing value?

- **What are our value creation strategies?** How do we make sure we execute them in meaningful ways with our customers? How do we leverage them to drive differentiation? How do we increase our importance to customers and markets?

- **How do we fit in the organization?** Where do we have critical dependencies? Who depends on us? How do we align, how do we work most effectively? How do we work them?

- **What is our Go-To-Customer strategy?** What's the right deployment model? How should we be organized and structured to most effectively achieve our goals? Within this, there are a number of fundamental issues around "who is our customer," what is our "sweet spot?" What's our Total Addressable Market? Will it continue to be large enough to support our ambitions? Should we look at expanding into additional markets?

- **In assessing the strategies, executives will be concerned with the market ecosystem.** Beyond just customers, who are their customers, what trends and issues do we see with those, how big is the market, how is it structured? Who are partners and influencers important to customers or us? Who are the competitors, not only direct competitors, but distant and emerging competitors? How are our solutions positioned in terms of the maturity of the markets?

- **What are top performing sales organizations in the world doing?** What should we learn from them? What should we adapt for our own organization? Who should we benchmark, how to we make sure we are best of breed?

- **How do we make sure we have and develop the right talent to achieve our goals?** What type of people do we need to attract and retain, how do we grow and develop them, how do we maximize performance? What kind of culture do we want to have? What do we, as managers, need to do to build and reinforce that culture?

- **How do we establish a growth mindset and a culture of continuous learning and improvement?**

- **How do we measure and track sales productivity and effectiveness?** What processes, programs, systems, tools, and training do we need to put in place to maximize productivity, effectiveness, and performance? What goals do we need to establish?

- **What are the day to day, week to week, month to month, quarter to quarter tactics, and programs the organization needs to execute to achieve its goals?** How do we assure we are executing as effectively and efficiently as possible?

- **What does the leadership team need to do to keep on track with our goals and performance?**

We'll explore some of these in the following chapters.

If you noticed, most of these were very strategic. However, the top management team will also be very execution focused. They will be concerned about where you and your team are in terms of achieving your numbers. They will want to make sure you are putting the right goals, strategies, plans and programs in place and that you are executing your plan. Finally, they will want to make sure you are identifying problems and executing plans to correct them.

SALES MANAGEMENT ECOSYSTEM

Having a framework or an ecosystem to understand how all the "pieces/parts" of the sales function fit together is critical in making sense in developing and executing strategies and leading the organization.

Make sure you visit the web site www.salesmanagersurvivalguide.com. In the resources section, I've provided comprehensive materials to help you establish this Sales Management Ecosystem.

54

ENTERPRISE STRATEGY

Sales executes the corporate strategy with customers. While various marketing, communications and other programs may play part in creating awareness of the enterprise and its general strategies, it's sales that implements the strategy with customers.

It's important to recognize this is much more than simply making the numbers. Each organization is concerned about positioning, how they are perceived, what they stand for. Organizations have goals for specific markets and product lines. They want to achieve share in certain markets or with certain types of customers.

Your manager (or you, if you are the top sales executive,) is concerned with the issue, "What does this mean for the sales organization? How do we do this?"

Let's take the simplest example of what this means. Imagine that you work for a $100M company. There are four primary product lines, each expected to generate $25M. One of the product lines involves going after a completely new market segment or industry vertical. Another involves opening a new geographic segment, where you have little presence. These two product lines represent the company's future. But since they are relatively new, it will be tough achieving the $25M goals for each.

The other two product lines represent the traditional business the sales people have sold for years. But they address maturing markets and solutions.

I'll add one final twist: The top sales executive believes the team can sell $100M in its traditional products, doing very little with the two newer products.

If you were the top sales executive, what would you do?

1. **You might go for the sure thing: You'd go after the $100M.** After all, if the corporate goal and the sales goal is $100M and you can achieve it, you are helping the organization achieve one of its most important financial goals.

2. **You might develop a plan that says, "How do I balance the organization's performance across all four product lines?"** As a sales executive, you might look at product/market training on the two newer product lines. You might look at redeploying resources to the new geography or building a channel organization, you might look at establishing sales specialists. Your goal would be to achieve each of the four product line goals, selling $25M of each to achieve $100M, even though you know it will be tough.

3. **You might do (2), but also look at, how much you can overachieve on the two traditional product lines, so you dramatically overachieve our revenue number.** There are some resourcing challenges, because you have to figure how to make the goals for the two newer product lines, perhaps you could make an argument for increasing total sales resources to pursue the strategy that might enable you to make $150M, but you know the key goal is to make at least $25M in each product line.

Which would you choose?

The "right answer is (2) or (3), or some variant of it.

The wrong answer is (1). Recently, I fired a sales VP. He was making his numbers, but basically, he was implementing the strategy outlined in the first example. When I had the tough discussions leading up to his termination, he kept saying, "I don't understand, I'm making my number!"

He was right, he *didn't* understand. His job was to make the number and execute the corporation's strategy. By not focusing on the new product lines, he was threatening the entire future of the organization. Those divisions would not make their goals, the company could no longer afford to invest in those divisions, and they might be scaled back or even shut down. All this could have devastating consequences to the future growth strategy of the company.

We see these challenges in the real world every day. Large companies don't exist, because sales execution did not align with the company growth strategies.

In my own career, I was a sales manager at IBM as the shift from mainframes, to minicomputers, to desktops, to software/services was going on. In the early years of the transition, it was very easy to make my goals just by selling mainframes. For every mainframe we sold, we would have to sell five to ten minicomputers— and the sales efforts weren't that much different.

Many of my peers thought the same thing. IBM struggled for some years, realigning its resources and focus to continue to grow. Sure, there were a lot of other issues in IBM in that shift of the business model, it wasn't just sales. But the slowness of sales in making that shift was one of the big challenges.

Sales executives are constantly facing the challenge of not only making the number, but doing it in a way that reinforces the overall organizational strategy.

Your job is to make sure both you and your team understand the company strategy and your roles in supporting and executing it in your day to day efforts with your customers.

55

CUSTOMER CENTRICITY

What does your company think of its customers? No I don't mean the lip service that's in your website, in all your press releases and brochures. I mean what do you really think of your customers?

Are they merely a vehicle to generating revenue? Are they long term, highly valued relationships key to your growth? Is their success key to your success?

Who your customer is, how you hold the customer, what kind of customer experience you want to create, is a critical element of your sales strategy and will drive the structure, priorities, programs, goals, and metrics of the organization.

The issue of how you hold the customer is not just a sales issue, it's a corporate issue, and everything the company does has to be consistent with the views of the customer and the experiences the organization wants to create.

Somehow, though, it has more urgency and immediacy with the sales organization. In many ways, it is through the sales organization we first begin our relationships, creating those first customer experiences.

If we want to have deep, rich relationships with customers, developing them for their long term value, a sales organization that is only concerned about "getting the order" would behave in ways that are inconsistent with that goal.

If our Go-To-Customer and deployment strategies are to leverage channel and other partners, we want to make sure those partners created a customer experience consistent with our strategies.

Customer experience starts long before we first see customers. It starts with the customer's very first encounter—it may be a billboard, a Google Adwords ad, a press release, an interview with an executive, the website, or marketing materials. It continues through every interchange the customer has with people representing our company, whether sales, a partner, a retailer. It continues through the buying process and long after they have purchased, their experience of using the products/services, getting support, even buying again.

All of these create a customer experience. Customers share their impressions of us with each other, possibly through referrals in social networks. Those can be positive or negative.

As a result, how we hold the customer and the experiences we and the rest of the organization create are critical to our success in achieving our sales goals.

Defining how we hold the customer, what that customer experience should be, tracking and measuring it through the entire life of their relationship with us is critical. Defining how the sales organization engages with customers, making sure our engagement models and behaviors are consistent with the experience we want to create is critical. It shapes our success with the customer not just for this deal but through the lifecycle of that relationship.

Increasingly, this issue, mapping the customer experience through the lifecycle of the customer is consuming more of top executive time, across the organization.

Make sure you understand the customer experience strategies, what that means in how sales people engage customers, the behaviors they should be exhibiting, and the relationships they should establish.

Whether you manage a team of field sales people, inside sales, SDR's, channel partners, it's your job to make sure your people both understand and execute your organization's customer experience strategies.

You need to train, coach, reinforce the right behaviors. You need to find sales people doing the right thing, recognizing and reinforcing that behavior with them and the team. You need to catch and correct errors quickly.

Many think customer experience is the competitive battleground of the future. I think it always has been. Customers have always voted with their wallets. We in sales, marketing, and across our organizations are only recognizing this as it becomes tougher and tougher to attract, retain, and grow our customers.

56

SALES AND THE REST OF THE COMPANY

In many organizations, it seems as if sales is isolated from the rest of the company. In some organizations, we wish that sales were more isolated from the company. Bottom line, we can't exist alone. Our success and ability to achieve our goals is dependent on everything else "working right."

Likewise, others in the organization depend on us "working right," so they can do their jobs, which in turn enables us to do our jobs. (Funny how what goes around comes around).

Sales executives and sales operations people spend a lot of time on these issues. Understanding the dependencies, the workflow, how the diverse pieces/parts fit together to enable the entire organization to get work done is important for the organization and each part of the organization to achieve the goals.

When things go wrong, as they inevitably do, it's usually a failure in one of the components in this complex workflow. Perhaps there was an error, perhaps someone dropped the ball, perhaps there was confusion and several people did the same, but conflicting things, perhaps no one had the responsibility and something fell through the cracks.

When these issues start becoming systemic, when they are not just chance happenings, executives start examining the workflow, roles, and responsibilities, to identify where the breakdowns occur, and what to do to fix them.

Part of the issue executives are concerned about is: "Does everybody have the right information at the right time to do their jobs?" Let's take one of the "favorite" problem areas in sales—forecasting.

Most sales people, even most first line managers, despise forecasting. It seems to be a process where top management is seeking to torture or harass sales people with, "When are we getting the business?" Usually, we want to respond, "We're trying as hard as we can," or "We'll get it when we get it." In reality, a lot of people in the organization depend on accurate forecasts to do their jobs. Procurement needs to make sure they understand when parts will be needed and have ordered the right ones. Manufacturing needs to know what their build plan will be, so they can schedule the line appropriately. Logistics needs to be making sure they can ship the products to get to the customer when committed, and customer support needs to install the products or be prepared to onboard and support new customers.

Additionally, all of these groups need to accomplish their tasks as effectively and efficiently as possible. They need to be responsive, while at the same time managing costs.

Cost management, meeting commitments within budget, making sure each part of the organization is being as effective and efficient as possible is a big concern of executives at the top of the organization. They are constantly examining things: Is every part of the organization working as effectively as possible? Are they working as efficiently as possible? What should be changed to improve the impact we as an enterprise have? How can we eliminate/reduce barriers and road blocks? And very importantly, how do we reduce the costs of delivering these products and services?

Finally, top management recognizes the world is constantly changing. In order to grow and compete, the company must constantly refine its strategies, offerings, processes, workflows, everything. So a lot of executive time is spent looking at what needs to be in place to support our goals tomorrow—and how we manage the change in moving from today's environment to tomorrow's.

Top management across the company is constantly looking at functional and cross-functional workflows. They are constantly tuning them to improve the results they produce, and reduce costs. They are constantly balancing the needs of supporting today's requirements with tomorrow's.

Sales people, great ones at least, know how to get things done in organizations. Often, the way they do things is not the way things should be done. Exceptions happen, there may be good reason. But sometimes it's dysfunctional. While the salesperson may be doing the easiest thing to achieve their goals, sometimes it causes difficulty for others in other parts of the organization.

As managers, we have to manage the dichotomy. Sometimes going around the system is the right thing to do. But each time that happens, it may be creating other problems. As much as possible, we have to make sure our people are working the system—the way it's designed. Where there are systemic problems, we need to work with other organizations to understand and fix them.

57

WHAT'S OUR GO-TO-CUSTOMER STRATEGY?

This is an area that consumes huge amounts of time and thinking with top sales executives. It focuses on the issue of how do we reach our customers most effectively and efficiently—while still achieving our goals both from a revenue generation and affordability point of view.

Today there are so many routes to your customers, including field direct, inside sales, web sales, channels of all shapes and sizes. Each of those have a number of different implementations, including SDR's, outsourced lead qualification, account management (global, major, others,) new account development, territory coverage/management, specialists and overlays—for traditional company sales organizations. Channels are even more varied with VAR's, distributors, resellers, agents, retail, catalog/web, integrators, manufacturer's reps, partners, alliances, and on and on.

And then, there are the hybrids, the combinations of some or all of the alternatives listed above.

The Go-To-Customer, deployment or overall organizational strategy can be very complex. Figuring out the right way to most effectively reach the customer, evaluating the pros, cons, risks, costs, of each strategy is very complex.

Plus, the evaluation never ends, as markets and competition changes, our Go-To-Customer strategies need to evolve and change. Here is where we confront the very tough issues of transformation and change management.

The whole process is like changing a tire on an F1 racer while it is still on the track going 200 mph!

This is tough in small organizations, the challenge and complexity grows exponentially with the size of the enterprise, the breadth of solutions, the breadth of markets.

The good news and the bad news is there is no right answer. Looking to competition, emulating their approach to their sales deployment strategy is a race to second place or worse.

Let's look at the core issues in our Go-To-Customer strategy. Basically, we are answering a few key questions to ensure we've optimized both the coverage and customer engagement models:

- **How do we find and engage all the customers in our target market?**

- **How do we engage them as effectively as possible?**

- **How do we do this at the lowest possible cost and risk? (Total cost)**

To answer the first question, we have to know who our customers are. The answer is never "everyone." We have to identify our sweet spot. By that, we have to answer the questions, "What problems are we the best in the world at solving?" And (we have to be honest,) "Who has those problems?"

Anything as we move to the fringes of that sweet spot, our win rates plummet, our costs for those sales we get skyrocket.

In answering the second question, "How do we engage them as effectively as possible?" we too often use inside-out thinking. That is, we focus on how we would prefer to engage them, what we want to do. Usually, we get it wrong. It's far easier, to use an outside-in approach, "How do the customers want to buy, what does their buying process look like?" While it seems simple, asking the customers gets us to the right answer much faster, much cheaper, and with much greater success.

It's here where you start looking at different deployment models. Do they buy from integrators; do they like to deal with the vendor directly? What other products do they buy at the same time? There are dozens of questions, the answer to which help you evaluate the different deployment models.

There is seldom a clear-cut right solution. There are usually several alternatives, each with its own pros and cons, each with different costs and risks.

Here's where the third question comes in, "How do we do this at the lowest cost and risk?" In reality, you make a decision based on balancing cost and risk. The lowest cost alternative is seldom the lowest risk alternative.

Now, the real work begins. You thought it was tough getting to this point? You've developed your Go-To-Customer strategy or strategies—remember you may have differing strategies by market segment, product line, or other factor.

But now you have to dive into the detailed work of designing the organization, strategies, plans, programs, people, resources, systems, tools, processes and so forth needed to put the capability in place. Then you have to make it happen in execution.

I'll stop here. This is just a thumbnail sketch of some of the issues top management looks at in developing the Go-To-Customer, deployment, organizational strategies. Clearly, it's something that doesn't change every day or even every year—unless there have been huge changes in the markets or the solutions you bring to market.

Generally, they evolve over time. Most often, organizations move too slowly, recognizing the need to change only after they have failed to meet their goals for a number of years, or are seeing huge share loss or other things.

Sharp leaders are always watching the signs; they are always thinking of where they need to be in a year or two years. They're putting plans in place to move the organization where they need to be.

You will have the opportunity to participate in this planning (if you are the top sales exec, it's one of your responsibilities.) Within your own team, you will be looking at your coverage models—do you have the ability to reach every customer in your sweet spot, do you have the right coverage of your territory, whether it's geographic, segment, or account oriented? Are your people engaging the customers in the most effective manner?

Additionally, undoubtedly, your company will have a hybrid strategy. That is not a single approach but a combination of approaches. It's important for you and your people to understand the overall approach and how you fit into the overall Go-To-Customer plan.

Finally, you will want to pay attention to the deployment of your people. You won't be changing the overall deployment strategy of the structure of the organization, but you will be looking at your coverage plan within your own "territory," maximizing the growth and performance of your own team.

58

MARKET ECOSYSTEM

This is very closely tied to the previous chapter, Go-To-Customer Strategies. Where that chapter focuses on how to most effectively reach and engage the customers in your sweet spot, this is a broader perspective on the business.

To be honest, depending on the dynamics of your company, your customers, their markets and their customers, the amount of time top executives spend on the general market ecosystem, business climate, and business strategies varies.

Some industries, engaged in radical restructuring or disruption, require executives to spend a lot of time completely rethinking the business, your positioning and your business model.

For example, in recent years in technology businesses, the move to the cloud has disrupted many of the traditional enterprise software companies including SAP, Oracle, Microsoft and dozens of others. They've had to rethink their business strategies, product lines, how they market and sell.

Financial services industries are undergoing huge restructuring as payment methods like PayPal, Apple Pay, even new "currencies" like BitCoin emerge.

Automobile industries are being reshaped at various levels with things like Driverless cars, Green/Electric cars, and competition from nontraditional companies like Tesla. Even the market and need for cars is being shifted by companies like Uber, Lyft, and Zipcars.

Markets and customers mature; the demand and need for your solutions change.

Again, these are issues that drive the core business strategies and models of your organization. Top executives spend a lot of time behind closed doors in meetings trying to figure things out (By the way, that's the wrong thing—they should be out in the markets with customers).

What does this mean to you and your team?

First, you and your team are probably the first to see the changes and disruptions going on in the markets. You see new types of customers, you see your customer changing how they do business, perhaps changing the need for your products or services. You see new competitors—not the same old familiar faces. If you are looking more broadly, you see the things impacting your customers, the things they should be worrying about.

It's critical to feed this information back into your company. Your management needs to be aware, product and market managers need to see what's happening with customers, your company's business strategists need to be aware. Marketing, customer service, and other functions all may have a stake in understanding what you and your team are observing happening with customers.

Some companies have formal mechanisms for getting feedback from sales, too few don't. You may recall early in the book I suggested you get to know lots of people in the company. Make sure you continue to do this, spend time with product planners, managers, strategists, and so forth, to let them know what you see in the market place. Invite them to visit customers so they see it firsthand.

It's not just the right thing to do in helping drive (however indirectly) the strategies and directions of your company, but it's critical for you and your team. If you don't have the products and solutions your customers need, if you don't have a business model that enables you to compete with the disruptors, your and your team's ability to be successful is seriously compromised.

The final thing is that all this means change—disruption. I'll spend more time on change later, but realize your organization is constantly evolving. If you haven't gotten the message yet, as a leader you will constantly be facing and driving change. The moment the organization stops learning, changing, and improving is the first moment on a journey to irrelevance.

Make sure you are prepared for this, that you welcome and embrace it. Make sure your team understands it, internalizes it, and owns it for themselves.

59

TALENT AND CULTURE

The success of the sales organization has little to do with the products and services it sells. It has little to do with your strategies or the power of your brand. The processes, systems, tools, programs, and training all contribute to improving success.

But the success of the sales organization is rooted in the talent, that is the people who make up the sales organization and the culture of the organization.

Peter Drucker was quoted as saying, "Culture Eats Strategy for Breakfast." I'd add, "Talent Finishes It Off at Lunch."

Watch where the top executives in organizations you admire focus their time. It's on talent and culture. Business publications are filled with stories about the culture at Google, Apple, Zappos, Amazon, and other companies. Organizations like GE, IBM, and Nordstrom's have long been known for their investment in talent.

Absent these, no company can expect to be a top performer.

Ideally, this is a top priority of your management team and you. Ideally, you are constantly examining and understanding the culture of the organization—what do we stand for, what are our values? How do we want to be perceived by our employees, customers, suppliers, investors, community? What are the attitudes and behaviors that reinforce these? How do we, as a leadership team, set the example and constantly reinforce and leverage the culture.

The right people, fully bought into the culture, will overcome any obstacle.

There are those words, the right people—talent. To buy into the culture to be fully onboard and take ownership of what the organization is trying to achieve, you have to have the right talent.

While it sounds trite, the organization is only as good as its people and their combined efforts. All the surrounding things: strategies, processes, systems, tools, programs, training support people in achieving the goals. Weaknesses or flaws in any of those probably won't be devastating, but the wrong talent or absence of talent is devastating.

If you don't mind my getting a little philosophical for a moment, I get concerned about attitudes I see in many businesses. Attitudes where people are a commodity, we can swap them in and out just like we might change machines in an assembly line. The seeming ease many managers have with wholesale layoffs and reductions in force is both shameful and wasteful. The declining loyalty to the people that make up the organization, and their resultant declining loyalty to the organization, doesn't bode well for business.

There are organizations that stand out, organizations that realize people and talent are the ultimate differentiators and take great care in attracting, developing, growing, and retaining that talent. These organizations tend to consistently top the list of best performers, most innovative, highest growth, most admired.

It's even more important in sales. By its nature, sales is a people business. It's ultimately human beings—our customers—trusting us to help them grow their business. It's them trusting us with their careers. After all, what we lose is an order. If the customer makes a wrong decision, it could mean their jobs, the jobs of others, and even their businesses.

Talent and culture trump everything else.

The greatest compliment that can be paid to any leader is they are great spotters, developers, and retainers of great people. That they can mobilize teams to achieve extraordinary goals.

I'm sorry for this philosophical diversion, but this is probably the single most important skill for any leader. It's the skill that will drive your success and enable you to grow your own career. By being great at talent and building a strong culture, you can hire the smartest people in the world to develop the greatest strategies, you can hire the very best to execute those strategies and get things done.

This is also the most fun part of the job—it is all about people.

60

CONTINUOUS LEARNING
AND CONTINUOUS IMPROVEMENT

You've seen me constantly referring to these concepts throughout the book. Simply stated, the moment you stop learning and improving, you, your team, and your company are on the path to irrelevance. It's not a matter of if you die; it's only a question of when.

The world, our customers, their customers, our competitors are constantly changing. The pace of that change seems to be accelerating.

Look at your own company's product life cycles; they are probably getting shorter and shorter. That's a reflection of the pace of change.

The very nature of selling is convincing our customers to change—change the way the run their business, change to address new opportunities, change their current supplier.

Recently, the Chairman and CEO of AT&T made a bold statement to all AT&T employees. Paraphrasing him, he said, "If you don't invest a minimum of five to ten hours a week in learning and developing new skills, you have no future with this company."

It starts with learning—both formal and informal. Your top leaders and you will put in place formal programs to provide specific skills critical to doing the job. But learning doesn't stop there. It continues informally, reading books, professional literature, blogs, attending conferences, wandering around customers and learning their business.

We need to think as individuals: How do we develop new skills to improve our capabilities? As leaders, we need to look at our organizations and look at what new capabilities our organizations need to grow and perform.

Continuous improvement is tightly coupled with learning. Learning by itself is nice, but we need to apply it to our businesses. How do we get better? We aren't looking for huge breakthroughs and quantum leaps forward. Those are nice, but rare, and many fail miserably. It's the little improvements accumulated across the organization that drive sustained growth.

How do we reduce onboarding time by a day, a week, a month? How do we improve win rates by 5%, 10%? How do we increase customer retention by a few percent, how do we improve opens on emails by a few percent?

How do we decrease the number of customer meetings required to close by a day, two days…

Years ago, our company took that on as a project. We looked at the number of meetings typically needed to move a deal through the entire buying/selling process. We weren't looking at the calendar time—for example we qualify a deal in January and close it in December for a 12-month cycle—we actually looked at the hours and days spent in meetings with customers. Over an 18-month period, we reduced that time by 60%! It enabled us to more than double our productivity with no increase in workload or staffing! (I won't tell you our secret, you can hire us to help you figure out how to do this.)

Results from inspecting how you do things or improve don't have to be that dramatic, a single percent improvement here, a couple there drive huge differences across the organization.

Top sales executives are constantly looking at this. They may have task forces driving improvement initiatives.

The cool thing about continuous improvement is that it doesn't have to start at the top of the organization. Each of your sales people can look at what they do, how they spend their time. Exploring the simple question, "How do I get more accomplished in each meeting with a customer?" (That's part of the secret we discovered in our own efforts.)

Within your team, you can drive improvement initiatives. How do we make one-on-ones more effective and impactful? How do we make team meetings more productive? How do we learn from each other to improve our performance?

As a leader, regardless the level, you need to have a written plan in place for two things:

1. What are your learning goals and how are you going to achieve them?

2. What are your continuous improvement goals and how are you going to achieve them?

As a leader you need to make sure each person on your team has a similar plan in place. It's your job to help them through coaching, providing learning and development experiences, and constantly challenging them to do more—better.

PART NINE

YOUR FUTURE AS A SALES MANAGER—AND BEYOND

61

YOU AND YOUR FUTURE

We're getting to the end of the book. Most of this book has focused on your people and the overall organization. That's as it should be: Great leaders focus on serving their people and organization.

But it's important to spend a few chapters focusing on you and your future. There are things you are rightfully concerned about—your relationship with your manager, your own development and career, what to do when things go wrong, and your legacy as a leader.

By now you've learned how to think about things important to your performance and effectiveness as a leader. You've learned how to coach and develop your people in helping them learn how to "figure things out." These tools are fundamental to your development and your own career, so you have a strong foundation on which to build.

62

MANAGING YOUR MANAGER

Hopefully, you have a strong manager, one who knows her job is to get things done through her people—that is you and your peers. Hopefully, she recognizes her role is to coach, challenge, and develop you.

Some managers don't know this—they may have never been trained. Give them a copy of this book as a not so subtle hint about their role.

But you also have to think about managing your manager.

How do you do this, what does it mean?

UNDERSTANDING PERFORMANCE EXPECTATIONS

First, you have to understand the goals and priorities of your manager. The best way is to understand their performance plan. Managers all the way up the food chain have performance expectations and performance plans.

As CEO, my board has set my performance plan. I've always found it useful to share it with my direct reports. It's important for them to know what is driving me, what drives my priorities, what I'm expected to accomplish. They understand their performance plans are driven by my performance plan. In turn, their performance plans drive those of their subordinates, all the way through the organization.

It's important to understand your manager's own plan. As a result, you will know what's important to her.

Leverage this in working with your manager in developing your own performance plan. Just as you learned how important it is to work with your people in developing their performance plans, making sure you they understand it, they own it, and they know how they will be evaluated; you need to do the same with your manager.

Sometimes your manager may not know she needs to be doing this with you. She may not even put a formal plan in place, just evaluating you at the end of each year because HR says she has to. You are really cheating yourself if you let this happen.

If your manager isn't driving the process, write it up yourself. Take the time to develop it, then sit down with your manager to make sure you and she are aligned, and that you have the expectations documented. Just like there should be no surprises between you and your people, there should be no surprises with your manager.

If you remember back that far, recall I mentioned that I periodically pull my performance plan out and review myself against it. It's important that you pull your plan out periodically, and make sure you are still focusing on what's important on your plan and to your manager. In the rush of everyday business, it's too easy to get distracted by crises and what appears to be urgent, forgetting to focus on what's important. Your own performance plan should keep you centered on what's important.

If your manager isn't initiating periodic checkpoint reviews, make sure you seize the initiative. Make it a point to sit down for a review once a quarter. Make sure your perception of how you are doing is aligned with your manager's.

COMMUNICATING WITH HER

Much earlier we talked a little about Behavioral/Communications styles. Make sure you understand yours and that of your manager. Just like you want to communicate effectively and impactfully with your people, you want to do so with your manager.

One of the people on my team has a behavioral style that is diagonally opposed to mine. As I mentioned, often it's people in the diagonals that we have the most difficulty connecting with. His style drives me crazy. You already know I'm a "net it out person." He likes to tell me the story. Fortunately, we've reached a happy medium.

He knows my style; he knows he can drive me crazy. Likewise, I know his style, and that my own behavioral style may drive him crazy. Fortunately, since we both understand this, we are able to work together in a very productive way, have fun with each other, and deeply respect each other's capabilities. His differences really drive strength in our organization, and help me understand things I might otherwise be blind to. Hopefully, my different way of looking at things contributes to his growth, as well.

In addition to understanding your manager's behavioral style, understand her communication needs. What information does she need to know? How does she understand what's going on in the organization? What frequency of information does she expect? Daily (hopefully not), weekly, quarterly?

How does your manager want to get information? Does she want reports? Is she more comfortable with a conversation? How detailed does she want the information to be?

DEALING WITH PROBLEMS

You are going to have problems. Things will go wrong. One of the worst things you can do is hide them from your manager. Just as you don't want your people hiding things from you, your manager doesn't want you hiding problems from her. Your manager doesn't want to be surprised.

You've probably heard the expression, "Don't bring me problems, bring me solutions." In a lot of senses, as a manager and leader, that's something to think about in reporting problems and issues to your manager.

Think about the coaching approach you take with your people. You know you shouldn't be telling them what to do. You want to develop the capability for them to think through things, to figure things out themselves.

One of the reasons you are a manager is probably because you have that ability. So as you have problems and crises, make sure you've thought them through. Think about solutions, and how you might approach and solve the problem.

As you present these issues to your manager, review your plans and approaches. Make sure they understand your analysis, reasoning, and your action plan.

While, I may seem to be reversing myself, sometimes there are no easy answers. Don't be hesitant in asking for help. The problems we deal with at managerial levels are often not easy problems. They test even the best leaders. For example, the executives we work with are among the smartest and highest performers in the world. But they face very difficult challenges and don't hesitate getting other experienced people to help them address them.

Your manager is probably much more experienced and her job is to help you. So use her as a sounding board for different approaches. Use her to find the holes in your solution so you can develop a stronger solution.

While this may sound excessively political, make sure you and your manager are aligned in the approach to the solution. You want your manager in the same boat with you; you want her to support and reinforce what you are doing. As she explains to her own manager what's happening, you want her to have great confidence in what you are doing and to pass that confidence along to *her* manager.

HOW MUCH MANAGEMENT TIME DO YOU TAKE?

You've probably experienced this with your own team. Some of them just take a lot of management time. Perhaps they are low performers; we already know they take a lot of time. Even some of your best performers may "need" a lot of management time—they may lack confidence, may be looking for help or advice, or are just very communicative. But you expect your higher performers and more experienced people will need less management time. If you've developed them correctly, they are figuring things out, and being proactive in identifying what they need to do to stay on course.

As a manager, you should need "just enough, but not too much time." I know that's obscure, but if you need a deeper explanation, you may be in trouble as a manager.

I'm involved in two completely different situations with key managers in two organizations. Both are experienced and seasoned managers. One is a bad performer. He's having terrible problems achieving his goals. He has the wrong team. He's not doing the things he needs to be doing. He's failing miserably. He needs daily supervision in the simplest things.

Clearly, he's in the wrong job. He's on a Measured Mile, unfortunately, he's not going to make it. His manager and I shouldn't have to be spending the amount of time we are, and he isn't getting better.

Another case is a very senior leader who isn't a team player. He's out for his own objectives. He consumes huge amounts of resource. He is a terrible leader and coach. His people aren't developing; he uses them as glorified assistants, swooping in to save the day on the biggest deals. He's making commitments to customers that are not necessarily things we want to be doing and at pricing levels that are unacceptable.

Naturally, he's doing these things on his own, never informing his manager. We have to sit down with him daily, and force him to keep us informed. His manager shouldn't have to be doing this. We're having serious talks with him about this, he needs to correct his behaviors or we will move him out of his job.

In both of these situations, the amount of time we have to spend with these managers is excessive. This is a real problem. Your manager is probably managing a number of other managers and critical issues: If you require too much time, it adversely impacts what she is trying to achieve.

You are in your job because you can think, lead, and figure things out. You need to spend time with your manager and she wants to spend time with you. It has to be just enough and not too much.

YOU NEED COACHING

Just as the most important investment of your time is coaching and developing your people. Your manager needs to invest time in coaching you.

Hopefully, because you are both leaders, it's more collaborative. You should identify areas where you could really use help and your manager's coaching. Your manager will also have areas where she will want to focus your development.

The nature of the coaching and frequency may be different from that you give your people. You are hopefully spending time doing deal and call reviews, as well as one-on-ones every week with each person.

Ideally, your manager is using the same approach with you, leveraging the business reviews with you as opportunities to coach and develop you.

COLLATERAL ASSIGNMENTS

As you develop as a manager, your manager will be giving you additional responsibilities. She may ask you to serve on task forces or special project teams. You will be drawn into strategy and other discussions. You may be given additional responsibilities. These are good for your own personal development, so it's important to do these. But remember, you only achieve your goals if your people achieve their goals. Your highest priority and time allocation is with your people.

Guard your time carefully, don't let your time be sucked away, don't spend all your time on collateral assignments.

TEAM PLAYERS/LOYALTY

This is one of those subjects I shouldn't have to talk about but need to. As a senior executive, I expect my management team to be team players. This means they can't be out for themselves, but must have as their highest priority the success of their teams and entire organization.

Being a team player isn't about blind compliance. In fact it's the opposite; it's challenging each person on the team to stretch further. It's facing tough situations together and celebrating together. It means good give and take. It means we have to compromise and align what we are doing with our peers and others in the organization.

The higher you go in an organization, the more you realize your abilities to achieve both your goals and the organization's goals is dependent on successful and collaborative relationships with your peers. The most dysfunctional organizations I see are those where the top executives have their own agendas and are not working collaboratively with their peers.

Tied to this is loyalty—loyalty to what your team, your manager, and your organization is trying to achieve. Again, your own personal agenda is not important. What is important is what the organization is trying to achieve. If you aren't aligned with this, then you aren't living up to your responsibilities as a leader.

Like being a team player, loyalty doesn't mean *blind* loyalty. Sometimes the best "loyalty" involves appropriately challenging the thinking of your team, your peers, your manager, and your organization. As an executive, it's important that managers working for me challenge me. I may be missing something; I may be just wrong. Having managers with the confidence to push back, keeping the entire organization on target is critical to each of our success.

We aren't talking at all about a team of "Yes" men and women. We are talking about a team fiercely dedicated to each other's success, to the success of the whole organization, and to achieving the organization's goals. Hidden agendas and power plays have no place in successful, growing organizations.

YOUR MANAGER'S MANAGER

Your manager's priorities are driven by her manager. It's always useful to understand your manager's manager and how you can best support your manager in her own performance with her manager.

Again here, the goal is not going around your manager, but understanding what she faces and helping her be more successful.

SOMETIMES YOUR MANAGER IS A JERK!

Sometimes your manager is pretty bad, I know you've had them before. They lack the skills. They don't invest time as they should. They may be very politically motivated. These managers aren't a whole lot of fun to work with.

But if we are to be successful, we have to figure something out. The mistake too many make is one of "avoidance." This is probably the worst thing you can do.

With jerks, it's really critical to understand their expectations of you, their need for information and communication, and behavioral styles. Understanding these won't make it any easier, but it will help you manage your relationship a little better.

Sometimes, the manager isn't a jerk; he may just be inexperienced. He may not know what he should be doing as a manager. This is where you can leverage the skills you've developed in working with your team. The same skills for coaching, the same skills you've used in reviews, can all be applied to your manager.

We've talked about setting performance expectations. But think about some of the reviews you might have with your manager: pipeline reviews, Quarterly Business Reviews (QBR's). The same principles apply to these. Have clear objectives going into the review, perhaps provide an agenda in advance. Make sure you are prepared, perhaps send your manager an overview in advance. Walk through the review, answer your manager's questions, make sure they get what they want. Ask your manager for coaching or feedback. He may not be comfortable, but at least give him the opportunity. Make sure you agree on next steps.

Managing a manager who is a jerk or inexperienced is always a challenge, but the approaches and methods are the same that you use in effectively managing your team.

63

WHEN THINGS GO WRONG

Things will go wrong, it's the natural order. Despite everyone's best intentions, your best planning and execution, things will go wrong. Murphy seems to be a member of every organization and each of our teams.

Hopefully, by now, this book has given you some tools to leverage, both to identify when things are going off course and how to put things back on course. Skills you've developed in coaching, managing performance, recruiting/hiring/onboarding, and in managing the business are all things you will need when things go wrong.

You have the tools to manage and correct performance with the individuals on your team.

But things will go wrong.

FIND PROBLEMS WHEN THEY ARE SMALL

It's far easier to deal with problems and challenges while they are very small. That's why having the right metrics in place is so important. Identifying issues as early as possible enables you to eliminate or minimize the impact. You may want to re-read the chapters on Metrics.

The biggest mistake I see managers making is depending too much on trailing metrics. We've already talked about the problem of measuring only quota performance or revenue. By the time you realize you have a problem, it's either too late to do anything about it, or the time to develop and implement a solution is excessive.

Make sure you have the right leading metrics in place.

Likewise, things like the sales process, leveraging reviews and one-on-ones are critical in identifying individual performance issues very early and addressing them before they become catastrophic.

AVOIDANCE IS NOT A PROBLEM SOLVING TECHNIQUE

By avoidance, I mean, burying your head in the sand, wishful thinking, not paying attention; wishful thinking is not a problem resolution approach.

Yet too many managers adopt this approach. They don't address problem performers, choosing to ignore them until it's too late. Performance problems don't go away, and they don't solve themselves. Generally, they get worse! You have to identify them and jump on them as early as possible. You have to do something—it's your job, and if you aren't addressing them, then you aren't doing your job!

YOU HAVE TO HAVE DATA

You can't know that you are having a problem and you can't begin solving problems unless you have data. Data—the right data is your friend. Facts are always better than opinion, instinct or gut reaction. Data tells you when you are failing and when you are improving. It gives you clues about what you might do to clearly define the issues and develop solutions.

But make sure you have the right data and that it is accurate. Tracking the wrong things or using bad data can cause you to solve the wrong problem. If you aren't collecting the right data, if you haven't established the goals and metrics, you may be totally unaware there is a problem until it's too late.

MAKE SURE YOU ARE SOLVING THE RIGHT PROBLEM

If you aren't careful and brutally honest with yourself, you either miss being aware of problems or you solve the wrong problem.

For example, a couple of years ago, an executive called me saying his team had very serious closing problems. According to him, the win rates were way down, and his people weren't closing enough deals to make their numbers. The way he determined this was they had missed their quarterly goals for a few quarters. His management was putting him under tremendous pressure.

When I started looking at the situation, it turned out they actually had very good closing skills and very good win rates—with customers in their sweet spot. The problem ended up being a qualifying problem. The sales people were letting a huge number of bad deals into the pipeline. They were deals outside the target markets or where the customer clearly had no intention of buying. Yet sales people would chase these bad deals, wasting lots of time. For well-qualified deals in their sweet spot, their win rates were actually well over 50%.

Had I accepted the exec's assessment, I would have been helping him solve the wrong problem—we would have had no impact. Once we understood the issue and focused on improving qualification skills, the results skyrocketed.

Often, we get executives asking us to fix a sales skills issue. But the real problem is they have the wrong people. No amount of sales skills training will help if you have the wrong people.

Sometimes, we've had CEOs call us to fix the "sales problem." Usually, they think they have a sales problem because they aren't making their numbers. In one case, after doing research and analysis, we found it wasn't a sales problem, but a product problem. The product was uncompetitive. Even the best sales people in the world can't fix a bad product problem.

Too often, because we don't take the time to really look at the data, because we are collecting the wrong data, we end up trying to solve the wrong problem. Take the time to dig into your numbers to make sure you understand what the real problem is, solve that problem.

In our experience, too many managers and executives don't take the time to do the analysis and identify the core or root problems. Instead, they react to symptoms they may be seeing. Inevitably they end up trying to solve the wrong problem, and are upset when they don't see the results they wanted.

SOMETIMES A LOT OF DIFFERENT PROBLEMS ARE ACTUALLY RELATED TO ONE UNDERLYING PROBLEM

The other thing about solving the right problem is that by doing so, you may actually solve several additional "symptom" problems.

Sometimes we walk into organizations that seem to have lots of little—but important problems. Win rates may be down, sales cycles up, there's more discounting than normal, pipelines are never big enough, and the list can go on. Managers are desperate, saying, "We have all these problems, we have to solve them now!"

Perhaps they've tried to solve each of these problems, but the solutions may not stick and the problems don't seem to go away.

When we take some time to look at them and analyze them, almost all the time we find the problems are interrelated, they all trace back to one underlying issue. In the set of problems above, it may be no sales process or the wrong sales process. It may be huge changes in their markets and customers.

By trying to find the root or core problem and fixing it, you will eliminate many of the "symptom" oriented problems. But the reverse is never true; you will never eliminate the core problem by solving the symptom oriented problems.

AS BAD AS IT LOOKS, YOU CAN ALWAYS SOLVE THE PROBLEM

This is somewhat related to several of the previous issues. Too often, we see organizations struggling, nothing seems to be working, or the fixes are seldom sustainable.

Typically, they are not using data to understand the problems, instead they are just reacting. Alternatively, they are not identifying the right problems, or they are dealing with symptoms and not root issues.

Sometimes when they get to the core problem it looks terrifying, there is a natural tendency not to face reality or avoid these critical issues.

Once, I was called into an organization whose leaders were frightened. They had a lot of problems, and not much was going right. They had tried all sorts of solutions, but nothing was working.

We started looking at a number of things. We looked at the pipeline. It wasn't great to start with, but after analyzing the deals they were chasing and problems with the deals, we eliminated 85% of the opportunities in the pipeline—things that looked bad before, looked disastrous now.

But we identified the root problems. All the work they had done before had never enabled them to solve their problems because they never identified the root problems and never really faced reality—partly because reality looked so bad.

As bad as it looked, we had a clear course of action. We could begin solving the problems and driving improvements in results. It wasn't long until they started seeing huge progress.

The lesson we all learned: As bad as it may look, face reality. Once you understand the root problems, you can always find a solution. If you refuse to be brutally honest, if you refuse to face reality, you will never identify and fix the problems. Of course, then your management always has the option of finding someone who will.

DRIVING CHANGE

We've spent enough time talking about problems. Once you've identified the problems, you have to fix them. This usually involves change. Change is always scary. Through this book, we've talked a lot about change, usually focusing on changing individuals' behaviors or performance.

Our change efforts fail for a number of reasons.

We try to do too much at one time. No individual or organization can focus on executing more than two or three major change efforts at a time. There's a lot of scientific research about the human mind, and it all gets back to the same numbers: We can't do more than two or three things at one time (and two is much better than three).

As you look at your change initiatives, you may have a long laundry list and all are "A" priorities. You cannot do all of them at the same time, you will fail.

This is where focusing on the root problems and the solutions to those problems is so important. You have to prioritize the change initiatives—focus on the two or three most important, not most urgent. As you address those, move to the next two or three, then the next, and so on.

The second big issue is making sure people understand their roles in the change process, and that they own it. Part of the reason so many change initiatives fail is that they are "imposed on us." None of us like to be told, "Do this!" If you've built the right team, they will be very resistant to something being imposed or mandated.

One of the first things you must do in driving any changes is to make sure people understand what the change is, why the change is necessary, and what success looks like. This can't be abstract; it has to be personalized to them and what it means to them.

As we ask people to change, we have to make sure they understand their role in the change and that they have internalized that role, and own if for themselves.

As we go through the change process, there will be rough spots. We have to continually adjust and refine our plans. We have do continue to reinforce what we are trying to achieve and why it's important. Don't forget to celebrate success once you've made it to the other side!

OTHER THINGS TO THINK ABOUT

As managers, sometimes we think it's our responsibility to figure things out and develop the solution. It may be pride, or it may be an attempt to hide our problems from others.

This is a certain path to failure, both in fixing problems but in your career as a manager and leader.

Today's business world is very complex. The problems we face are seldom simple or have easy fixes. We need to utilize all the resources available to identify and fix the problems. We need to collaborate with our managers, our peers, our people. We need to work together in solving them. The very worst thing you can do is to try to do it by yourself!

Leverage the collective brain power of the people on your team and in your organization. Leverage their knowledge, experience, and creativity. The solution the team develops is almost always better than one you develop by yourself. You also get more people engaged in owning the problem and solution, so the change process becomes much easier.

BEING A LEADER IS ABOUT SOLVING PROBLEMS

If you are uncomfortable in addressing big challenges and solving tough problems, you won't succeed in management. The core part of our jobs is about addressing problems and opportunities. Whether they are the challenges of getting each individual to perform, or overall organizational challenges, our jobs are to address them.

You need to be comfortable with this; you need to be energized by the opportunity.

64

POWER IS NOT WHAT YOU THINK IT IS

We have a lot of ideas about power and influence. Too often, they are wrong and misguided. Perhaps driven by watching terrible movies or TV shows, bad stereotypes, or bad examples set by those perceived to be "in power."

Non-managers, new managers, and bad managers tend to have very naïve or bad views of power. The latter group is probably clueless and will never care, so this is directed to the former two and others who want to think about it differently.

To be honest, I've learned this over a long time, with some painful experience.

Growing up, I had some fleeting experiences with what I thought was "power," president of a school class, captain of a team, things where I was put in some sort of nominal leadership position.

When I moved into my first management job, I thought, "Wow, I'm the boss!" With that thought came some vague ideas of power—at least over my team.

As I got moved to other roles—Director, Vice President, Executive Vice President, CEO—each with the increased responsibility, for a few moments, thoughts of increased power might have flown through my mind. It's a very natural reaction.

- **I have 10 people to manage and am responsible for $50M in sales.**

- **I have 100 people to manage and am responsible for $100s of millions.**

- **I have 1000s of people in my organization and lead a $2B organization.**

The numbers of people, the dollar volume of sales, perhaps budgets, number of facilities, total assets—all contribute to ideas of power.

In reality when you "get there," you suddenly realize where all the power really resides—it's with every person in the organization.

It's impossible to produce the outcomes for which we are responsible by ourselves. As leaders, we are dependent on each individual performing at the highest levels, each achieving their goals, each one making a contribution. Without that, it's impossible to achieve our collective goals.

Yet too many managers and executives get this wrong. They think the people are there to serve them. To do their bidding. They think they hold some sort of power over the individuals because they can "fire" someone or eliminate the job. Some use their positional authority to try to get people to do things.

But jobs are easy to find. Current data, in fact, shows people (at least high performers,) taking control over their careers, moving from job to job every three years.

In reality, we don't "give people jobs" or "give them the privilege to continue to be employed." They manage their own careers and choose to work for an organization in which they can contribute, grow, and be recognized.

Power resides with the people doing the work.

If we are to be effective as leaders, then we must serve the people doing the work. We must coach and develop them. We must remove roadblocks and help them perform at the highest levels.

We have to create a compelling vision, direction, and strategy, that challenges them, excites them, and makes them want to be a part of that achievement. We have to create a culture that encourages them to stay, grow and contribute. We need to create exciting workplaces and be doing something they want to be part of.

Power is a strange thing. Just when you think you have it, you suddenly realize you probably never had it.

65

WHERE DID THE TIME GO? MANAGING YOUR OWN PERFORMANCE AND DEVELOPMENT

If you've been reading this from start to this point, we've covered a huge amount. We've focused on how you get started as a new manager, talked a little about how you should spend your time on the job, spent a lot of time talking about coaching (don't worry, there's still more to come,) and done deep dives into leveraging reviews to both keep up with what's going on, manage the business and coach your people.

By this point, it's reasonable to start feeling a little overwhelmed.

And there's a lot more to go!

So it's worthwhile to pause and regroup. It's time to think a little about ourselves. How we most effectively use our time. How we maximize our own performance. How we develop as managers.

Earlier, I talked about the 50-25-25-25-25-time allocation. Yes, I remember I allocated 150% of your time. The reality is that's what it takes, sometimes more.

By this point, you've probably modified that recommendation to fit your specific circumstances and style. That's perfect—I do hope the time you've allocated to work with your people is no less than 50%, perhaps even a little more.

If you've gotten below 50%, think about it a little. The only way you will achieve your goals is if your people are achieving theirs. Getting your people to perform at the highest levels possible, achieving their full potential is the most important contribution you can make to the business, as well as your own personal success and growth.

You aren't measured by the number of "cool," even interesting meetings you sit in. You aren't (or shouldn't be) measured by the amount of time you sit behind a desk analyzing whatever it is you are analyzing.

You are only successful if your people are.

CONTINUOUS LEARNING AND IMPROVEMENT

But you should also be thinking about your own personal development. You should be thinking about how you grow and continually improve your own skills and capabilities.

Hopefully, you have a great manager who is taking the time to coach and develop you. Hopefully, you are paying attention, being coachable, and continuing to develop.

Whether you do or don't have one of those great managers, it's important for you to continually learn and improve. You should make sure you actively look for ways to learn and apply those lessons.

Take advantage of formal leadership and development programs your company may offer. Consider some outside your job and pay for them yourself. It is the single best investment with the highest return you can achieve.

Don't restrict yourself to formal programs. Read books, blogs, other publications. Talk to your peers. Look outside your company, talk to people who do very different things. One of the things that tends to happen is we become prisoners of our own experiences. We see the same people every day. We do the same things every day. We look at the same competitors, the same issues, and on and on.

Sometimes we start to get blind—we are less sensitive to what's going on, simply because we see it every day.

Sometimes, we keep coming up with the same answers, not realizing there may be a different way of doing things.

So networking outside our "traditional space," looking at different businesses, industries, and people keeps us fresh with new ideas.

Most of my work tends to be in High Technology, Industrial Products, And Professional Services. But for some reason, I also got involved in doing work in Powersports/Motorsports and Extreme sports. I also serve on the board of an entertainment company focused on Hip-Hop, RAP, and Urban artists.

Exposure to these diverse groups, different ways of thinking, different ways of doing things, keeps me on my toes. I'm always learning. I'm taking lessons from the RAP artists I've met and thought, "What does this mean to enterprise software?"

So develop your own plan for learning through formal and informal means. Consciously expand your network to ensure that you get exposed to fresh and new ideas. It's also huge fun!

Block time on your calendar and make it habit.

TIME MANAGEMENT AND YOUR CALENDAR

By now, you've probably seen that your calendar isn't yours. As a salesperson, you had reasonable control over your time and calendar. But now, as a manager, that control has probably diminished.

Your people need to meet with you, so they schedule meetings. Your manager puts meetings on your calendar. Your peers and colleagues put meetings on your calendar.

Pretty soon, you find your calendar completely booked. Soon, you realize you probably aren't spending your time doing the most important things.

There's another thing I see happening with managers. Somehow, they seem to measure their worth or importance by how busy they are. The more meetings, the more activities, the more pressured, the more important they must be.

Being hard to get to, having every moment booked with openings for ad hoc meetings needing to be booked weeks in advance. Or meetings constantly being cancelled or shuffled,

Soon we discover we're busy, but not accomplishing much.

A number of years ago, I was working with a Fortune 25 company. It was one of those companies where everyone was always running to a meeting. Trying to get something done was tough. They were facing huge challenges, but they didn't have the time to sit down and work on fixing them.

I happened to run into the CEO in an elevator. It was one of those opportunities every salesperson dreams of. It was just the two of us, in a very tall building—Yes, his office was on the top floor.

I reintroduced myself—we had actually met a few times in meetings, and I'd done some good work at his previous company. He was very cordial; he was aware of the project I was working on. He complimented me on the results.

We paused for a few seconds of uncomfortable silence. Then he turned to me, "Dave, you're a consultant, what is the one thing I should do to change the performance of this company?"

It turns out, I already knew the answer, so I was ready. "George, I think I know something that will have a huge impact. Do you have 15 minutes? Can I show you something in your office?"

He agreed, though I could see him steeling himself for a sales pitch. We walked into his office. I asked him to sign on to his calendar—calendars for the top executives in the organization were shared. I had actually seen his calendar and knew the problem.

He was a heavy multitasker. His executive assistant would typically schedule three meetings simultaneously. He'd choose the meeting he wanted to focus on, spending most of his time in that meeting, but running to the other two, and just "showing up."

I then asked him to look at the calendars of his direct reports. They were doing the same thing—emulating his behavior. We looked one level further down (at the EVP/SVP level) and saw the same thing.

I could tell he was beginning to get the issue, but I told him, "This behavior permeates the organization. It turns out people in this organization have less than a 30% chance the right people will be in meetings and something can be accomplished. So huge amounts of time are wasted with going to meetings that can't accomplish anything. Then those meetings are rescheduled, so they can have, once again, less than a 30% chance of having the people that need to be there."

We had looked at enough calendars for him to see what was happening. He asked, "What do I do?"

"Cancel 70% of the meetings on your calendar immediately," I replied.

"Which ones?" he asked.

"It doesn't matter. The right ones will surface," I said.

Thirty days later, his assistant searched me down, saying George needed to see me immediately. I started wondering, seeing my whole consulting relationship with this huge company flashing before my eyes. It was a multi-million-dollar relationship, I was thinking, "What do I tell the team and my board about screwing up one of our most important relationships?"

I screwed up the courage and walked into George's office expecting the worst. He apparently saw the concern on my face and, laughing, said, "Dave, that recommendation has turned things around in ways you can't imagine. I can see in just the past few weeks we are accomplishing more and we are spending time on the most important issues."

I was relieved and happy as I left his office, but thought, "Gee, the best piece of consulting I've given this company took me ten minutes and I gave it away for free...."

Actually, we ended up being locked in with the exec team and booked millions more in projects over the following years.

I wish I could make this stuff up, but it is a true story. We stop paying attention to how we spend our time, soon our calendars and our lives are no longer our own.

We are busy, but not accomplishing anything.

Be vicious about your time. Protect it, don't give it up without very good reason. Your priority is time spent with your people. For all other meetings, insist on clear agendas before putting a meeting on your schedule.

THREE THINGS THAT MUST BE ON YOUR CALENDAR

Even with the most disciplined time management skills, there are three things that have to be on your calendar. Without these, you have no chance to succeed:

1. **Keep at least 15% of your daily agenda unscheduled.** Typically, we try to schedule every hour of the day, thinking we are being productive and efficient. Yet much of our time is spent firefighting or reacting to something that just came up. A customer situation, a request from a senior manager, something your people need.

We can't push it off, we have to respond. Everything in our calendar gets destroyed, meetings are cancelled and rescheduled—impacting the time and productivity of those people that needed to meet.

You can't anticipate the requests you'll get every day, so it's critical that you keep 15% of your time unscheduled, giving you the flexibility to deal with the realities of your job.

Don't worry how you will fill that time. It will be filled for you.

2. **Schedule "think time."** It's natural to get caught up in everyday activities and the sheer momentum of the business. Pretty soon, you find yourself and your team lost. You are no longer focused on your goals, but on your day to day activities. You focus on getting through the day, not making progress.

It gets worse. Not only are we diverted from what we need to do to achieve our goals, we don't have the time to think further out, to look at what you and your team should be doing, to assess changes in your markets, customers, and territory, to look at the business differently (perhaps some salesperson who's recently gone through Insight or Challenger sales training, will try calling on you with insights.)

It's critical to schedule thinking and planning time. Time where you can reflect, where you challenge yourself to look at what's happening, question what you are doing, and think about what you should be doing.

Depending on your work habits, perhaps you can find a quiet place in your office—a conference room, or maybe a bench outside—if you work on a corporate campus.

I get physically away from the office. Since I live right next to the Pacific Ocean, I'll go for a walk on the beach. Or I'll sit at a table with a notebook and pen to write ideas or doodle.

Yes, I know you promise you will do this, but block it on your calendar. A few hours every two weeks.

3. **Schedule exercise time every day.** Selling and sales management is very demanding. It's about thinking and engaging. It's tough stuff, and you won't be at the top of your game if you aren't physically in shape.

Make sure you schedule time every day for some exercise. Even if it's only 30 minutes for a good walk, or a bike ride, or a quick workout. You need to be physically prepared to do your job.

DON'T TAKE YOURSELF TOO SERIOUSLY

Finally, I see this with all sorts of people, but particularly new managers. As we start getting consumed by the job, as everyday activities take control of our lives, we start to take ourselves too seriously.

We have to always be attentive. We have to have our hands in everything that's going on. We have to always be moving, in meetings, always acting.

What we do is not life or death. Even in the most challenging of circumstances, or the most difficult of times—things can work out. If we are focused, if we clearly understand the issues, if we can clearly define the problem, we can always figure out approaches to solve these problems.

If we've done the right job with our people and our colleagues, hopefully, they don't need you watching over everything. If we've done the right job, they are figuring things out.

No one is indispensable.

Recently, I had lunch with an outstanding manager. But he was starting to become overwhelmed. He was working increasingly long hours, finding himself carrying the weight of the world—or at least his team on his shoulders.

I asked him, "What would happen if you died today?" He looked at me quizzically, but he was used to my strange questions. Upon reflection, he said, "They'd figure out how to make do.... Jason would start doing this, Greg would focus on that, Max would handle these things."

Things will always go on. They may not be quite as effective, but people will figure it out. You people will carry on, your manager will carry on.

You are, hopefully, important because you are having an impact. But you aren't indispensable.

So lighten up. Have a little fun, take time to laugh with your team and colleagues.

Free yourself to look around.

66

WHAT MAKES YOU A GREAT LEADER AND MANAGER?

At some point in your career as a leader and manager, hopefully you pause to reflect, "What makes a great leader and manager?"

More specifically, "What makes you a great leader and manager?"

Sometimes, we think it's our track record in making the numbers and achieving our objectives. Sometimes, it may be the awards we've gotten, or the bonuses, or the promotions.

As managers, leaders, coaches, we are entrusted with the development of our people. How we develop and grow their capabilities, how we get them to grow in their own careers, stepping up to bigger responsibilities becomes our legacy.

Ultimately, this is the greatest measure of our success and impact as managers and leaders.

I've learned that lesson, many times over, from great people that have managed me. But nothing is more vivid than watching the example set by my wife, Kookie.

She was a front line manager with a very successful high technology company. She built the highest performing team in the company. Somehow she had an instinct for people. She was wickedly smart in selling but rather than focus on the heroics of closing deals herself, she tried to pass her knowledge on to her sales people, helping them become better.

Her goal, as it is with all great leaders, was to maximize the success of her teams. Her greatest joy was to see her people win very tough, complex deals.

As a result, she spent all her time coaching, developing, working with her people. With virtually everything we have covered in the book, she just naturally did them as part of her job. She was a tough manager; she set high expectations for herself and her team. She wouldn't let people off the hook, but would coax, goad, coerce, and sometimes threaten them into higher levels of performance. She could get them to do things they never thought they could do.

She left her last sales management job about 20 years ago, shifting her career to pursuing her dream—becoming a chef.

Fast forward to today. Every month, something remarkable happens. The phone will ring and one of the people she managed during her career will ask for her, "Dave, I need to talk to Kookie about this deal…. Dave, I'm struggling with this issue in my organization, can you put Kookie on the phone…."

After more than 20 years, her people still call her for coaching and advice. Most of them have gone on to much bigger things in their careers. Some are running sales organizations, some are running companies, some are great sales people.

But the calls still come, at least one a month, sometimes more.

Each of them knows they can reach out for help and ideas from Kookie. I listen to the conversations (at least Kookie's side of them). She doesn't know a lot about the companies, their products, or the specifics of the deals.

Most of the time she's listening, asking questions, and getting people to think about things differently. She's helping them figure out what actions they should take.

Isn't that what great leadership is really about? Isn't it about empowering your people with the skills, knowledge, capabilities, and confidence to execute in their jobs?

Isn't the joy we get in doing our jobs, seeing those things take hold?

As you ponder the question of, "What makes you a great leader?" ask yourself this:

Will your people still seek you out for your coaching and advice 10, 15, 20 years later?

Your legacy as a manager has little to do with the titles you hold, the awards you have gotten.

Your legacy is the impact you have had on your people.

It is how you have helped change their lives, helped them grow, helped them be successful.

That is the true legacy of the Front Line Sales Manager/Leader.

APPENDIX

Throughout the book, I've mentioned a number of resources to help with the ideas presented in this book. They are all available at the book website

http://salesmanagersurvivalguide.com

Registration at the site is free for anyone who has purchased this book. You will immediately have access to:

- **Sample Sales Competency Model**

- **Roles and Responsibilities Model**

- **First 30 Day Front Line Manager Checklist**

- **Sales Manager Checklist**

- **Sales Management Ecosystem**

   Over time, we plan to add additional tools to this site, and your registration will ensure that you're notified as new material appears.

   For any special issues, questions or needs; as well as to get in direct contact with me for consulting, coaching, training, or speaking, feel free to reach out at **dabrock@excellenc.com**

ACKNOWLEDGEMENTS

There are thousands of people to acknowledge. This book is a result of my experiences both in being managed/led, and my own experiences in managing/leading. It's the result of experiences with thousands of individuals, great people in companies I've worked for, and great clients. My thoughts have been influenced by colleagues, fellow consultants, and others.

Some truly outstanding managers and leaders who inspired me, and from whom I learned valuable lessons. However, I won't forget some horrible managers. Perhaps, some of my most important lessons in leadership and management came from them. Not because of what they did, but because of the sharp contrast between them and the great leaders. I learned important lessons from the bad examples they set—though I think those lessons are not things they would have been proud of.

Even more important in my personal development as a manager, coach, and leader, are the people who worked for me or in my organizations. They put up with me and all the mistakes I made. For the most part, they were patient and forgiving. Most of all, they cared enough to teach me and help me be a better manager, coach, and leader. Many had the courage to push back, saying, "Dave, you need to clean up your act!" It's through them, that I really developed and learned what it takes to be successful.

We've been blessed with a very diverse client base, and with the managers for those clients. They come from every imaginable industry, from over 60 countries, and range from very small family owned businesses, to exciting start-ups, up through the very largest corporations in the world.

They have provided our company a real-world lab to develop, test, and apply many of the concepts outlined in the book. Many of these clients have been world class leaders themselves, sharing their approaches, experiences, and ideas.

As a consultant, I've had the privilege of working with and sharing ideas with many others in the consulting community, learning from them, debating, and sharing experiences. They contributed and enriched this book.

Many colleagues in the consulting world have been very encouraging in getting me to write a book, and advising me on the process. One stands out, Charles Green of Trusted Advisor Associates has long encouraged me. As the book reached publication, he provided great advice and insight helping make this better.

There are the people that literally made this happen. My wife Kookie has been an inspiration as a sales leader—helping me learn what great sales leadership is. Tactically, however, she literally put me on a Performance Improvement Plan in writing the book and getting it done.

Publishing this book has put me in touch with a whole new world of people— editors and graphics artists who have taught me more about publishing a book than I thought I needed to know. At the head of the pack is Keith Ferrell, who did a masterful job of guiding me from a lot of ideas and pieces into putting together a cohesive, and, I hope, impactful book for readers. Keith did a great job in editing and making my ideas readable. It was great fun working with him, and learning about writing books (and a few other life lessons). Jennifer Melzer undertook the tedious task of the final copy-editing, making me look smarter—at least grammatically and spelling-wise, than I really am. KS Rives Revivo is responsible for the stunning cover design and the graphic treatments of the website, all the promotional materials associated with the launch of the book. Angie Hodapp did a wonderful job of transforming a complicated manuscript's messy pages into this book's attractive and readable pages.

Finally, my Mom, Janellen Decker Brock. As the proud son, I sent her some early drafts of the book. Little did I know her background in journalism and writing caused her to pull out a red pencil and start editing and correcting the manuscript.

Writing this book has been a work of pure joy. If it provides you just a fraction of what I got from writing it, I will have achieved my goal.

INDEX

21762911R00198

Printed in Great Britain
by Amazon